LET'S GO BUDGET

FLORENCE

Research Manager
Billy Marks

Managing Editor
Chris Kingston

Editor
Michael Goncalves

Contents

Discover Florence 3

Planning Your Trip 9

Accommodations. 32

Sights 48

Food 76

Nightlife 95

Arts and Culture 111

Shopping 117

Excursions 124

Essentials 172

Florence 101 193

Beyond Tourism 201

Index 213

Discover Florence

The Medici. Botticelli. Dante. What do these names, familiar to anyone who has studied history, art, or literature (or a combination of all three), have in common? All of them were natives of Florence, and their presence survives in the city today. As the birthplace of the Italian Renaissance and an epicenter for high culture, Florence has become one of the artistic treasure troves of the world. You can barely walk along the streets and *piazze* without running into famous works (or their replicas), and the myriad museums are rivaled in number by dozens of churches, which house priceless artwork and frescoes all their own. One might think that being a tourist in Florence would get old, once the splendor of walking through yet another museum with yet more artistic landmarks wears off. But this city is so much more than that: you can sip regional Chianti at the many cafes and bars, enjoy traditional Tuscan cuisine in trattorias and *ristoranti,* and view spectacular live performances of everything from music to theater. What's more, if the city begins to wear on you, the quaint, relaxing cities and towns of Tuscany are just a train ride away, allowing you to venture into the countryside and return to the city with renewed fascination. This is a city of purely Florentine sights, tastes, and customs, and if you allow yourself to embrace that culture, you'll no doubt leave feeling like a true *fiorentino.*

Budget Florence

PANINI FOR PENNIES

You don't have to limit yourself to gelato to save a few bucks in Florence. There are many cafes and *ristoranti* that offer pizza, sandwiches, and pasta for less than €10. The trick to snagging an affordable meal goes beyond the menu—many restaurants charge cover fees for table service, so munching on the go or at the bar can satisfy your hunger and your bank account.

- ▶ **PIZZERIA DEL DUOMO:** The slices are so large that you might actually ask for a smaller piece, which is quite the bargain for €2 (p. 78).

- ▶ **THE OIL SHOPPE:** Grab a stool quickly—this sandwich joint is constantly filled with hungry study abroaders on a quest for cheap panini (p. 89).

- ▶ **NERBONE:** This century-old *ristorante* serves *primi* and *secondi* for as little as €2.50, or go for a glass of house wine—it's only €1 (p. 84).

- ▶ **MESOPOTAMIA:** Take a walk on the Turkish side with these affordable (and delicious) kebabs (p. 77).

- ▶ **MERCATO CENTRALE:** San Lorenzo's famous market is your ticket to cheap meats, cheeses, and even pizza and sandwiches (p. 84).

Freebies

- ▶ **DUOMO:** Although you have to pay extra to climb up to the top, the city's most visible landmark is free to enter (p. 49).

- ▶ **PIAZZALE MICHELANGELO:** It's quite the hike, but the view is almost unparalleled, and there's even a(nother) *David* reproduction (p. 75).

- ▶ **CHIESA DI SAN SALVATORE A OGNISSANTI:** Come here to view Botticelli's tomb, or the very convincing balcony painted on the ceiling (p. 61).

- ▶ **CHIESA DI SANTA MARIA DE' RICCI:** If you want to satisfy your visual and auditory senses, come to this small church for a free organ recital (p. 112).

BUNKING ON A BUDGET

Florence isn't the kind of city where hostels put up signs on every corner raving about low prices and the phenomenal amenities that come with them. However, if you know where to look, there are definitely places that cater to the penny-pinchers instead of the luxury-seekers. If you visit in any month that isn't summer, prices can drop as much as €20 per night.

- ▶ **ACADEMY HOSTEL:** A prime location near the Duomo makes this one of the best values in Florence (p. 33). Quick, reserve now, the €30 beds fill up fast!

- ▶ **SOGGIORNO PITTI:** It may be out of the way in West Oltrarno, but this upscale hotel doubles as a hostel, so you get the comfort without the price tag (p. 41).

- ▶ **HOSTEL PLUS:** This is probably the only hostel in Florence (or in Italy, for that matter) that gives you a bed, gym, Turkish bath, and pool for only €25 (p. 42).

- ▶ **OSTELLO ARCHI ROSSI:** Not only do you get a cheap room, but you can score a plate of pasta every night for a mere €2.50 (p. 39).

▶ **FLORENCE YOUTH HOSTEL:** Art enthusiasts will love the location next to the Uffizi, while night owls will appreciate P. della Signoria's array of nightlife (p. 35).

THE ART BURGLAR

No, we aren't encouraging you to break into one of Florence's famed galleries and sell the pieces to alleviate your budget altogether (it probably wouldn't end too well for you anyway). Rather, we want you to know that seeing famous artwork, whether it's housed in a museum or a church, can be a real steal. Travelers can get into many museums for under €5, and some even offer joint tickets with other locations for a single low rate.

▶ **MUSEO DI SAN MARCO:** It's not the Accademia, but it's right next door (p. 66).

▶ **BASILICA DI SAN LORENZO:** Pay the small entrance fee to see Filippo Brunelleschi's rendition of the night sky, or sneak a free peek from the prayer area (p. 64).

▶ **MUSEO DEGLI INNOCENTI:** This former orphanage is now home to an extravagant art collection that charges an affordable €4 entrance fee (p. 68).

▶ **BASILICA DI SANTA MARIA NOVELLA:** This is one of the most awe-inspiring churches outside the famed Duomo, and it only costs €3.50 (p. 60).

▶ **PALAZZO PITTI:** You may have to cough up €10, but the resulting ticket gets you into three museums as well as the Boboli Gardens—you do the math (p. 71).

What To Do

RENAISSANCE REPOSITORY

"Florence" is practically synonymous with "Renaissance art." As the arguable birthplace of the Italian Renaissance, it's no wonder

the city is home to some of the most notable art pieces known to man. You'll find a museum full of them at the **Uffizi Gallery** (p. 52), which houses Botticelli's *The Birth of Venus* among 35 other rooms of noteworthy works. You'll finally see Michelangelo's real *David*—no replicas here—in the **Galleria dell'Accademia** (p. 64). Or you can become acquainted with the least famous Ninja Turtle in **The Bargello** (p. 55).

WALKIN' AFTER MIDNIGHT

You might think that the only (admittedly attractive) nightlife option in Florence is a glass of wine by the Arno. While its scene isn't as vibrant as Rome's or Milan's, Florence does have a few places that will amp up your excitement. Take advantage of unique drinks at **James Joyce Pub** (p. 109) or enjoy one of the city's *libreria caffès*, like **Volume** (p. 108). Plus, many bars become live music venues on select nights—party with Nessie to some live tunes at **Lochness Lounge** (p. 104). Or you can get a conventional club experience, sadly including the price tag, at **Space Electronic Discotheque** (p. 100).

GET OUTTA TOWN

Even if you love art history more than life itself, you might want to introduce a little variety into your trip. Fortunately, Florence isn't an artistic island within a barren Central Italian wasteland—it's at the heart of scenic Tuscany. Head to **Pisa** (p. 138) to see that notorious 3.99° tilt, or journey to **San Gimignano** (p. 162) for a scenic daytrip. **Lucca** (p. 150) earns the coveted *Let's Go* 🖋**thumbpick** for its neverending Puccini Festival and gorgeous views, while **Siena** (p. 125) will surely wow you, whether through the crazy Palio or the beautiful Duomo complex.

BEYOND TOURISM

Although it's great to visit Florence as a tourist, why not channel your desire to see the city into something more worthwhile? Italy is the perfect place to study abroad, volunteer, or earn a paycheck. You could improve your Italian skills at the **Istituto Italiano** (p. 205) or put your love of animals to good use helping injured horses at **Fondazione Flaminia da Filicaja** (p. 208). Plus, it'll give you something to do when the Uffizi line is 3hr. long and you really don't feel like waiting.

Student Superlatives

► **MOST LIKELY TO CAUSE SEVERE NECK PAIN:** The Baptistery of San Giovanni and its elaborate, mesmerizing ceiling mosaic (p. 51).

► **MOST UN-CONVENT-IONAL:** If you're staying overnight in San Gimignano, stay at Foresteria Monastero di San Girolamo, where you'll get a room inside a functioning convent (p. 163).

► **MOST LIKELY TO SUCK UP ALL YOUR TIME:** La Cité Libreria Cafe has everything you'd ever need: food, cheap beer, live music, and comfortable seating (p. 111).

► **MOST MISLEADING:** While it's not actually a celebration, you'll rejoice after tasting the frozen fare at Festival del Gelato (p. 80).

► **MOST LIKELY TO BECOME A WORKAHOLIC:** The Puccini e la Sua Lucca festival runs 365 days a year to celebrate the local opera legend (p. 159).

Planning Your Trip

Welcome to Florence, land of the Renaissance. Painted, carved, and frescoed half to death, Florence's famous art practically bursts out of its ornately sculpted windows. Amid solemn churches and posh palaces, restaurants and accommodations often have to get creative, squeezing into tiny windows, alleyways, or abandoned monasteries. Many of these patterns repeat themselves across the city, so you might not notice that much distinction between neighborhoods. Don't tell the residents that, though: local pride is fierce.

Our coverage of Florence is divided into neighborhoods that roughly correspond to the major church districts. You'll most likely arrive at Santa Maria Novella Station in the western half of the city. This area is not especially different from stations in any other city; cheap restaurants and clustered accommodations await weary travelers. Follow the crowds to the city's geographical focal points: the ostentatious Duomo that dominates the city center and the River Arno that separates the city from the Oltrarno, a greener land that feels like a whole separate world. Between the Duomo and the river, Piazza della Signoria blends seamlessly into the Duomo neighborhood to form a hub for high-end shopping and tourism. The eastern third of the city looks after the student population with cheap pubs and kebab shops.

Icons

First things first: places and things that we absolutely love, sappily cherish, generally obsess over, and wholeheartedly endorse are denoted by the all-empowering 👍 **Let's Go thumbs-up.** In addition, the icons scattered at the end of a listing can serve as visual cues to help you navigate each listing:

👍	Let's Go recommends	☎	Phone numbers	🪧	Directions
i	Other hard info	[$]	Prices	⏰	Hours

WHEN TO GO

The best times to visit Florence are the spring and mid-fall. You might think that summertime on the Mediterranean is the perfect vacation fantasy: low rainfall, beautiful sunshine, and as far away from wintry chills as possible. However, take it from the locals—many Florentines leave the city during August to escape the blistering heat in an area with few cooling breezes. You should probably follow suit; not only will you be glad to be out of the sun, but with the locals cleared out, you'd have been stuck in a city full only of tourists and long lines. That said, late fall and early winter see an increase in rainfall as well as a drop in temperature, with averages in the mid-50s. Although many sights have reduced hours during these chillier months, you may prefer to deal with this rather than sizzling in the summer sun.

NEIGHBORHOODS

The Duomo

Florence's distinctive Duomo is perhaps the most helpful feature for wandering tourists—it's easy enough to find your way back here, so learn the route from the Duomo to your hostel and you'll never be lost. If you imagine a *piazza*-compass, the **Baptistery** points west and the Duomo points east. The tall tower just south of the Duomo is the **Campanile.** While the streets south off P. del Duomo run straight, the northern ones veer eastward. This huge, bustling *piazza* is full of tourists during the day, but the incredibly diverse crowd makes it a surprisingly cool place to people-watch. As with any heavy tourist zone, though, there are a few things to watch out for. Ignore the fake designer brands on the street, or risk being slapped with a fine far higher than the real deal would have cost. Check the signs before joining the snaking lines, or you could find yourself paying to climb hundreds of stairs when you meant to be poking around the free church. You can safely assume that street vendors and beggars are trying to rip you off. As always, keep an eye out for pickpockets. P. del Duomo isn't just a tourist hub, though—locals come here to drink and mingle once the sun and crowds have gone.

Piazza della Signoria

Near the **Uffizi Gallery** and Arno River, this *piazza* is perhaps the best part of the city to wander. Cheap food and accommodations are tucked away among the many ritzier options, but the eastern portion of this neighborhood is the best bet (near the abominable **Casa di Dante**). Take V. Calimala toward the Mercato Nuovo to observe the daily chalk art creations that are wiped clean by the noisy street-cleaning trucks. Outside the Uffizi, you'll often find human statues and other street performers, while **Piazza della Repubblica** is the place for live music. A block north of the river along Borgo Santi Apostoli, you'll find designer clothing shops with tempting window displays. Along the Arno, you'll primarily find unaffordable hotels, expensive home decor, and fancy leather.

Piazza Palooza

When looking at a map of must-see places in Florence, the word *piazza* is likely to show up often. The word refers to a paved public area, usually in front of a significant building or shopping area. If the dizzying number of *piazze* is overwhelming, put a pep in your tour-ridden step by asking about the stories behind your favorite square. For example, in 1869, architect Giuseppe Poggi solidified his man crush on Florence's greatest sculptor by erecting a monument in his honor, the Piazzale Michelangelo. Poggi's plan for a museum to accompany the park of statues was vetoed, with the building instead being transformed into a restaurant. This offers yet more proof that Italy's joy lies in not love of man or art, but of food.

Piazza della Signoria is the place to be as the evening cools and the sweaty tourist mobs retreat.

Santa Maria Novella

The Santa Maria Novella **train station** will likely be your first introduction to Florence, and the decision to venture east or south will color your earliest impressions of the city. To the east of the station you'll find the cheap accommodations and casual food joints that you'd expect near the train station of any major city. To the south, clustered around the church that gives the station its name, you'll find art galleries, modern museums, and a calm stretch of the Arno. Don't bother venturing north or west (unless you're trekking out to the Central Park nightclub) as you'll be leaving Florence's historic center before you've even set foot in it. Stop by in the evening to find happy young Italians smoking outside the entrance to their favorite bar or club.

San Lorenzo

Just east of the train station lies a land of markets and 99-cent stores. Come for the cheap accommodations on **Via Faenza** and **Via Nazionale;** stay for the food around San Lorenzo's vibrant outdoor market on **Via dell'Aviento** and the adjoining **Mercato Centrale.** If you're only here for a little while, these will be the most memorable sights in San Lorenzo, which is light on museums. Nightlife is more of the relaxed bar variety and a bit removed from the more happening Florentine clubs.

San Marco

By "San Marco," we mean pretty much everything between **Piazza di San Marco** and the northern edge of the old city. The primary draw of this area is the density of museums and bus stops, not to mention the (real!) statue of David in the **Accademia** (which, unfortunately, also comes with a block-long line of tourists). To the east, **Piazza Santissima Annunziata** has its own concentration of sights worth exploring. Late at night, stick to the southern edge of the area or travel with a friend—north of P. di San Marco is one of the quietest parts of the old city and can be unsafe after the buses stop running.

Santa Croce

Santa Croce is Florence's student and nightlife center and a great place to go exploring. The neighborhood spans the area east of the Duomo down to the river and is laced with cheap restaurants. Interspersed between the shops, food stations, and cultural venues, you'll find an exotic synagogue, the remains of many of Italy's greats, Michelangelo's house, and a once-a-year event where a bunch of guys in medieval garb beat each other up before a large audience. As you wander, note the neighborhood's walls—though plaques marking the water line of the 1966 Arno flood can be found all over Florence, the profusion of watermarks here show that Santa Croce was hit the hardest. **Piazza Santa Croce** is filled with clothing and leather shops, and the antique market under **Piazza dei Ciompi's** old arches is worth checking out even if you don't plan on lugging anything home. **Piazza Sant'Ambrogio** is the epitome of Florence's casual, *piazza*-based nightlife scene. If there were cheap accommodations in Santa Croce, it would be the best budget base in the city.

West Oltrarno

This is the cool, artsy half of the Oltrarno, the area on the south side of the Arno. With a concentration of pharmacies, supermarkets, and dogs, it feels more authentic and lived-in than the other side of the river but still has a high density of hostels, museums, and study-abroad students. The main tourist draw is the **Palazzo Pitti** complex, but let the young and trendy vibe take you a few steps further to eat in **Piazza Santo Spirito** and explore the jewelry boutiques, art galleries, and studios nestled in the residential streets.

East Oltrarno

The most common reason to trek to East Oltrarno is for the unbeatable view of Florence from the **Piazzale Michelangelo.** This generally quiet residential area is laced with some of Florence's most active nightlife, which makes crossing the river even more worth your while. We've set the Oltrarnos' dividing line at **Ponte Vecchio,** but you'll find a large residential stretch between the bridge and the lively evening entertainment around **Ponte San Niccolò.**

SUGGESTED ITINERARIES

A Cheap Date Paved in Gold

Here's how to spend an affordable afternoon (with a particularly metallic theme)with that cute hostel friend you finally asked out.

1. MUSEO ARCHEOLOGICO: Start off your date by looking at sphinxes, mummies, and statues, a welcome break from the typical Renaissance paintings (p. 68).

2. IL PIRATA: Grab dinner at this pirate-themed *ristorante*. You probably won't find buried treasure, but at least the buffet is only €7.50 (p. 85).

3. VESTRI CIOCCOLATO D'AUTORE: With gelato this good, you'll feel like you've struck gold (p. 77).

4. PONTE VECCHIO: There's no better place to conclude this golden date than the bridge that's lined with gold shops during the day. But you should really go there at night—it's far more romantic (p. 57).

Firenze on Foot

Trekking Florence on a walking tour does not seem like the most productive task since most of the "sights" are the artworks within the museums and churches. However, many *piazze* are sights in their own right, and the churches can be just as beautiful to look at from the outside as the inside.

1. SANTA MARIA NOVELLA: Start here to get to know the outer ring of Florence neighborhoods. There's not much to see other than the train station, although you can get an exterior look at the Basilica di Santa Maria Novella and Chiesa di San Salvatore a Ognissanti.

2. SAN LORENZO: Wave hello to the Basilica di San Lorenzo and take your time exploring the busy Mercato Centrale—grab a sandwich to munch on for the rest of your tour.

3. SAN MARCO: Look from afar: this is the museum hub of

Florence, so it's not exactly conducive for meandering the sights. However, at least you'll know where to spot the Galleria dell'Accademia and the Museo di San Marco.

4. SANTA CROCE: This student-filled neighborhood is great to wander through. If you don't want to take a pit stop in one of the many bars, you can just admire the city's glorious synagogue or the evidence of the devastating 1966 flood.

5. DUOMO: Enjoy one of the most spectacular collections of buildings anywhere in Europe. Even without climbing them, the dome and Campanile are impressive.

6. PIAZZA DELLA SIGNORIA: Like San Marco, Piazza della Signoria is home to museums, so scope out the Uffizi Gallery and the Bargello for future reference. But make sure to take your time in the P. della Repubblica and the P. della Signoria itself—these areas feature famous art and a host of street performances. When you're done, cross the river along the beautiful Ponte Vecchio.

7. THE OLTRARNOS: Forget walking—you'll be hiking up to the Piazzale Michelangelo. Once you've arrived, sit down, rest your feet, and admire the panoramic view of the city you just conquered on foot.

Three-Day Weekend

Here it is folks: the best of Florence in a long weekend. Hold on; it's going to be a bumpy, art-filled ride.

Day One

1. After grabbing breakfast at your hostel, set out for the center of the city to the **Duomo** (p. 49). Climb the Campanile or the dome for your first spectacular view of Florence, then stop at the nearby museum to see the art that used to be in the church.

2. Do a little people-watching in P. del Duomo before grabbing lunch a little to the south at **Da Vinattieri** (p. 80).

3. Stroll through the P. della Signoria and admire its collection of sculptures, including a replica of the famous *David*.

4. Pay a visit to **The Bargello** (p. 55). Or be on the safe side and nab a late-afternoon spot in line at the **Uffizi Gallery** (p. 52). to make a reservation for a few days from now.

5. Head for dinner at **Caffè Duomo** (p. 78) for a €9 multi-course meal, then have a low-key night with a few beers in P. della Signoria.

Day Two

1. Make the trek across the **Ponte Vecchio** (p. 57) to West Oltrarno early for the 8:15am opening of the **Palazzo Pitti** (p. 71) complex—whichever ticket you buy, you'll see a nice combination of museums. Grab lunch at **Dante** (p. 92), particularly if you're a student, in which case you get a free bottle of wine with any meal.

2. Head across the Arno to Santa Maria Novella to the **Museo di Ferragamo** (p. 59) to bring some sole to your weekend. Stop at the **Farmaceutica di Santa Maria Novella** (p. 120) to get a taste of 13th-century medicine (although actual tasting is probably a bad idea).

3. Trek across the city to Santa Croce—the synagogue might be closed already, but it's the food and entertainment at **Cibréo Teatro del Sale** (p. 89) that you're after.

4. If you can still move after the buffet and dinner show, you can stop by one of Santa Croce's many bars and clubs; we suggest **Caffè Sant'Ambrogio** (p. 105).

Day Three

1. Spend your last morning (or the whole day, if you have the stamina) at Florence's most famous museum, the **Uffizi** (p. 52) By arriving early, you'll beat the longest lines.

2. After conquering the Uffizi, head north to San Marco. Lunch today is at **Il Vegetariano** (p. 87), where the cuisine is so delicious you won't even miss the meat.

3. If the replica *David* wasn't enough for you, wait in line to see the real thing at the **Accademia** (p. 64). If you're museumed-out, have a relaxing afternoon in the **Botanic Gardens** (p. 67). Just try not to fall asleep on one of the benches.

4. To enjoy a true Italian dinner like the locals do, dine at **Trattoria Mario** (p. 84) in San Lorenzo.

5. San Marco and San Lorenzo aren't the greatest for nightlife, but one of the most happening block parties goes down every summer night at **Las Palmas** (p. 104) in Santa Croce.

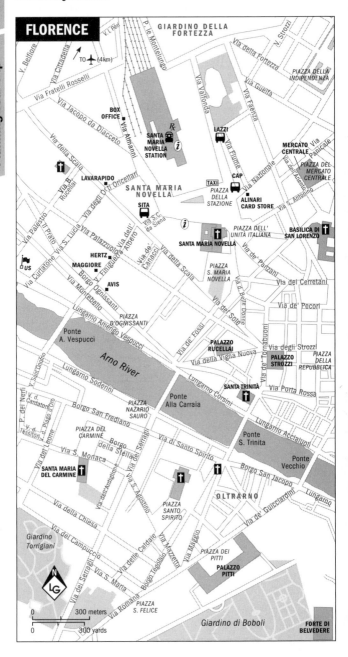

FLORENCE

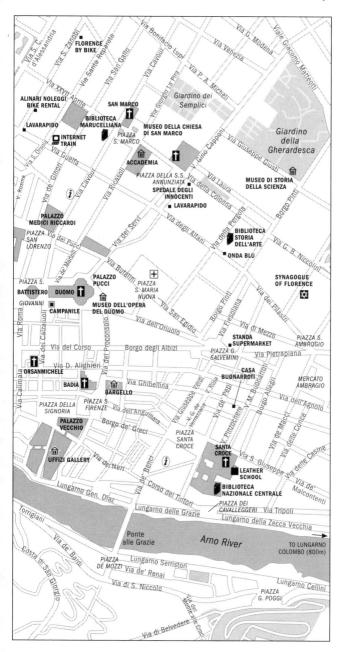

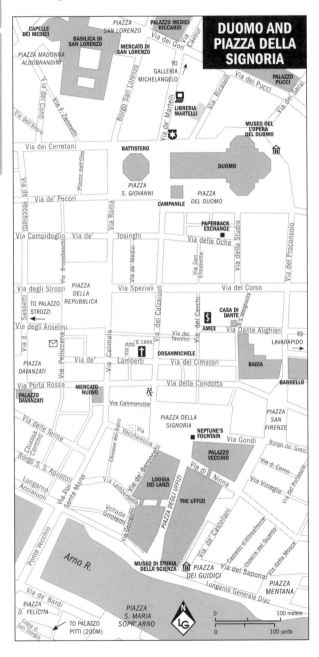

DUOMO AND PIAZZA DELLA SIGNORIA

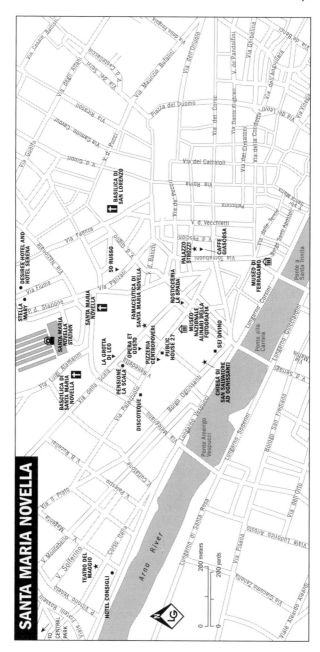

SANTA MARIA NOVELLA

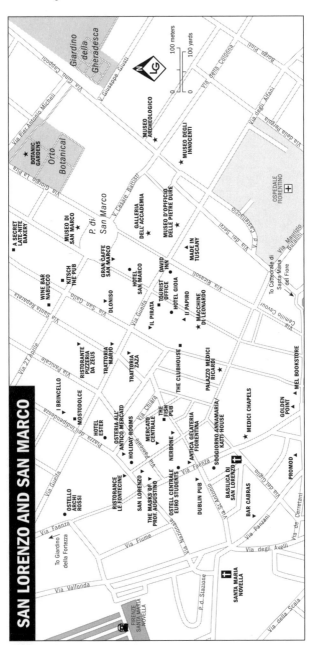

SAN LORENZO AND SAN MARCO

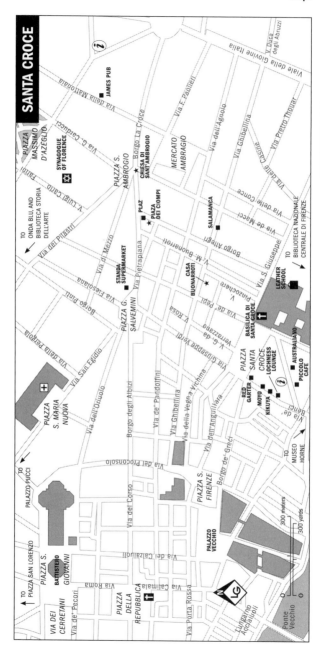

SANTA CROCE

TO
PIAZZA SAN LORENZO

TO
PIAZZA PUCCI

TO
ONDA BLU and
BIBLIOTECA STORIA
DELL'ARTE

TO
BIBLIOTECA NAZIONALE
CENTRALE DI FIRENZE

PIAZZA S.
CERRETANI

VIA DEI
CERRETANI

BATTISTERO
PIAZZA S.
GIOVANNI

Via de' Pecori

Via de' Pecori

PIAZZA
DELLA
REPUBBLICA

Via Roma

Via Calzaiuoli

Via del Corso

Via del Proconsolo

PIAZZA S. MARIA
NUOVA

Via della Pergola

Borgo Pinti

V. Luigi Carlo Farini

PIAZZA
MASSIMO
D'AZEGLIO

Via G. Carducci

Via della Mattonaia

JAMES PUB

SYNAGOGUE
OF FLORENCE

PIAZZA S.
AMBROGIO

CHIESA DI
SANT'AMBROGIO

Borgo la Croce

Via dell'Agnolo

Via F. Paolieri

V. Pietro Thouar

Viale della Giovine Italia

V. Duca
degli Abruzzi

MERCATO
AMBROGIO

Via Ghibellina

Via delle Casine

Via dei Pilastri

Via di Mezzo

Via Pietrapiana

STANDA
SUPERMARKET

PIAZZA G.
SALVEMINI

Via Fiesolana

Via San Egidio

Via dell'Oriuolo

Borgo degli Albizi

PLAZ

PIAZZA
DEI CIOMPI

SALAMANCA

Borgo Allegri

Via de Macci

Via delle Conce

V.M. Buonarroti

CASA
BUONARROTI

V. delle
Pinzochere

Via de' Pepi

V. Rosa

V. G. da
Verrazzano

V.M. Buonarroti

Via Giuseppe Verdi

Via Ghibellina

Via de' Pandolfini

Via dell'Anguillara

Borgo de' Greci

PIAZZA S.
FIRENZE

BASILICA DI
SANTA CROCE

PIAZZA
SANTA
CROCE

LEATHER
SCHOOL

Via S. Giuseppe

RED
GARTER

MOYO

KIKUYA

LOCHNESS
LOUNGE

PICCOLO
CAFE

AUSTRALIANO

Via de'
Benci

MUSEO
HORNE

PALAZZO
VECCHIO

Via del Corso

Via Porta Rossa

Lungarno
Acciaiuoli

Ponte
Vecchio

300 meters
300 yards

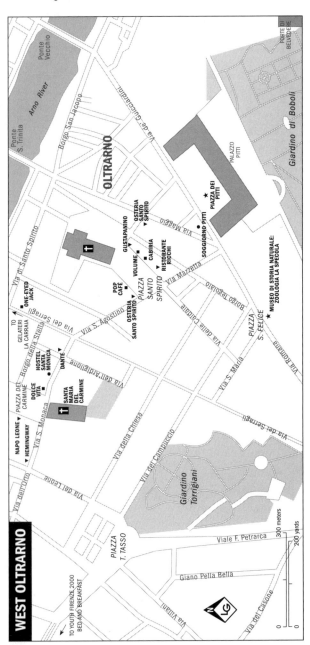

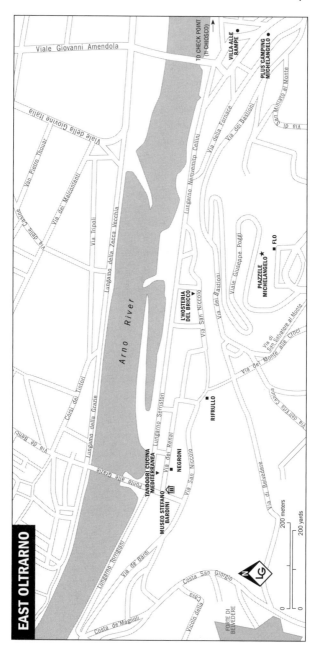

EAST OLTRARNO

Viale Giovanni Amendola

Viale della Giovine Italia

Van Pietro Thouar

Via delle Casine

Via dei Macianiani

Via Tripoli

Lungarno della Zecca Vecchia

Arno River

Lungarno Niccolò

TO CHECK POINT
(IL CHIOSCO)

VILLA ALLE ●
RAMPE

PLUS CAMPING ●
MICHELANGELO ■

Via di San Miniato al Monte

Via della Fornace

Via dei Bastioni

Viale Giuseppe Poggi

PIAZZALE ★
MICHELANGELO

■ FLO

Via dei Bastioni

Via di San Salvatore al Monte

Via del Monte alle Croci

Via delle Croci

Corso dei Tintori

Via de' Benci

Lungarno delle Grazie

Lungarno Serristori

Ponte alle Grazie

Via del Renai

L'HOSTERIA
DEL BRICO ■

Via San Niccolò

RIFRULLO ■

TANDOOR CUCINA
MEDITERRANEA ▼

NEGRONI ■

MUSEO STEFANO 🏛
BARDINI

Via San Niccolò

Via di Belvedere

Lungarno Torrigiani

Via de' Bardi

Costa San Giorgio

Costa de' Magnoli

Vicolo della Cava

FORTE DI
BELVEDERE

200 meters

200 yards

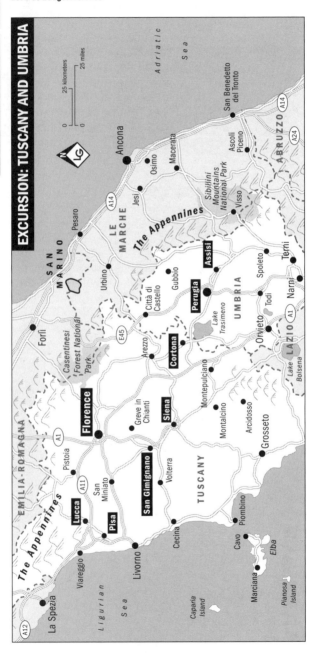

EXCURSION: TUSCANY AND UMBRIA

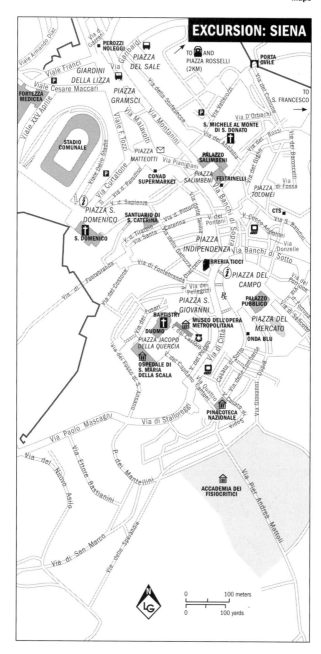

EXCURSION: SIENA

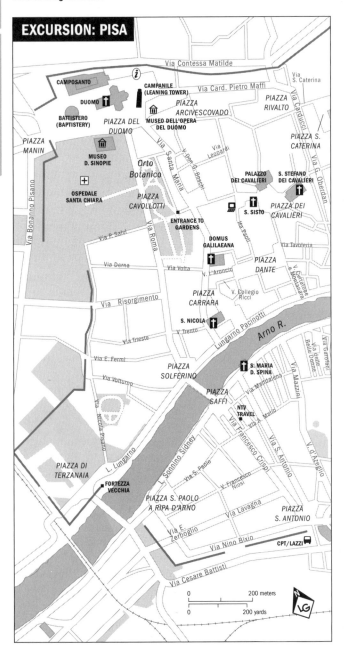

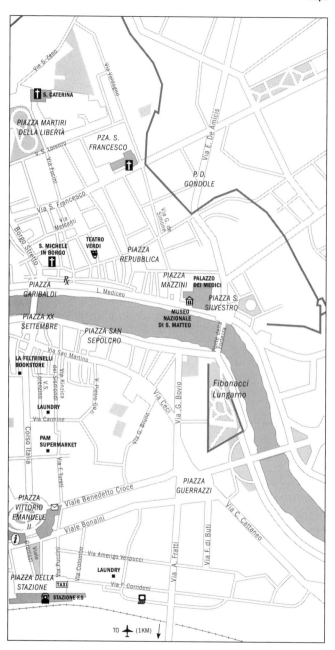

S. CATERINA

PIAZZA MARTIRI
DELLA LIBERTÀ

Via S. Zeno

Via Valdagno

Via S. Lorenzo

Via Fiumi

PZA. S.
FRANCESCO

Via E. De Amicis

P. D.
GONDOLE

Via S. Francesco

Via G. de Simone

via Metcanti

Borgo Stretto

S. MICHELE
IN BORGO

TEATRO
VERDI

PIAZZA
REPUBBLICA

PIAZZA
GARIBALDI

L. Mediceo

PIAZZA
MAZZINI

PALAZZO
DEI MEDICI

PIAZZA S.
SILVESTRO

PIAZZA XX
SETTEMBRE

PIAZZA SAN
SEPOLCRO

MUSEO
NAZIONALE
DI S. MATTEO

Ponte della
Fortezza

LA FELTRINELLI
BOOKSTORE

Via San Martino

V.S.
Lorenzino

Via Marica
dei Steinondi

V. Pietro Gori

Via Ceci

Via G. Bovio

Fibonacci
Lungarno

LAUNDRY

Via Carmine

Via G. Bruno

PAM
SUPERMARKET

Via F. Turati

Corso Italia

PIAZZA
VITTORIO
EMANUELE
II

Viale Benedetto Croce

PIAZZA
GUERRAZZI

Via C. Cattaneo

Viale Bonaini

Via Colombo

Viale Gamici

Via Amerigo Vespucci

Via A. Fratti

Via F. di Buti

PIAZZA DELLA
STAZIONE

TAXI

LAUNDRY

Via F. Corridoni

STAZIONE F.S

TO ✈ (1KM)

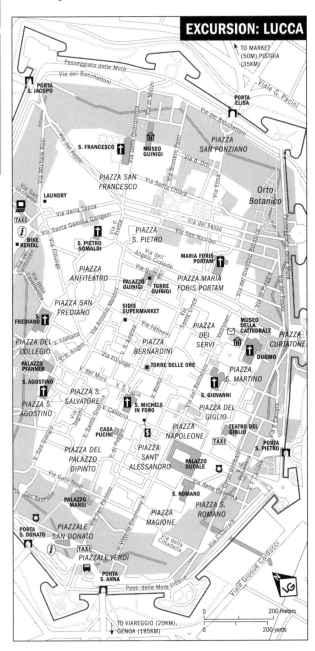

EXCURSION: LUCCA

TO MARKET (50M), PISTOIA (35KM)

Via G. Pacini

Passeggiata delle Mura

Via dei Bacchettoni

PORTA S. JACOPO

PORTA ELISA

Via dei Bacchettoni

Via della Quarconia

Via della Quarconia al Mezzo

S. FRANCESCO

MUSEO GUINIGI

PIAZZA SAN PONZIANO

Via Fratta Brunero Paoli

Via d. Orti

PIAZZA SAN FRANCESCO

Via Santa Chiara

Orto Botanico

Via San Leonardo

LAUNDRY

Via della Zecca

Via del Fosso

Via San Nicolao

Passeggiata delle Mura

Via San Giorgio delle Mura

Via Michele

Via Santa Gemma Galligani

TAXI

BIKE RENTAL

i

Via del Carmine

Via di Fratta

PIAZZA S. PIETRO

S. PIETRO SOMALDI

Via dell' Angelo Custode

MARIA FORIS PORTAM

Via dei Giardini delle Mura

Via della Cavallerizza

Via Filungo

PIAZZA ANFITEATRO

PALAZZO GUINIGI

TORRE GUINIGI

Via Guinigi

PIAZZA MARIA FORIS PORTAM

Via Santa Croce

PIAZZA SAN FREDIANO

S. FREDIANO

SIDIS SUPERMARKET

Via Arnolfo Moroni

Via Fatinelli

Via Cesare Battisti

MUSEO DELLA CATTEDRALE

PIAZZA CURTATONE

Via S. Andrea

PIAZZA DEI SERVI

PIAZZA DEL COLLEGIO

V. Fontana

V.n Angeli

PIAZZA BERNARDINI

Via Filungo

DUOMO

PALAZZO PFANNER

V. del Moro

TORRE DELLE ORE

Via Roma

PIAZZA S. MARTINO

S. AGOSTINO

V. S. Lucia

PIAZZA S. SALVATORE

S. MICHELE IN FORO

S. GIOVANNI

PIAZZA S. AGOSTINO

V. Santa Giustina

V. Calderia

V. del Battistero

PIAZZA DEL GIGLIO

V. San Paolino

V. Beccheria

V. del Poggio

CASA PUCINI

$

PIAZZA NAPOLEONE

TEATRO DEL GIGLIO

V. San Giorgio

PIAZZA DEL PALAZZO DIPINTO

PIAZZA SANT' ALESSANDRO

TAXI

PALAZZO DUCALE

PORTA S. PIETRO

Via Galli Tassi

Via Vittorio Emanuele II

Via della Caserma

Via S. Giustina

Via dei Giardini delle Mura

Via S. Tommaso

S. ROMANO

PALAZZO MANSI

Via S. Paolino

PIAZZA MAGIONE

PIAZZA S. ROMANO

Via A. Carrara

PORTA S. DONATO

i

PIAZZALE SAN DONATO

TAXI

Via della Cittadella

PIAZZALE VERDI

PORTA S. ANNA

Pass. delle Mura Urbane

Viale Giosuè Carducci

TO VIAREGGIO (20KM), GENOA (195KM)

N

VG

0 ————— 200 meters
0 ————— 200 yards

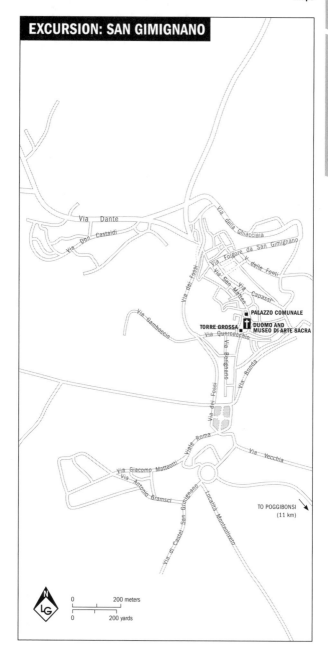

EXCURSION: SAN GIMIGNANO

Via Dante

Via Don Castaldi

Via della Ghiacciaia

Via Folgore da San Gimignano

V. delle Fonti

Via dei Fossi

Via San Matteo

Via Capassi

Via Gamboccio

PALAZZO COMUNALE

TORRE GROSSA

DUOMO AND MUSEO DI ARTE SACRA

Via Quercecchio

Via Berignano

Via Romba

Via dei Fossi

Viale Roma

Via Vecchia

Via Giacomo Matteotti

Via Antonio Gramsci

Via di Casoni San Gimideano

Località Montecchvetro

TO POGGIBONSI
(11 km)

0   200 meters

0   200 yards

Accommodations

The best way to get your money's worth in Florence is to travel in a small group, so if you're still hesitant to invite that slightly annoying friend with the buckteeth on this trip, remember that he could save you a fair deal of cash. Small groups can score gorgeous rooms in three-star hotels for the same price as a hostel, especially during the low season. Unfortunately, solo travelers with a fear of hostel showers are out of luck—singles in otherwise affordable hostels often cost almost as much as doubles. Those armed with flip flops and ready to brave the showers will find a few reputable hostels to choose from. If you're sticking around a little longer, consider commuting from a hostel outside the city, where you'll find better deals, cleaner air, and other travelers with similar priorities. Whatever you choose, you'll be glad to hear that prices drop significantly during the low season: you can save €10-20 per night when the city is less flooded with out-of-towners seeking beds. In our listings, we've stuck to high-season rates, so those of you traveling to Florence in February can silently gloat every time you read a price estimate and think about how much lower your rate will be.

Budget Accommodations

When it comes to accommodations, Florence doesn't have specific neighborhoods that are particularly less expensive than others, but like any city, heading farther out from the *centro* will lead you to cheaper places. So consider venturing north into San Marco or crossing the river into West Oltrarno if you're scrimpin'. There are at least a few cheap hostels just about everywhere, though, so you should be able to find a cheap bed. The best places fill up well in advance, so plan ahead.

THE DUOMO

While Florence is quite small, it's still expensive to stay right at its heart. There are a lot of options here, though none are super cheap. **Academy Hostel** is your best bet if you can book in advance. There are also many small hotels east and north of the Duomo that are surprisingly affordable considering their top-notch locations.

🞕 Academy Hostel   HOSTEL $$

V. Ricasoli 9

☎055 23 98 665; www.academyhostels.eu

Don't wait another minute to make a reservation at this hostel—with only 30 beds and the best value in the neighborhood, it's no surprise that Academy doesn't have many last-minute vacancies. The nightly "snack" of pasta and wine brings guests together, though the small plates mean that everyone will know if you're trying to turn this snack into a meal. Academy keeps clean with a lengthy lockout and laminated signs that say things like "We aim to keep this bathroom clean. Gentlemen: your aim will help. Stand closer—it's shorter than you think. Ladies, please remain seated for the entire performance." You'll find everything you need here: a stock of Italy guidebooks, large lockers, beds (not bunked!) with privacy screens, towels, a smoker-friendly balcony, and an awesome complimentary breakfast, which includes the best fruit salad we've ever tasted.

▶ 🕀 Less than a block north of the Duomo, on the left. *i* Breakfast included. Free Wi-Fi in reception. Complimentary pasta and wine "snack" 6:30pm. 🟊 Dorms €29-34. Credit card min. €150. 🕓 Reception 24hr. Lockout 11am-2pm.

Hotel Locanda Orchidea   HOTEL $$

V. Borgo degli Albizi 11

☎055 24 80 346; www.hotelorchideaflorence.it

For almost the same price as a bed in a bare-bones dorm elsewhere, you can get a spacious room at Locanda Orchidea. Rooms are adorned with paintings and have large, clean shared bathrooms. Amid the homey charm of tile floors, leather couches, and an overgrown terrace, you'd hardly believe you're just a few blocks from the bustling Duomo.

▶ ⚐ Take V. Proconsolo at the southeast edge of P. del Duomo and turn left onto Borgo degli Albizi. *i* Complimentary tea and coffee all day. Ⓢ Singles €30-60; doubles €50-80; triples €65-100; quads €75-120. Slight discount for stays over 2 nights. ⏰ Reception 8am-10pm.

Hotel Dalí   HOTEL $$

V. dell'Oriuolo 17

☎055 23 40 706; www.hoteldali.com

Located on V. dell'Oriuolo ("The Clock Road"), Hotel Dalí will persist in your memory not for its eccentric mustache but for the ornate wooden headboards on its pale orange beds. Simple rooms with rugs and stenciled walls overlook a small, verdant courtyard. Perhaps most surreal is Dalí's free parking in the middle of the Old City.

▶ ⚐ About a 5min. walk down V. dell'Oriuolo from the Duomo. Ⓢ Singles €40; doubles €65-70, with bath €80-85. Up to 20% discount on low-season rooms. Special offers listed online.   ⏰ Reception 24hr.

Hotel Casci   HOTEL $$$

V. Camillo Cavour 13

☎055 21 16 86; www.hotelcasci.com

This old Medici palace passed through the hands of composer Gioachino Rossini just a few centuries ago, but now one of the 24 unique rooms can be yours. At Casci you can find fresh fruit, eggs, toast, and homemade cakes, with modern amenities like cable TV and mini-fridges. The family rooms are a great deal for a small group.

▶ ⚐ Follow V. de' Martelli north of the Duomo to V. Camillo Cavour; Hotel Casci is on the right. *i* Breakfast and small lockers included. Free Wi-Fi. Ⓢ Singles €60-110; doubles €80-150; triples €110-190; quads €140-230. 10% discount for paying cash. Winter visitors get 1 free museum ticket for stays over 3 nights. ⏰ Reception 24hr.

Residenza Dei Pucci
B AND B $$$$

V. dei Pucci 9

☎055 28 18 86; www.residenzadeipucci.com

Each of the 12 doubles (and one panoramic suite) of this little bed and breakfast is different, but four-poster beds, glass-fronted armoires, and small balconies are common features. You can even bring the cereal, yogurt, and croissant to your room in hopes that a bribe of breakfast in bed will convince your traveling companions to hold your spot in line in the Duomo while you explore.

▶ 🏃 From north of the Duomo, follow V. Ricasoli and turn left onto V. dei Pucci. *i* Wi-Fi €10 per day. 💲 Doubles €80-150, superior €105-170; suite €120-250. €15 discount for single-occupancy doubles. 🕐 Reception 9am-8pm.

PIAZZA DELLA SIGNORIA

This area is the quintessence of convenience, but you'll pay for it with sky-high prices or fewer amenities. That said, it's prime real estate for a short stumble home or a couple nights of pretending you're filthy rich.

🗺 Florence Youth Hostel
HOSTEL $$

V. della Condotta 4

☎055 21 44 84; www.florence-youth-hostel.com

Roll out of bed and into the Uffizi—you can't get much more central than this. You may love the location during the day, but you'll be less of a fan at night when drunken student noise rises from the street. Here's what to do: down complimentary tea and coffee, (ET) phone home, and take advantage of the staff's uncommon willingness to give you advice about the city.

▶ 🏃 Coming from V. dei Calzaioli, the building is on the left. Florence Youth Hostel is on the top floor. *i* Wi-Fi, local calls and some international calls, maps, tea, and coffee included. No elevator. Breakfast M-Sa. 💲 Dorms €28; twins with bath €45; doubles €90; triples €105. Hot breakfast €2.50. 🕐 Reception 24hr.

Hotel Bretagna
HOTEL $$$$

Lungarno Corsini 6

☎055 28 96 18; www.hotelbretagna.net

Hotel Bretagna floods your senses in class from the moment you step inside with soft classical music, subtle incense, and a postcard-perfect balcony. The feast for the senses continues

Accommodations

with a literal feast in the palace-like breakfast room. Dream of ceiling frescoes in an unnecessarily large suite, or if you're frescoed out, the standard room's high ceilings are mercifully blank. Be sure to reserve a room with a corner bathtub or a view of the river.

▶ 🧭 Facing the river, it's 2 blocks right of Ponte Vecchio. ℹ Wi-Fi and breakfast included. Tell reception if you are arriving by car. [$] Singles €99-139; doubles €109-119. Prices vary by room and season, so check the website. ⏰ Reception 24hr.

Hostel Veronique/Alekin Hostel — HOSTEL $$

V. Porta Rossa 6, 2nd and 4th fl.
☎055 26 08 332

Be ready to explain yourself when you buzz for these two barebone hostels, because owner Alekin won't let just any old passerby into the building. Fewer rooms at Alekin Hostel (2nd fl.) mean less crowded bathrooms than in Hostel Veronique (4th fl.). The rooms here are all private, but what you're paying for a convenient place to crash.

▶ 🧭 Just north of Mercato Nuovo. ℹ Free Wi-Fi. [$] Private twins €34; doubles €67; triples €64; quads €78. Cash preferred. ⏰ Reception 24hr.

SANTA MARIA NOVELLA

As in most cities, there are plenty of budget hotels right next to the train station. If you roll into town late and are just looking for somewhere to crash, head straight to **Via Fiume.** The area between the station and the river offers mainly posh options; hostel-seekers should look in neighboring San Lorenzo. Whatever you seek, ignore the monstrous Majestic Hotel that is very visible from the train station—despite the building's valuable real estate, it is abandoned.

👍 Pensione La Scala — PENSIONE $$$$

V. della Scala 21
☎055 21 26 29

Bearded owner Gabriel, a stuffed crocodile, frescoed ceilings, and a nifty vintage radio (that sometimes works) set this quirky place apart from the generally yawn-worthy hotels in the area. With your room's abundant floorspace, you'll have space for a workout to burn off all that pasta, and you can shower in the full bath (so no one has to see your sweaty face afterwards).

▶ 🧭 Down from the train station, on the left. Look for the vertical Pensione sign; it's on the 1st floor. *i* All rooms with bath. $ Doubles €80-90; triples €120-135; quads €160-180. Cash preferred. ✇ Reception 24hr.

Hotel Consigli   HOTEL $$$$

Lungarno Amerigo Vespucci 50

☎055 21 41 72; www.hotelconsigli.com

The few extra steps it takes to get to Hotel Consigli are rewarded by a quieter area and an enormous rooftop terrace that overlooks the river. Small groups can score a 16th-century frescoed suite, though at this point you're probably wondering who doesn't casually offer old, original frescoes. In other news, Tolstoy stayed here, so you know they've done something right. And with the American consulate right next door, you're sure to be first in line for the airlift if Florence is invaded by zombies.

▶ ⚑ Follow the river west, just past the consulate on the right. *i* A/C. Wi-Fi, luggage storage, and breakfast included. $ Doubles €130-200; triples €170; family suite €130-170.   ✇ Reception 6am-midnight.

Desiree Hotel   HOTEL $$$

V. Fiume 20

☎055 23 82 382; www.desireehotel.com

Stained glass is common for the hotels in this building, but at the Desiree it has broken out like gorgeous colored-window chicken pox. Find your perfect combination of balcony, chandelier, big antique armoires, and floral bathroom tiling. Walking through the Christmas-colored hallways to the sunny mini balcony may confuse your sense of season, but a little holiday cheer never hurt anyone.

▶ ⚑ V. Fiume is parallel to the train station. *i* A/C. Breakfast and Wi-Fi included. $ Singles €60-70; doubles €75-100; triples €99-125; quads €115-150. ✇ Reception 24hr.

Hotel Serena   HOTEL $$$

V. Fiume 20

☎055 28 04 47; www.albergoserena.it

Hotel Serena is the standard hotel incarnate, give or take some stained-glass doors. Reasonable prices make this a practical option with no big surprises—the most stressful room choice you'll have to make is along the lines of "tiled floors or hardwood floors?"

▶ ⚑ From the train station, turn left onto V. Nazionale then left onto V. Fiume. *i* A/C. Breakfast and safes included. All rooms with bath. $ Singles €45-75; doubles €60-110; triples €105; quads €100-175. ✇ Reception 24hr.

Hotel Stella Mary

HOTEL $$$

V. Fiume 17

☎055 27 41 599; www.hotelstellamary.it

After a dizzying day of art, Hotel Stella Mary's institutional white walls and big windows (don't jump!) may be just what you need. You might have to dodge a crowd of students to get in, though, since the building shares an entrance with an Italian language school. Between the students and its location across from the station, this hotel isn't for the noise-sensitive.

▶ ⇆ Look for the McDonald's when you exit the front of the train station. V. Fiume is 1 street over in that direction, parallel to the station. *i* Breakfast included. All rooms with bath. Pay for plug-in internet. [$] Singles €60-70; doubles €70-83; triples €80-103. ⏰ Reception 24hr.

SAN LORENZO

Check out **Via Faenza** for San Lorenzo's primary hostel scene. Proximity to the train station and the cheap food at the **Mercato Centrale** make this neighborhood one of the best places to stay in Florence.

👍 Ostello Archi Rossi

HOSTEL $

V. Faenza 94r

☎055 29 08 04; www.hostelarchirossi.com

You'll have the best of times, you'll have the worst of times. The hostel's staff are sometimes too busy to care about your Wi-Fi difficulties or the miniature lake on your bathroom floor. But when you're strolling through the garden or past the graffitied walls gripping a free cappuccino and snacking on giant portions of pasta for a mere €2.50, your anger will melt away. Choose your room wisely—the lower the floor the better—to avoid the damp, overcrowded bathrooms on the upper floors. Lockers come with keys to keep out nosy roommates, but the luggage area is only under video surveillance. Despite its cons, this is definitely one of the best values in Florence, particularly for solo travelers on a budget.

▶ ⇆ From the train station, take V. Nazionale and turn left onto V. Faenza. *i* Breakfast included. Beer sold at desk. Wi-Fi available. Rooms are equipped with computers. [$] Dorms €21-27; singles €40. ⏰ Reception 6:30am-2am. Curfew 2am; some travelers report that if you ring the doorbell, the door will open regardless of the hour.

Accommodations

📋 Soggiorno Annamaria / Katti House   B AND B $$$$

V. Faenza 21

☎055 21 34 10; www.kattihouse.com

If you're traveling with friends and don't mind sharing queen-sized beds, don't hesitate to stay here. With exposed-beam ceilings, grandfather clocks, and an unusually enthusiastic staff, this bright bed and breakfast—which is split into Soggiorno Annamaria and Katti House—wants to be your home away from home. Plus, they keep it all in the family: the brother of the titular Annamaria puts his 30 years of culinary experience to use, serving local specialties in the on-site restaurant (*primi* €6-8, *secondi* €4-14; three-course meal €25-30).

▶ ⚓ On V. Faenza, look for the doorway with all the Let's Go stickers. *i* Breakfast of cappuccino, croissant, and *biscottini* included. A/C. Wi-Fi available only in Katti house, but those staying at Soggiorno Annamaria are welcome to use it. Ⓢ Soggiorno Annamaria singles €65-100. Katti House singles €75; doubles and triples €120-130.

Hotel Ester   HOTEL $$$$

Largo Alinari 15, 2nd fl.

☎055 28 09 52; www.roominflorence.com

Don't let the grimy stairs or flimsy-looking elevator of the building's shared entryway put you off of these clean, colorful rooms near the train station. Your feet will love the cool hardwood after a long day's trek, and the rest of your body will appreciate the kitchen, flatscreen TV, and air-conditioning. Inquire at reception, which is decorated with terrain maps of Italy, about special deals for larger groups.

▶ ⚓ From the train station, turn left at the McDonald's; Hotel Ester is about 1 block down on the right. Luna Rossa is across the street but shares Hotel Ester's reception. Ⓢ Mar-Oct doubles €75, with bath €90; Nov-Feb €55/60.

Holiday Rooms   HOTEL $$

V. Nazionale 22

☎055 28 50 84

Three rooms with double windows to keep out the street noise face V. Nazionale, while a fourth faces the courtyard with a view of monuments that casually peek over the back wall. Nothing says "holiday" like sunny-colored walls, flatscreen TVs, and computers (and nothing says "room" like the wooden armoires). You won't even need the communal kitchen thanks to free breakfast and the machine that dispenses hot drinks for only €0.50 each.

▶ Finding these aptly named 4 rooms is only slightly less difficult than the quest for the Holy Grail, but we've got you covered. On V. Nazionale, look for Hotel Nazionale on the right when walking away from the train station. Ring the bell to get in and climb the stairs until you see Holiday Rooms on the right. Enter Machia's on your left for reception. *i* A/C. Free Wi-Fi. [$] Singles €40-45; doubles €65-74.

Ostello Centrale Euro Students/Hostel Central HOSTEL $

V. Faenza 46r

☎055 41 44 54

Beware of cars when following the driveway entrance to this no-frills hostel. The beds are dorm-style without bunks, but what you gain in comfort you lose in floor space. The entrance is plastered with signs that read "No disturbing noise after 11"—you have to wonder if the owners were once the accidental audience to some travelers' tryst. There's something mystifying about this hostel: somehow, the tiny patio with potted plants lined up like a firing squad holds a certain charm.

▶ From the train station on V. Nazionale, take a right onto V. Faenza and look for the driveway with flags. [$] Dorms €20-22.

SAN MARCO

Staying in San Marco is convenience at its laziest for the greedy museum-goer. As you go farther north, San Marco gets increasingly quiet and residential, which is great for daytime peace of mind but eerie late at night.

Hostel Plus HOSTEL $

V. Santa Caterina d'Alessandria 15

☎055 46 28 934; www.plushostels.com

This chain hostel is better than chain smoking, chain mail, and maybe even daisy chains. The beastly gray building can feel empty without the tourist hordes, but this just means more room for you at the pool table, Turkish-style bath, gym, sauna, and tupperware-sized pool. When the place is crowded, be sure to bring your own lock, as the constant flux of people makes it easy for non-guests to walk in. Special offers include a pasta and wine dinner and all-you-can-eat breakfast combo (€10), day and night bike tours, and wine-tasting trips. Backpackers with a girly side will adore the pink all-female floor and hair straightener rental service. Pop into the rooftop terrace bar or the basement restaurant, where the disco ball doesn't care that no one is dancing.

▶ ♯ Follow V. Nazionale until it changes names. Hostel Plus is the big gray thing on your left soon after P. dell'Indipendenza. *i* Wi-Fi. Ⓢ Dorms €20-25. Ⓐ Reception 24hr. Walk-ins, come after noon to check availability.

David Inn   HOSTEL $$

V. Ricasoli 31

☎055 21 37 07; www.hostelfirenze.splinder.com

One of the few small hostels in Florence, the three rooms of David Inn sit on the top floor of a residential building and provide you with somewhere to sleep, but not much else. There's no common space except a few squishy couches against an orange wall, and the dorms are your basic bunk-bed situation. But the small hostel scene in town is fairly dire, so if Academy is full or too posh for your hosteling tastes, try David Inn.

▶ ♯ About 5min. north of the Duomo, on the right. It's the door with the funny pull knob doorbells. *i* Luggage storage. Wi-Fi. All-female room available. Cash only. Ⓢ Dorms €27. Ⓐ Reception 24hr.

Ostello Gallo d'Oro   HOSTEL $$

V. Camillo Cavour 104

☎055 55 22 964; www.ostellogallodoro.com

San Marco's other small hostel lies in the quiet northern part of town. Ensuite bathrooms mean you might stand a chance at the shower being free when you want it. A sign at the reception desk reads "No partying on the balcony," as if you could somehow fit both a beer and yourself out there.

▶ ♯ 5min. up V. Camillo Cavour from P. di San Marco, on the right. *i* Breakfast included. A/C. Wi-Fi. Room cleaning 10am-noon. Ⓢ Dorms €26-28; doubles €60; triples €96; quads €120. Ⓐ Reception 24hr.

Hotel Gioia   HOTEL $$$$

V. Camillo Cavour 25

☎055 28 28 04; www.hotelgioia.it

If you're hopeless at finding hostels tucked discreetly into shared buildings, then this hotel's video-monitored, private entry from the street will be your favorite kind of conspicuous. The 28 rooms here are reminiscent of an American chain hotel—they must've ordered the bedspreads from Holiday Inn's supplier. Four couches make up Gioia's social scene, unless the TV is on.

▶ ♯ Easy to find. It has its own door! *i* Breakfast included. Ⓢ Singles €95; doubles €140. Ⓐ Reception 24hr.

Accommodations

Hotel San Marco

HOTEL $$$

V. Camillo Cavour 50

☎055 28 18 51; www.hotelsanmarcofirenze.it

You pay dearly for location at this small hotel, but at least you get a wooden dining room and a fully equipped kitchen. If you're lucky, you can catch an Italian soap on the common TV.

▶ 🚏 Just past the Gran Caffè from the *piazza*. ℹ A/C. Wi-Fi. [$] Singles €50; doubles €80. ⏰ Reception 24hr.

Hotel Benvenuti

HOTEL $$$

V. Camillo Cavour 112

☎055 57 21 41; www.benvenutihotel.it

This hotel is nothing exceptional—just plenty of rooms and in the quiet northern part of San Marco. Expect quite a few common sitting rooms, breakfast in a yellow and white dining room, and bedspreads that could get second jobs as tablecloths.

▶ 🚏 Walk north from P. di San Marco on V. Camillo Cavour. Pay attention to the doorbells on the right side as you near the end of V. Camillo Cavour. ℹ Breakfast included. [$] High-season singles around €64; doubles around €74. ⏰ Reception 24hr.

SANTA CROCE

Looking to minimize the stumble home after a night out? Unfortunately, you're out of luck. Affordable accommodations in Santa Croce are difficult to come by, so you may be better off looking in the adjacent Duomo neighborhood and just walking from there.

Hotel Arizona

HOTEL $$$$

V. Luigi Carlo Farini 2

☎055 24 53 21; www.arizonahotel.it

If you're studying at the university and your parents come to visit, this is a good place to put them; otherwise, you'll do better in another neighborhood. Rooms feature mini-fridges and often have tables or small balconies overlooking the street.

▶ 🚏 To the right of the synagogue, on the corner. ℹ Free Wi-Fi. [$] Singles from €102; quads €145. Discounts for stays over 4 nights. ⏰ Reception 24hr.

Hotel Ariston

HOTEL $$$

V. Fiesolana 40

☎055 24 76 980; www.hotelaristonfirenze.it

Ariston has two things to offer: space and convenience. Well, that and a mini plaster David (in case you haven't seen enough of that guy around Florence already). If you're desperate for a place to crash in Santa Croce, Ariston will do, but it's not the most affordable option in the city.

▶ ✠ Look for the neon hotel sign from the intersection with V. Pietrapiana. *i* Breakfast included. Free Wi-Fi. Ⓢ Singles from €45; high-season doubles €60-70. ⏰ Reception 8am-9pm.

WEST OLTRARNO

The hostels on this side of the river aren't significantly cheaper than more centrally located ones; they're best if you intend to spend the majority of your time in West Oltrarno.

Hostel Santa Monaca   HOSTEL $

V. Santa Monaca 6

☎055 26 83 38; www.ostello.it

This former monastery is massive enough to feature a 22-bunk dorm room. Follow the laminated, rainbow WordArt signs to your room. The simple kitchen, small balcony, and picnic-tabled common room are all kept clean during a strict lockout. Perks include free Wi-Fi, a refrigerator, and satellite TV in the common room. If you're not a light packer, don't expect your bag to fit into the lockers. The "kitchen" is poorly equipped and can get overcrowded during meals, but the proximity to P. Santo Spirito means you have plenty of dinner and after-dinner options nearby, as long as you manage to stumble back before the 2am curfew. This place is perfect

Accommodations

The Emperor's New Retirement Home

You probably don't spend much of your free time visiting retirement homes. So as you flit around Florence, keep in mind that the city was originally established in 59 CE as a retirement home for Caesar and his veteran troops. The average Roman soldier retired around age 40, when the time was just about ripe to buy that shiny new leather tunic and saddle. In their last conquest, these old timers named this city *Conolia Florentice,* or the Flourishing Colony. Though it's questionable how much these early residents flourished after settling here, the city they founded hasn't done too badly for itself.

for people who intend to spend the day without frequent trips back to the hostel.

▶ ⚡ From P. Santo Spirito, turn right onto V. Sant'Agostino and left onto V. Santa Monaca. *i* Free Wi-Fi. Ⓢ Dorms €18-21. Laundry €6.50 per 6kg. 🕐 Reception 6am-2am. Curfew 2am. Lockout 10am-2pm.

Soggiorno Pitti   HOSTEL, HOTEL $
Palazzo Pitti 8
☎055 39 21 483; www.soggiornopitti.com

Soggiorno Pitti is a posh hotel with a hostel alter ego. You won't find their handful of dorm beds on the website—that might scare off customers looking for majestic doubles with a view of the *piazza,* which go for a hefty price. In the affordable range, you may have to deal with tiny stairs and shared bathrooms, but at least you've got the best location in West Oltrano and a big common room TV.

▶ ⚡ Across the street from Palazzo Pitti. Ⓢ Dorms €20; singles with bath from €45; doubles with bath €70-100. Cash only. 🕐 Reception 8am-11pm.

Youth Firenze 2000 Bed and Breakfast   B AND B $$$
Viale Raffaello Sanzio 16
☎055 23 06 392; www.cheap-hotel-florence.com

This bed and breakfast is anything but central, and by "breakfast" they mean sweet jam and fruit. It's on a busy road far from the main drag, but if you want to be somewhere more residential, Youth Firenze is about as local as it gets.

▶ ⚡ From Santa Maria Novella train station, board the #12 bus and ask for the 1st stop in Viale Raffaello Sanzio. Ⓢ Doubles with bath €60. Credit card €60 min. 🕐 Reception 7am-7:30pm.

EAST OLTRARNO

Unless you have a reason to stay in this neighborhood, you might as well book a room at a nice bed and breakfast a few kilometers away in Bagno a Ripoli. Either way, you'll still have to take a bus to reach the sights.

Plus Camping Michelangelo   CAMPING $
Viale Michelangelo 80
☎055 68 11 977; www.camping.it

Camping sure sounds nice, doesn't it? A bit of the great outdoors, some greenery, roughing it a little? Don't be fooled. Whether you're packing a tent or renting a bungalow, this campsite has all the appeal of the neighboring Piazzale Michelangelo—which is to say, of a parking lot. The bungalows sleep two or three in bunk beds. You have to share a key, and there's no locker in the tent, so we don't recommend going halfsies on one with a stranger. The bathroom facility at the top of the hill is akin to the locker room at a large gym, Wi-Fi is expensive and limited, and the cafe is your only option for dinner that doesn't require a good walk. You'll only see Florence from a distance as a stunning view. Still, the low prices and relative isolation mean a crowd of other cheap travelers are always hanging around the outdoor bar, and for a small group the price couldn't get much better.

▶ To the left of Piazzale Michelangelo, stay on the left side of the road and look for a small sign with a tent on it next to a steep downward path. Alternatively, take bus #12 to the Camping stop. *i* Safe deposit boxes for rent at reception. Ⓢ 2-bed tents €29; 3-bed €36. Reception 24hr.

Villa Alle Rampe   B AND B $$$

P. Francesco Ferrucci 6/7

☎055 68 00 131; www.villaallerampe.com

If you have reason to be staying way over in East Oltrarno, the small and modern Villa Alle Rampe should do just fine. The rooms feel like an Ikea catalogue, there's a small garden, and you're just off the river.

▶ Straight ahead from Ponte San Niccolò, across the street from James Joyce Pub. *i* Wi-Fi included. Ⓢ Singles €60-75; doubles €70-100.

Sights

This section can be summed up in a single word: Renaissance.
Part of being in Florence is reaching the day when you've officially seen more of Jesus's face than your own mother's. You may
be surprised by just how few Renaissance artists stray from the
biblical theme, but they'll still manage to wow you again and
again. If you think the religious theme means paintings of stern
guys in robes, check out any rendition of Judgment Day, in which
humans are skewered, devoured, or burned according to the hor-
rifically inventive imaginings of the artists' twisted minds. Florence's architecturally masterful churches and fancy palaces attest
to an age when the only people making it into the handwritten
history books were religious authorities, the absurdly rich, and
the artists they commissioned. Because the art collection is so
vast, attempting to see too much too quickly will leave you with
nothing but a devalued mush of crucifixes and semi-attractive
women. It's best to choose a few select spots and take your time.
When you've had enough Medici and Michelangelo for one day,
there are a handful of unusual spots that aren't rooted in the 16th
century. You can also check out www.firenzeturismo.it for information regarding current expositions, festivals, and other events
in Florence.

Budget Sights

With so many sights, Florence can be a little overwhelming for your eyes—and very overwhelming for your wallet. Luckily, students and EU citizens under 26 often get discounted admission to museums, so make sure to bring your ID. Otherwise, most tourists bump into or trample over many of Florence's famous free sights without even knowing it. On your way to the Uffizi, you'll run into the Duomo, Piazza della Repubblica, and Piazza della Signoria; crossing over the Arno, you'll accidentally get the chance to marvel at Ponte Vecchio; and climbing up to Piazzale Michelangelo, you'll get to see yet another *David* replica. For the best free sight of all, take your eyes off *David's* beautiful body and turn around to see what your calves really paid for.

THE DUOMO

The Duomo-related sights (the church and its complex) are pretty much the main event in this neighborhood.

Duomo   CHURCH

P. del Duomo

☎055 23 02 885; www.operaduomo.firenze.it

Construction of Florence's Duomo began before anyone had come up with a solution to actually build and support the signature red dome that now pokes its head above the city. A man named **Filippo Brunelleschi** claimed he could build the largest and tallest dome ever made, and would do so without scaffolding. Though most called him a lunatic, he won the dome's commission in a contest without ever revealing how he actually planned to build it. Somehow, he came through in one of the greatest triumphs of Renaissance architecture. Just as beautiful as the dome is the shock of pink and green laced into the Duomo's stunning marble facade. Most tourists don't realize, though, that the facade was left unfinished until the 19th century (last Thursday by Florentine standards). The line to enter the free interior advances quite swiftly. Unfortunately, all the Duomo's artwork has been moved to the Museo Opera complex (see below), and to get a real view of the Duomo fresco you'll need to pay for the separate climbing entrance. Still, the 24hr. clock by **Paolo Uccello** that runs counter-clockwise is worth a look, and if you don't mind odd-smelling spaces, you

Sights

can take the stairs in the middle of the church's floor down to the basement and pay €3 to see the archeological remnants of the Duomo's previous site.

▶ ✝ Come on, you can't miss it. *i* Audio tour available in English. Ⓢ Free. Archeological site €3. Audio tour €5, students and under 18 €3.50. Ⓞ Open M-W 10am-5pm, Th 10am-4pm, F-Sa 10am-5pm. Holidays open 1:30-4:45pm. 1st Sa each month open 10am-3:30pm.

Campanile and Dome   CHURCH

P. del Duomo

☎055 23 02 885; www.operaduomo.firenze.it

Endless lines not tiring enough? Try climbing hundreds of stone steps! The Campanile's 414 steps are steep, not too crowded, and lead to a view of the Duomo's exterior. The Duomo's 463 are less strenuous, wider, and have a separate exit path, but their best feature is that they lead right past the bright Judgment Day fresco inside the dome. (How 16th-century painters Giorgio Vasari and Federico Zuccari managed to paint better 340 ft. above ground than most people can in a luxury studio, we really don't know.) Both climbs offer worthwhile views of Florence and the surrounding hills. But if you're going to do that corny thing from the movies and meet your lover on top of the Duomo, make sure you settle on whether to meet at the dome or the tower. Otherwise, you might be staging your reunion via shouting and Semaphore flags.

▶ ✝ Enter the dome from the north side of the round part of the Duomo. Enter the Campanile at the base of the big tower. *i* Not for the out-of-shape. Ⓢ Dome €8. Campanile €6. Tour of the dome and the cathedral's terraces €15. Ⓞ Dome open M-F 8:30am-6:20pm, Sa 8:30am-5pm. Campanile open daily 8:30am-6:50pm.

Museo Opera di Santa Maria del Fiore   MUSEUM

P. del Duomo

☎055 23 02 885; www.operaduomo.firenze.it

If the Duomo seemed a little empty to you, that's because all the art was moved here. Thankfully, this means an escape from the Duomo's crowds and a chance to get up-close and personal with some big-name artwork. Unlike many church museums, this one doesn't fade into a blur of chipped noses and column fragments. Instead, Donatello's *Maddalena* successfully dresses herself using nothing but her own hair, and *Mary of the Glass Eyes* makes up for her lack of pupils with her excessive creepiness. Unfortunately for him (and fortunately for you), you'll

Sights

What Not to Wear

See that strip of naked brick around the base of the Duomo? As you might have guessed, plans for the cathedral included decoration that would cover this portion of the structure. In 1506, **Baccio d'Agnolo,** a talented young woodcarver, won the commission to complete this section of the cathedral. Unfortunately, only one side of the dome's octagonal base was covered with his design before Michelangelo dubbed it a "cage for crickets" and shut down construction. At least d'Agnolo was saved the acid comments Mickey G reserved for his own apprentice, **Bartolomeo Ammannati.** Upon viewing the Neptune Fountain Ammannati had constructed for the P. della Signoria, Michelangelo is rumored to have said to his pupil, "What a beautiful piece of marble you have ruined." Who knew *David's* daddy was the Simon Cowell of the Renaissance?

also find Michelangelo's *Pietà* here, even though the artist had intended it for his own tomb. Get a good look at Nicodemus—his features are sculpted to resemble the sculptor's own. On the second floor, models and sketches of the Duomo detail the long genesis of its 19th-century facade, displayed alongside the fixed pulleys and hoists used to construct Brunelleschi's dome.

▶ On the south side of the Duomo. *i* Most texts in Italian, but the important ones are also in English. Ⓢ €6. Audio tour €3.50. Open M-Sa 9am-6:50pm, Su 9am-1pm.

Baptistery of San Giovanni   MUSEUM

P. del Duomo

☎055 23 02 885; www.operaduomo.firenze.it

Though there's little else to see besides the Baptistery's magnificent doors, the mosaic ceiling could keep you staring upward until your neck gets stuck that way. Judgment Day scenes separated by columns on a sparkly gold background surround a massive Jesus, whose awkwardly shaped greenish toes dangle over the edge of a decorated circle. Until the 19th century, his stern visage presided over the baptism of Florence's infants, including **Dante.**

▶ The octagonal building next to the Duomo. Ⓢ €4. Open high season M-W 12:15-6:30pm, Th-Sa 12:15-10:30pm, Su 8:30am-1:30pm; low season M-Sa 12:15-6:30pm, Su 8:30am-1:30pm. 1st Sa of every month open 8:30am-1:30pm.

Sights

Cut to the Chase

If there's one thing that can ruin the experience of seeing Florence's amazing art, it's long lines. Fortunately, the wait is totally avoidable. Avoid spending your whole trip in a sweaty queue by making a reservation beforehand. You can do so online, over the phone, or in person for both the Uffizi and the Accademia. Booking online is the priciest option since you'll pay at least a €4 reservation fee upfront. If you're staying in a hotel, ask your hotelier to book for you, generally at no extra cost. The best option is to call the Florence Museums telephone booking center at ☎055 29 48 83. With a reservation booking number in hand, you'll be ready to jump the line at both museums—definitely worth the extra €4 you'll pay when you purchase your ticket at the "reservations only" window. And, if it turns out there is no line when you arrive, you won't have paid any upfront reservation fee, so you can buy an unreserved ticket at the normal price.

PIAZZA DELLA SIGNORIA

Piazza della Signoria is one of the most beautiful parts of Florence. Home to the city's most famous museum, the **Uffizi Gallery,** the area also holds innumerable noteworthy outdoor spaces from the **Ponte Vecchio** to the **Loggia.**

🏛 Uffizi Gallery   MUSEUM

Piazzale degli Uffizi 6

☎055 23 88 651; www.firenzemusei.it

Welcome to the Uffizi. The first thing you should know about this museum is that Michelangelo's *David* is not here—he's on the other side of town, in the Accademia. Also, the *Mona Lisa* is in France, and de Nile ain't just a river in Egypt.

You're going to wait in line for what seems like an eternity. Consider passing the time by drawing terribly unflattering portraits of the people around you and trying to sell them for a euro. Alternatively, attempt to recreate Venus's hairstyle, guess the nationality of the others waiting in line, or convince everyone that you are the reincarnation of Botticelli and should be getting in for free.

If you're looking for an art history lesson, don't expect to find one in this listing. You won't find one in the galleries' texts either: although the explanatory panels are in both Italian and English, they're not hugely informative. Your best bet is to take an audio tour (€5.50) or to stick with *Let's Go.* The Uffizi's rooms are numbered; look to the lintel of the doorway to figure out what room you're in.

Start the Uffizi from the top. Don't crumple up your ticket at the bottom of your bag because, after climbing two flights of the Uffizi's grand staircase, you'll be asked to flash your *biglietto* once more. At this point, you're standing in an enormous hallway lined with statues and frescoed within an inch of its life.

Room 1 is on your right, but you can't enter. **Room 2** begins the long parade of Jesuses that you'll be visiting today. **Rooms 3-4** are particularly gilded. In Martini's *Annunciation,* Gabriel literally spits some Latin at Mary, who responds with the mother of all icy stares.

In **Room 6,** take some time with Fra Angelico's fun *Scenes From the Lives of Hermits.* Who knew hermits could be so social? If you're with a friend, try narrating some of the little vignettes or see if you can identify which clusters of hermits match the following made-up titles:

"And if you buy this one now, you'll get a second miniature stone FREE!"

"Not dead yet!"

"It rubs the lotion on its skin."

"The lion sleeps tonight."

"Psychiatric advice, five cents please."

"Questionably Appropriate Activities With Animals"

Room 8 is all about Fra Filippino Lippi. In the center of the room, his two-sided panel of a rather homely couple staring longingly at one another gives confirmation that even ugly people can find love.

Our second big-name artist is in **Room 9.** On your left, the seven virtues—which woman is which?—are lined up like dating show contestants, all painted by Pollaiolo. Well, all except for *Fortitude,* on the left. She is one of the earliest documented works by his student, a fellow by the name of Botticelli.

Rooms 10-14 are the main event. Where there be crowds and benches, there be the postcard works. Not that we need to tell you this, but Botticelli's *The Birth of Venus* is on the left— that's right, behind all those people. Push your way to the front to enjoy all the little details that don't come across in the coffee mug and mousepad reproductions, like the gold trim on the trees; the detail of the fabrics; the luminous, sleepy expression;

and the weave Venus stole off Rapunzel. Look to the opposite side of the room for a big triptych with some seriously wonky perspective courtesy of Hugo Van Der Goes.

Room 15 is another example of the student surpassing the teacher. Examine the painting by Andrea del Verrochio across the room on the right. Several of the painting's figures—it is still contested which ones specifically—were painted by his student, Leonardo da Vinci. Maybe you've heard of him? The two paintings to the left are fully Leonardo's.

Odds are, you're going to start speeding up at this point, so to keep pace, you might want to take a break at the **cafeteria**—go out into the main hallway and follow the signs. This is your typical overpriced museum cafe, give or take a balcony view of the Palazzo Vecchio. Take some snacks with you or buy an espresso at the bar (stand outside to avoid the pricey table service) and refresh your brain.

Right then—where were we? **Room 19** has Pietro di Cosimo's depiction of Perseus tackling Andromeda, a monster with a serious under-bite. If you're getting sick of Catholicism, skedaddle to **Room 20** to view a couple rare portraits of Martin Luther. Ninety-five theses, three chins. **Room 22** has an Andrea Mantegna triptych on the right with a curved center panel that makes it seem 3D. **Room 25** proves that Salome knew how to get a head.

There's a seriously ginormous baby in **Room 29's** Parmigianino painting, which is called *Madonna of the Long Neck* for obvious reasons. A painting of a woman bathing hangs on the right wall of **Room 31.** What do you look at first? Don't be shy, we know you're eyeing her luscious breasts. And then you probably look at her legs and thighs, and perhaps the rest of her. And then, if you haven't yet turned away, maybe you will notice King David in the top left corner. The woman is Bathsheba, and Brusasorci's painting is remarkable for making the viewer mimic the intensity of David's ogling gaze.

Leda and the swan have finally gotten a room—**Room 32** to be exact. On the left in **Room 35** is a *Massacre of the Innocents* by Daniele Ricciarelli. Despite the pile of dead babies in this painting, *Let's Go* does not condone the making of dead baby jokes.

Finally, you'll reach the **Room of Niobe,** an impressive palatial space full of statues posed as if frozen in horror. These statues were discovered in the Villa Medici gardens and are supposed to be the unfortunate children of Niobe about to be slain by the gods as revenge for their mother's pride in her progeny.

If you have time and energy left at this point, the last few rooms are refreshingly different 18th-century stuff. If you don't, no one has to know. Congratulations on finishing the Uffizi; now you can go act like a Botticelli expert, even if the only thing you remember is Venus's terrible haircut.

▶ ⚲ It's the long narrow part of P. della Signoria. Enter (or stand in line) on the left, reserve tickets on the right. To avoid the lines without paying for a reservation, arrive late in the day, when your time in the museum will be limited by closing. *i* Expect to wait 2-3hr. to enter. Ⓢ €10, EU citizens ages 18-25 €5, EU citizens under 18 and over 65 and the disabled free. €4 reservation fee. Audio tour €5.50. ⏰ Open Tu-Su 8:50am-6:35pm.

🖾 The Bargello   MUSEUM
V. del Proconsolo 4
☎055 23 88 606; www.firenzemusei.it

For a change of pace, the Bargello offers a nice dose of 19th-century eclecticism. Though you'd never know it from the inside, the Bargello was once a brutal prison. The statues here seem to know this—most are mid-kill, mid-struggle, or mid-sprint.

In the **courtyard,** once the site of public executions, be sure to look up. The ceiling frescoes are much more interesting than the old crest collection along the walls. Meanwhile, the meanest-looking fish you've ever seen awaits you to the left of the entrance, and several statues remain from an old fountain in which the three figures compete for who can place their spigot in the most suggestive location. In truly eclectic style, there's also a huge cannon and some Lion Kings from before Disney made them cool.

Pass the (very *Narnia*) lions to find a hall full of pagan (not so *Narnia*) sculptures such as Adonis and Bacchus as well as Musticci's *Madonna and Child.* Of all Florence's renditions, Musticci's is perhaps the most touching, human, and just plain adorable.

The courtyard stairs bring you to some stone fowl and a series of numbered galleries. **Room 4** is evidence of what you can make out of a little elephant tusk and a lot of skill—the minutely carved ivories range from tiny portraits to a giant chessboard. **Room 6** holds a huge collection of Maiolica, an earthenware pottery that is decorated before being glazed. **Room 8** will introduce you to the Ninja Turtle you know the least. This *Salone di Donatello* was designed for the artist's 500th birthday in 1887, and has remained unchanged ever since.

Room 9 contains probably the only Arabic script you'll see in Tuscany. This chamber is devoted to Islamic ceramics and textiles. **Room 10** is a true Victorian *Wunderkammer* (wonder-cabinet). There's the case of pipes, the case of bottles, and the collection of keys and locks. There are even table settings, scientific instruments, metalwork, jewelry, and that 17th-century spork you've been missing. On the third floor, check out the fantastic tiny bronzes in **Room 15. Room 13's** glazed terra cotta in blues, greens, and yellows creates a color scheme that will make you feel as if you've been sucked into a game of *Oregon Trail*.

▶ ⚑ Behind the Palazzo Vecchio. Ⓢ €7, EU citizens ages 18-25 €3.50, EU citizens under 18 and over 65 free. Cash only. ⏰ Open daily 8:15am-4:50pm. Last entry 4:20pm. Closed 2nd and 4th M and 1st, 3rd, and 5th Su each month.

Sexiest Artwork Alive

Italy has more than its fair share of beautiful people—both real and imaginary. Of course, no one wants to end up creepily falling in love with a statue, but here are *Let's Go's* picks for the five sexiest artworks in Florence.

5. **Giambologna's Mercury.** He may not have the six-pack abs or bulging biceps of Hercules, but you've got to admit that this is a messenger god with poise. He's got a pretty cute butt, too. Ogle him at the **Bargello.**

4. **Cristofano Allori's Judith.** Judith would be higher up on our list if she wasn't holding a severed head. Still, with her sultry gaze, she's downright sexy. Word has it Allori modeled Judith after his mistress and the head after himself. Ogle her at the **Palazzo Pitti.**

3. **Venus de' Medici.** Exiled from Rome by Pope Innocent XI in 1677 (perhaps because her provocative nudity was making him feel less than innocent), this lovely lady has been a famously titillating highlight of European tours ever since. Ogle her at the **Uffizi.**

2. **Botticelli's Venus.** It's hard not to be dazzled by this early bloomer. (Really, who comes out of the womb with hair like that?) Ogle her at the **Uffizi.**

1. **Michelangelo's David.** This choice is obvious but unavoidable. The symbol of Renaissance humanism, *David* oozes with the kind of charisma only an icon of human perfection can. He beats out Venus for our number one spot thanks to being in three dimensions rather than two. Ogle him at the **Accademia.**

Piazza Della Signoria   PIAZZA

P. della Signoria is the place to go if you want to see sculptures without the museum prices. The **Loggia,** a portico full of statues that's as legit as any room in the Uffizi, is free. Don't be fooled by the *David* in front of the **Palazzo Vecchio**—the real deal is in the **Accademia.** The reproduction in the *piazza* stands just as proud as the original did when he was installed in this exact location to celebrate Florence's dominance over Tuscany. The Loggia does one-up the Accademia by being the true home of Giambologna's spiraling **Rape of the Sabine Women.** To the left of the *David* is a giant fountain that Michelangelo despised so much that he called it a waste of perfectly good marble. This bustling daytime *piazza* full of tour groups, art students sketching, and street musicians gets calmer and more pleasant in the evenings as music spills out of the square's restaurants.

▶ ⚜ This is the main *piazza* north of the Uffizi.

Ponte Vecchio   BRIDGE

Looking for El Dorado? Here it is. On the Ponte Vecchio, the streets are paved with gold! And that gold is in the tons of gold shops that line this bustling bridge. It has been called the "old" bridge for, oh, 400 years or so, ever since the Florentines built a second bridge over the Arno and had to find a way to distinguish this one from their new *ponte.* When the Nazis evacuated Florence, Ponte Vecchio was the only bridge they didn't destroy. Come on a weekend afternoon and you are guaranteed to be in the wedding photos of at least half a dozen bridal parties. Visit at night for a romantic view of the river—and of other couples seeking the same.

▶ ⚜ From the Uffizi, walk to the river. It's the one with the shops on it.

Piazza della Repubblica   PIAZZA

For hundreds of years, this was the sight of the walled Jewish Ghetto, but when Florence's Jewish population was finally permitted to live and work elsewhere in 1888, the Ghetto was razed and paved over to create this spacious *piazza.* Now it's just another place to hang out, featuring a carousel (€2) and street performers. The restaurants surrounding the square are pricey, but their live music drifts into the open space for all to enjoy. Head to the northwest corner of the *piazza* where there is a large raised map of the city with streets labeled in Braille.

Sights

Evenings in P. della Repubblica are more upbeat than in the more subdued P. della Signoria.

▶ From P. della Signoria walk north up V. del Calzaioli and turn left on V. Speziali

Palazzo Vecchio

MUSEUM

P. della Signoria

☎055 27 68 465

The real draw here is that it's the only museum you can visit post-*aperitivo.* As you proceed through the palace, framed paintings on the ceilings and walls might make you feel like you're trapped in a fine-art Rubiks cube, and the fact that the finest paintings are on the ceiling takes a toll on your strained neck. Not that you'll know what you're looking at—explanatory panels are as rare here as tour groups of wallabies. Just enjoy the overall beauty. And keep your eyes peeled for the man with long, droopy whiskers like Jar Jar Binx that appears all over the walls and ceilings throughout the palace. Some of the highlights are the Room of the 500s, which features worryingly aggressive statues for a room that used to hold a political council; a fleur-de-lis room that might as well have belonged to Louis XIV; and a map room walled with yellowing maps of Italy. The palace also has some impressive views: the **Salon of Leo X** provides a great photo op of the city and the surrounding hills, and the **Sala dei Gigli** boasts a spectacular view of the Duomo. Finally, don't forget to call ahead and book a free Renaissance reenactment!

▶ The huge building in P. della Signoria. *i* Activities and tours with costumed actors available; call for times. $ €6, ages 18-25 and over 65 €4.50. Tours free if requested at time of ticket purchase. ⏰ Open M-W 9am-midnight, Th 9am-2pm, F-Su 9am-midnight.

Casa di Dante

MUSEUM

V. Santa Margherita 4

☎055 21 94 16; www.museocasadidante.it

If you want to read about Dante from a wall instead of a book, this is the place for you. It isn't really Dante's house; it's a reconstruction of how Dante's house probably looked in the place his house probably was, with a few artifacts from Dante's time that have no specific connection to him. The slow-paced historical panels are easy to tune out—but if you do, there's really nothing left. If this place were free, we'd say why not. But we can't in good conscience send you to pay €4 for a kitschy giftshop and a Dante-esque robe.

▶ ⚑ On the corner of V. Dante Alighieri and V. Santa Margherita; it's very well marked. Ⓢ €4, under 6 free—but they won't get anything from it at all. Cash only. 🕑 Open Apr-Sept daily 10am-6pm; Oct-Mar Tu-Su 10am-5pm.

SANTA MARIA NOVELLA

Clustered around some notable churches, you'll find a few more modern museum collections here, like photography and shoes. These can provide a much-needed balance to all the Jesuses. For an additional off-beat option, check out the **Farmaceutica di Santa Maria Novella** (see **Shopping**).

🖾 Museo di Ferragamo   MUSEUM

P. Santa Trinita 5r

☎055 33 60 456; www.museoferragamo.it

Ferragamo was like the Leonardo da Vinci of shoes: he brought anatomy, chemistry, and engineering into the creation of footwear. The shoe molds of famous people might make you feel like Bigfoot, and Ferragamo's elegant designs may make your own shoes feel clunky and out-of-place. But you don't have to be Carrie Bradshaw to appreciate a fashion and culture exhibit as thoughtfully assembled as this one, which includes video and painting. The gift shop is surprisingly tiny, but check out the real Ferragamo store upstairs to ogle shoes you can't possibly afford.

▶ ⚑ Enter at P. Santa Trinita on the side of the building that faces away from the river. 𝒊 Ticket proceeds fund scholarships for young shoe designers. 1st and 2nd rooms are permanent; the rest of the exhibits change annually. Ⓢ €5, under 10 and over 65 free. 🕑 Open M 10am-6pm, W-Su 10am-6pm. Closed Su in Aug.

Palazzo Strozzi   MUSEUM, PALAZZO

P. degli Strozzi

☎055 27 76 461; www.palazzostrozzi.org

While this may seem like yet another old palace, no more impressive than any of the others, it isn't the seen-one-seen-'em-all Renaissance decor that makes Palazzo Strozzi worth visiting. The **Center for Contemporary Culture Strozzina,** which produces recent and contemporary art exhibits in the palace's halls, is the main draw here. To give you an idea, the likes of Dalí, Miró, and Picasso recently graced these halls, as did an exhibition on

5 Ways to Survive Art Museums

Woe is you—you've accidentally befriended (or worse, started dating) an artsy type. As they gush and stare riveted at the walls, you're checking your watch for the 56th time. Never fear! Here's a quick list to help you avoid getting crushed by the incredible weight of your own boredom:

1. Frescoes are a race against time to paint everything before the plaster dries—try and guess which area the painter was on when he started running out of time.

2. Pretend to be a statue. Stare uncomfortably intensely at everyone that enters. If reproached, claim you are just trying to relate to the artwork.

3. In museums that allow cameras, take pictures only of one specific thing, like noses.

4. Lay down across the whole span of possible seating and close your eyes. When the museum proctor asks you to stop, open your eyes widely and tell them you just had an art-coma epiphany, and have now attained nirvana. Extra credit if you seamlessly segue into singing "Smells Like Teen Spirit."

5. Walk over to whatever painting your friends are looking at and pretend to be their tour guide. See how many other visitors you can get to eavesdrop on your extensive knowledge of how Leonardo, Raphael, Donatello, and Michelangelo had a secret society with a fighting turtle as its symbol, or how Michelangelo's *David* is actually a self-portrait from the waist down.

Sights

social media. The programming changes regularly, so check the website or stop by if you want to shake a little 21st century into Florence's 15th-century aesthetic. Free events often take place on Thursday evenings.

▶ ♯ West of P. della Repubblica. *i* Prices and hours vary; check website for details.

Basilica di Santa Maria Novella   CHURCH
P. Santa Maria Novella
☎055 21 59 18; www.chiesasantamarianovella.it

If you're only going to bother with one of the non-Duomo churches, consider making it this one. Between the checkered floor and plethora of 3D figures, this church could be a giant's chessboard, and in the morning or early evening, sunlight streaming through the stained glass may remind you of last night's disco. Upon entering the church, you'll see a fresco of God doing the *Titanic* pose with Jesus on the cross. Do you notice anything strange about this picture? If God is standing on that back platform, how could he be leaning far enough forward to be touching Jesus in the front? Rather than believe that Masaccio could have made such a salient perspective error, some art historians argue that this is symbolic of God's capacity to be everywhere at once. Cappella Strozzi on the left has a sadly faded fresco of Purgatory (inspired by Dante), where goblins, centaurs, and less familiar mythological figures like the man-dove hide or torture people. If the frescoes are too much for you, check out the giftshop postcards for bite-sized morsels.

▶ 🧭 Just south of the train station; you can't miss it. Enter through the P. Santa Maria Novella entrance. $ €3.50; over 65, visitors with disabilities, and priests free. Audio tour €1. ⏰ Open M-Th 9am-5:30pm, F 11am-5:30pm, Sa 9am-5pm, Su and religious holidays 1-5pm.

Museo Nazionale Alinari della Fotografia MUSEUM

P. Santa Maria Novella 14A

☎055 21 63 10; www.alinarifondazione.it

Despite the somewhat ambiguous name, this is not just a museum *of* photography, but a museum *about* photography. This means you can walk a giant roll of film like a red carpet through a hall of cameras from different time periods. Ornate albums accompany a fascinating range of pictures of everything from camels to early 19th-century Florence to an albino sword swallower. Flip through 3D binocular images, or feel the tactile versions of some photographs that have things like wigs attached to render them accessible to the blind. Check if there's a temporary exhibit—we attended one on the history of photographic controversies that was awesomely outrageous.

▶ 🧭 Across the *piazza* from Santa Maria Novella. ℹ Audio tour €4. Braille texts, audio tour, and 3D reproductions of some images available for the blind. Sign language tour guides available on request. $ M €6, Tu €9, Th-Su €9; students and over 65 €7.50. ⏰ Open M-Tu 10am-6:30pm, Th-Su 10am-6:30pm. Last entry 6pm.

Chiesa di San Salvatore a Ognissanti CHURCH

P. Ognissanti 42

☎055 23 96 802

Stop by this church to pay your respects to **Botticelli,** who

Keeping Up With the Medici

It's impossible to tour Florence without hearing about the Medici, the family that ran the show here between the 15th and 18th centuries. While the Medici are best known for their banking skills, political prowess, and patronage to the arts and sciences, no family is without its eccentricities. Here's a crib sheet that'll help you keep the multi-faceted Medici men straight:

1. The first Medici to make it big was **Cosimo the Elder.** He was incredibly wealthy due to his father (Giovanni di Bicci) having founded the Medici Bank. He established his family's de facto rule in Florence by appealing to the working class, buying favors, and raising taxes on the wealthy. The players may change, but politics stays the same.

2. Cosimo had a son who was nicknamed **Piero the Gouty** because of the infection in his foot. He found it difficult to rule Florence with a swollen big toe, so he didn't last very long.

3. Despite their power, the Medici weren't always the coolest kids in the cafeteria. Rival families and a priest conspired to "sacrifice" Piero's son **Lorenzo** during a church service. After a brief period of expulsion (it's a long story), the Medici made a comeback in the early 1500s, helping to patronize artists like Leonardo da Vinci and Raphael.

4. **Cosimo I** de Medici is famous for establishing the Uffizi and Palazzo Pitti, ruling Florence, and patronizing the arts. He also deserves props, though, for embodying the "work hard, play harder" motto. In his free time he managed to father 15 children with four different women.

5. **Cosimo II** established the Medici family as patrons of science and technology. Cosimo *numero due* was Galileo's sugar daddy, supporting his research, giving him a place to stay, and offering him the chance to schmooze with the upper classes. In return, Galileo dedicated his books to the Medici, named some stars after them, and allowed the family first dibs on his new inventions, like the telescope.

probably never imagined his own *St. Augustine* would adorn his final resting place. The solemn mood is set by the monks' chants wafting in from the neighboring monastery—oh wait, no, it's from the speakers on the wall. The church's simple architecture is masked by a great deal of imaginary additions, from the trompe-l'œil molding to a fairly convincing balcony painted on the ceiling. And, of course, the 2D balcony also has a fresco, which presents a ceiling painting of a ceiling painting. Try to wrap your head around that one.

▶ 🚶 1 block north of the river. $ Free. ⏰ Open daily 7am-12:30pm and 4-8pm.

SAN LORENZO

Palazzo Medici Riccardi — MUSEUM

V. Camillo Cavour 1

☎055 27 60 340; www.palazzo-medici.it

Welcome to the Medici's not-so-humble abode. The tiny chapel is flooded with frescoed Medici faces attending the Adoration of the Magi. Downstairs, motion sensor technology lets you point at a projection of the chapel's frescoes and, without touching anything, cue explanations in Italian, French, or English. If you're excessively tall or short, be prepared to flail unsuccessfully until the guard adjusts the camera. The palace also hosts the current provincial government. The members of this council can zone out during dull meetings to the image of fleshy angels in the **Sala Luca Giordano,** which are more impressive than the modern projection screen, conference table, and rows of plexiglass chairs. *Let's Go* does not condone taking water from the conference room dispenser.

▶ 🚶 From San Lorenzo you can see the back of the huge brown palace. Enter from the reverse side on V. Camillo Cavour. $ €7, ages 6-12 €4, people with disabilities and their assistants free. ⏰ Open M-Tu 9am-7pm, Th-Su 9am-7pm.

Medici Chapels — MUSEUM

P. Madonna degli Aldobrandini 6

☎055 23 88 602; www.firenzemusei.it

Even a dead Medici is bathed in more wealth than most of us will ever touch. The **Cappella Principe,** begun in the 16th century, should be a Guinness World Records runner-up for slowest project of all time—the frescoes weren't painted until the 1870s, and the fancy altar wasn't completed until 1937. Some statues were commissioned by still-living Medicis, while others (the empty slots) they expected their sons to fill for them. The ceiling in here is higher than the sky outside; we started counting how many dozens of us we would need to build a human pyramid to the top. The **New Sacristy** is smaller and less color-ful, but we'll forgive its designer, a fellow named Michelangelo. And not to be crude, but goodness, someone should give the statue of *Night* a sweater, because she's clearly finding it a bit nippy, if you know what we mean.

▶ 🏛 It's the roundish building to the right of Basilica di San Lorenzo. *i* Likely visit length: 30min. tops. ⓢ €6, EU citizens ages 18-25 €3, EU citizens under 18 and over 65 free. 🕐 Open daily 8:15am-4:50pm. Closed 1st, 3rd, 5th M and 2nd and 4th Su each month.

Basilica di San Lorenzo   CHURCH
P. San Lorenzo
☎055 26 45 184; www.sanlorenzo.firenze.it

The Basilica di San Lorenzo is just over 1600 years old. Its Old Sacristy has a small cupola painted with gold constellations on a midnight blue background that represent the sky over Florence on July 4th, 1442. You could save your €3.50 and instead peruse the night sky for free every 24hr., but there's no way Filippo Brunelleschi's version of it can be blocked by clouds or tall buildings. If you're determined to not spend any money, you can take advantage of the free private prayer section and sneak glances at the church, but you'll have to deal with your guilt when you then blow your money on a large gelato instead. If you're truly shameless, you could then take that gelato back to the church and eat it in the pleasant, and unusually green, cloister to the left of the basilica.

▶ 🏛 In P. San Lorenzo, just a little north of the Duomo. ⓢ €3.50, under 10 free. 🕐 Open M-Sa 10am-5pm, Su 1:30-5pm.

SAN MARCO

Around P. di San Marco, museum density and diversity soar, so choose your own adventure!

🖼 Galleria dell'Accademia   MUSEUM
V. Ricasoli 60
☎055 23 88 612; www.firenzemusei.it/accademia

Leonardo da Vinci once said that Michelangelo's figures re-semble "a sack full of walnuts," but in a classic size comparison, whose masterpiece comes up a tad short? At an easy 17ft., it's no wonder the *David* can't find any robes in his size. Do you see those veins on his hand? The guy's a beast. Four unfinished statues by Michelangelo share *David*'s hall, trapped in the

Will the Real David Please Stand Up?

You've heard about the *David*. You've read about the *David*. You've seen coffee mugs and aprons and boxer shorts emblazoned with the *David*. And now you're ready to see the real deal. So you're making your way through Florence and wow! There he is! In all his naked *contrapposto* glory, chilling in the P. della Signoria. Not quite as impressive as the hype made him out to be, but then few tourist traps are. You snap a few pictures, pretend to grab *David's* well-sculpted posterior, and congratulate yourself—you saw the statue. Your work here is done.

Think again. Do you really believe they'd keep the world's most famous statue outdoors? You can be forgiven for being fooled, though—that replica in the *piazza* rests right where the real statue originally stood before it migrated indoors in the 19th century. The replica is far from the only copy of the *David*—the world is swarming with models of the Michelangelo masterwork. Head up to the Piazzale Michelangelo to see another replica—and you haven't even left Florence yet. There's a replica at Caesar's Palace in Las Vegas and one at Ripley's Believe It or Not in Florida. The campus of California State University, Fullerton, has one whose buttocks are traditionally rubbed by students seeking good luck. At the Victoria and Albert Museum in London, a strategically placed fig leaf was once hung for visits from Queen Victoria and other delicate ladies.

So who needs to see the original, if replicas are a dime a dozen? Head to the **Accademia** and see the difference for yourself. Can't see it? At least you can feel superior to the amateurs who were tricked by the statue outside.

remaining block of marble like Han Solo encased in carbonite. You may understand on an intellectual level that the master's statues are carved from a single piece of marble, but seeing these unfinished works (who go by *The Slaves*) drives it home. One man. A bunch of chisels. One big rock.

If you've saved room for dessert after staring amorously at the *David,* head to the right of the entrance for a musical instrument gallery. Check out serpents, trumpet marines, and hurdy gurdies, but let someone else try the water spring bowl—same great sound, no need to get grimy hands. In the next room on the left, you may notice the adored gnomish son about to pick his nose, or, we don't know, the enormous *gesso* model of *The Rape of the Sabines.*

Past the *David* gallery on the left is a 19th-century workshop overflowing with sculpted heads and busts. Notice the little black dots freckling the pieces? In the Accademia's days as an actual academy, the dots served as reference points for students making copies for practice. Upstairs, you'll see Jesus's face more times than you've seen your own mother's.

Tip: It's worth noting that visiting the Accademia generally won't take more than an hour. Bear that in mind when weighing the choice between paying extra for a reservation or waiting in a line that lasts far longer than you'll spend in the actual museum.

▶ 🚏 Line for entrance is on V. Ricasoli, off of P. di San Marco. *i* Make reservations at the Museo Archeologico, the Museo di San Marco, or the Museo del'Oficio. The non-reservation line is shortest at the beginning of the day. Try to avoid the midday cruise ship excursion groups. $ €6.50, EU citizens ages 18-25 €3.25, art students EU citizens under 18 or over 65 free. Reservations €4 extra. ⏰ Open Tu-Su 8:15am-6:50pm. Last entry 6:20pm.

Museo di San Marco MUSEUM

P. di San Marco 3

☎055 23 88 608; www.firenzemusei.it

Florence is hardly lacking in religious artworks, but Museo di San Marco packs in more than most. The themes may become repetitive, but the artistic importance of the works is impressive. The entrance courtyard features barely-there frescoes and some unattractive portraits that only get sadder when you imagine they are probably flattering. Enter the first room on the right for our favorite judgment day portrayal: on the hell side, people are eating what appears to be feces while others chew their own arms and *Lord of the Rings* style orcs string a man who appears quite content. Gold offsets dark paint in dozens of especially apathetic baby Jesuses (maybe Renaissance babies just looked like that), and when he's not an ugly baby or busy suffering for our sins, Jesus even randomly pokes his head into a study of drawing hands. Even Italian *paintings* use lots of hand gestures.

Upstairs, the museum is divided into the former cells of monks, each with its own painting on the wall. Pop inside and imagine spending four decades copying manuscripts by hand in there. Then look at Fra Angelico's famous fresco **The Annunciation** and imagine what it would be like if an angel arrived to announce that you were about to experience an unplanned pregnancy. In the last cloister on the right, note that the guy on Jesus's left doesn't appear to be suffering. This is because, five seconds before dying, he announced that God is his master, and as we all know, God practices the five second rule.

▶ ⇆ The north side of the *piazza.* ℹ Approximate visit time: 30min. $ €4, EU citizens ages 16-25 €2. ⏰ Open M-F 8:15am-1:50pm, Sa 8:15am-4:50pm, Su 8:15am-7pm. Closed 2nd and 4th M and 1st, 3rd, and 5th Su each month. Last entry 30min. before close.

Botanic Gardens

GARDENS

V. Micheli 3

☎055 23 46 70; www.msn.unifi.it

Listen. There are way more impressive botanical gardens in the world. Don't come here to learn about horticulture or to feel transported to a Chinese bamboo forest. Do come to sit somewhere green and relax. It is probably the best-smelling place in historic Florence outside of the Boboli Gardens, especially after it rains. Grab a bench to rest both your feet and your nostrils. Some say the Botanic Gardens are also a fine place to sneak a siesta, if you don't mind getting poked on the shoulder when a guard reluctantly decides to enforce the anti-vagrancy rules.

▶ ⇆ Continue past P. di San Marco; the gardens are on the right (and kind of obvious). $ €6. ⏰ Open Apr-Oct M-Tu 10am-7pm, Th-Su 10am-7pm; Oct-Mar M 10am-5pm, Sa-Su 10am-5pm.

Museo dell'Opificio Delle Pietre Dure

MUSEUM

V. degli Alfani 78

☎055 26 51 11; www.opificiodellepietredure.it

If the word "mosaic" makes you think of your elementary school walls, you are in for a surprise. Here, mosaics are slabs of stone cut to fit together like colored, unimaginably detailed puzzle pieces. Sure, a lot of the themes are pretty standard. You've got your typical birds, fruit, crests, and flowers—but you've also got LOL (Lots of Lions!), side-by-side paintings and mosaics of the same scene, and countrysides and faces you won't believe are made of stone. Upstairs, you can see the tools and process laid out, in case you thought you might actually recreate these masterpieces. A good look around won't take you more than 30min., but it's a change of pace from the Jesus paintings.

▶ ⇆ From P. di San Marco, head 1 block down Ricasoli then left onto V. degli Alfani. $ €4; EU citizens ages 18-25 €1; EU citizens under 18 and over 65, students and professors of architecture, art, or even literature or philosophy with an inscription certificate free. ⏰ Open M-Sa 8:15am-2pm.

Museo Degli Innocenti

MUSEUM

P. della Santissima Annunziata 12

☎055 20 37 323; www.istitutodeglinnocenti.it

In 1251, Florence decided that a guild of silk workers would protect and educate Florence's abandoned children. Foundlings, silk... the connection is obvious, right? This massive, terracotta-adorned hospital, where unwed mothers once served as wet nurses in exchange for being assisted in childbirth there, is now a UNICEF center, so you're bound to see some miniature Italians ushered through the courtyard by their impatient mothers. The museum portion is home to the orphanage's absurdly rich art collection, from standard oversized religious paintings to dioramas that will throw you back to your middle school book report days—including one that shows off the actual bones of St. Marcus. This place has some crazy history, but if your wallet's not feeling it, or for some reason you don't have a burning desire to see the birthplace of artificial nursing, you could always just read about the place. Ask at the desk about temporary exhibits in the cavernous basement which can make the €4 fee less painful.

▸ 🚏 On the right in P. di San Marco. It's the one with the babies on it. $ €4, children and seniors €2.50. ⏰ Open daily 10am-7pm. Last entry 6:30pm.

Macchine di Leonardo

MUSEUM

V. Camillo Cavour 21

☎055 29 52 64; www.macchinedileonardo.com

No, these models were not built by Leonardo da Vinci's own hand. Yes, this means you can touch them. The museum is a collection of realized models of Leonardo's many ahead-of-his-time blueprints. Get your money's worth by watching the Italian or English series about the artist's life, which—despite reading the English translations of notebook excerpts in a cheesy Italian accent—reveals lesser-known sides of the artist, from his cooperation with a pillaging lord to his love of autopsies.

▸ 🚏 5min. up V. Camillo Cavour from the Duomo, on the left. $ €7. ⏰ Open daily 9:30am-7:30pm.

Museo Archeologico

MUSEUM

P. Santissima Annunziata 9B

☎055 23 575; www.archeotoscana.beniculturali.it

Florence is admittedly a strange place for the Ancient Egyptian knickknacks that begin this exhibit, but if you were impressed by how old the rest of Florence's art was, this place will floor you. Browse sphynxes, mummies, and statuettes displayed on shelves like they were a child's figurine collection. The space is way too large for the number of objects on display, so there's twice as many posters as actual artifacts. If you like eerie rooms with old things and don't care much for background information (or if you know something about archeology), this is the place for you.

▶ 🐾 Facing P. Santissima Annunziata, it's on the right. ⓢ €4, EU citizens ages 18-25 €2, EU citizens under 18 and over 65 free. 🕐 Open Tu-F 8:30am-7pm, Sa-Su 8:30am-2pm.

SANTA CROCE

Santa Croce is a little out of the way of the main attractions, but its scattered sights are some of Florence's most memorable.

🔲 Synagogue of Florence   SYNAGOGUE, MUSEUM
V. Luigi Carlo Farini 4
☎055 24 52 52

This beautiful building definitely doesn't fade into the surrounding Florentine architecture. Its conspicuousness was a bold choice: when it was built, the Jewish population still lived in a walled ghetto in the city center and most synagogues were designed to blend in to avoid drawing attention to the community. Constructed in 1868, it's young by Florentine standards, but has still managed to have quite a life. The Nazis used it as their headquarters during the occupation of the city, and when they evacuated, they rigged the temple to explode. Somehow, all but one of the bombs failed to detonate, which is why the building is still standing today. The beauty of its exterior is matched by the abstract and colorful geometric patterns of the interior, making it so different from other places of worship in the city that you'll wish you didn't have to leave your camera behind the metal detector at the entrance.

▶ 🐾 From the Basilica di Santa Croce, walk 7 blocks north on V. dei Pepi. Turn right onto V. dei Pilastri and left onto V. Luigi Carlo Farini. 𝒊 Yarmulkes required and provided. Check bags and cameras at lockers before entering. ⓢ €5, students €3. Cash only. 🕐 Open Apr-Sept M-Th 10am-6pm, F 10am-2pm; Oct-Mar M-Th 10am-3pm, F 10am-2pm. The 1st fl. of the museum is only open during the 2nd half of every hr.

Basilica di Santa Croce   CHURCH
P. Santa Croce 16
☎055 24 66 105; www.santacroce.firenze.it

This enormous basilica has more celebrities than the Academy

Attention Body Snatchers

Step into a church in Florence and you'll likely run into a lot of saintly detritus. Thumbs, fingernails, femurs, and forearms are frequently enshrined as relics, often enclosed in carefully crafted and lavishly ornamented displays. Frankly, we don't understand why no one has thought to turn all these beatified bits into one Frankensaint. In case the mad scientist within you wants to run with our idea, here's a list of the relics worth reanimating:

- **At the Museo Opera di Santa Maria del Fiore:** This peaceful museum contains Donatello's shockingly grim statue of a haggard Mary Magdalene. In a glass case along the wall, find a finger reputed to belong to St. John the Baptist, Florence's patron saint.

- **At the Medici Chapels:** Glass cases of reliquaries are scattered about the entrance lobby, and in the Capella Principe, you'll find a treasure trove of elegantly displayed human odds and ends. Those greedy Medici weren't just content with collecting art masterworks—they wanted human flesh as well.

- **At the Basilica di Santa Croce:** Check out Saint Francis's cowl and girdle. Wouldn't they look great on a Florentine Frankenstein?

Awards. They happen to have been dead for hundreds of years, but no matter. Machiavelli lies in a chilling and understated tomb, Rossini under subtle decoration of treble clefs and violin bridges, and Galileo with a globe and etching of the solar system. Michelangelo's tomb explodes with color and features a painting of the statue he'd intended for his final resting place. Dante's tomb is just gray, but it holds some inordinately large statues. You'll even find Marconi, inventor of the radio. The complex also includes exhibits, cloisters, and gardens, which are full of dead people of the less famous variety. To the right of the entrance through the gift shop, the Santa Croce leather school awaits to instruct you in the ways of leatherworking or to sell you its students' handiwork. *Let's Go* does not recommend cheating Jesus, but some travelers report that it's not difficult to sneak into the basilica through the leather school's entrance at V. San Giuseppe 5r.

▶ 🏃 Take Borgo de' Greci east from P. della Signoria. 🌕 €5, ages 11-17 €3, under 11 and disabled free. Combined ticket with Casa Michelangelo €8. Audio tour €5. 🕐 Open M-F 9:30am-3:30pm, Sa-Su 1-5:30pm.

Casa Buonarroti   MUSEUM

V. Ghibellina 70

☎055 24 17 52; www.casabuonarroti.it

When Michelangelo hit it big, he did what any new celebrity would do: bought a bunch of houses and then never lived in them. Unlike the completely fabricated Casa di Dante, Casa Buonarroti is not a reproduction. It was home to several generations of Michelangelo's descendants, and, lucky for you, they were avid art collectors. The museum's collection includes Etruscan archeological fragments, rare sketches, models by Michelangelo himself, and 19th-century Michelangelo-themed kitsch produced during a Victorian burst of Michelmania. The relative lack of tourists means plenty of space to get up close and personal with Michelangelo's work, provided being followed from room to room by the museum staff doesn't put you off. Our favorite curiosity is the small model of the wooden contraption used to transport *David* from P. della Signoria to the Accademia. If you can only visit one Florentine palace, this one's a good bet.

▶ 🛱 From P. Santa Croce, walk 1 block to the left to V. Ghibellina. 🔉 €6.50, students and seniors €4.50. Cash only. 🕐 Open M 10am-5pm, W-Su 10am-5pm.

WEST OLTRARNO

Palazzo Pitti

The major sights of West Oltrarno are all condensed into the enormous Palazzo Pitti (www.uffizi.firenze.it/palazzopitti). It's not hard to find the complex: just cross Ponte Vecchio and walk until you reach the very obvious *palazzo*. The Palazzo Pitti museums are grouped into two ticket combos. **Ticket One** gets you into Galleria Palatina, Galleria d'Arte Moderna, and Apartamenti Reali. **Ticket Two** is for the Boboli Gardens, Museo degli Argenti, Galleria del Costume, and Museo della Porcellana. Overall, if you're choosing one ticket combo over the other, we recommend Ticket Two.

▶ 🔉 Ticket 1 €13, after 4pm €12; EU citizens ages 18-25 €6.50/6; EU citizens under 18 and over 65 free. Ticket 2 €10, EU citizens ages 18-25 €4.50, EU citizens under 18 and over 65 free. Audio tour €5.50, 2 for €8. 🕐 Ticket 1 sights open Tu-Su 8:15am-6:50pm. Ticket 2 sights open daily June-Aug 8:15am-7:30pm; Sept 8:15am-6:30pm; Oct 8:15am-5:30pm; Nov-Feb 8:15am-4:30pm; Mar-May 8:15am-6:30pm. Closed 1st and last M of each month.

Sights

▨ Boboli Gardens   GARDENS

www.uffizi.firenze.it/boboli

The Boboli Gardens feel like a cross between Central Park and Versailles. Imagine you're a 17th-century Medici strolling through your gardens—but don't imagine your way into a corset, ladies, because the gardens are raked at a surprising incline. They're also easily large enough for you to lose yourself for an entire afternoon. Head uphill from the palace for the porcelain museum and a stunning view of the valley where the city's packed red buildings give way to sprawling monasteries and trees. Further garden exploration results in the usual non-functioning fountains and mossy statues, but Boboli also features grottoes that look like drip castles, a sculpture of a fat man riding a turtle, and some colorful striped people added in 2003. As with any gardens, they are most fragrant and lovely right after the rain.

▶ *i* Ticket 2.

Galleria Palatina   MUSEUM

www.uffizi.florence.it/palatina

Gold, statues, and paintings of gold and statues deck every possible inch of this ridiculously ornate gallery. The permanent collection is housed in rooms named not for the displays, but for the ceiling art of figures like Saturn and Apollo. We are still in a *palazzo,* remember, so the organizational logic is still that of a rich royal wanting to clutter his brocaded walls with all the big-ticket masterpieces he could commission. The quirkiest object in the collection sits alone in a small chamber between the Education of Jupiter and Ulysses rooms. It belonged to Napoleon and proves that great conquerors come in small bathtubs.

▶ *i* Ticket 1.

Galleria del Costume   MUSEUM

www.uffizi.firenze.it/musei/costume

This fashion collection isn't just Medici-era vintage—it stretches all the way into the modern day. A true Italian knows that clothes are every bit as sacred as paintings of angels, so the couture is presented thematically. Pieces from the collection rotate, but the current exhibit categorizes styles by gimmick—one display includes classically inspired sheath dresses from 1890, 1923, 1971, and 1993. It's fascinating to see the same basic ideas get reinterpreted every other generation, and you can have fun playing the "guess the decade" game before reading the title cards (you'll be surprised how easy it is to confuse the

'20s with the '80s). The one permanent display is for the true Medici completist. The actual burial clothes of several dead Medici were torn from their rotting corpses and preserved for your viewing pleasure. You're welcome.

▶ *i* Ticket 2.

Museo degli Argenti   MUSEUM

www.uffizi.firenze.it/argenti

This museum is a pirate's dream. There's no getting lost in code or confusing markings: the treasure map is simply a sign that says, "To the Treasure." Visiting Museo degli Argenti is like wandering through a painted jewelry box. Lavish rings, minute ivories, precious jewels, dazzling crowns, and Chinese porcelain abound, and less traditional treasures like tiny shell statues of Arcimboldo's famous fruit people are also featured. Additional loot sometimes appears in temporary exhibits.

▶ *i* Ticket 2.

Apartamenti Reali   MUSEUM

The back end of the Galleria Palatina gets it right by doing away with the pesky art and sticking to the rich people's bedrooms; it's like a live version of MTV's *Cribs*. You can practically see lords nonchalantly strolling ahead of you through the marble columns and chandeliers as they chatter about some fresco or another. By the end, you'll definitely wish these apartments were listed in the Accommodations section.

▶ *i* Ticket 1.

Museo delle Porcellana   MUSEUM

www.uffizi.firenze.it/musei/porcellane

The top of that hill in the Boboli Gardens is home to a porcelain museum. Sounds dull, right? Turns out, whoever spent centuries amassing this collection of dishware really knew what he or she was doing. Even if you tune out all the floral plate motifs, there are some amazingly intricate painted scenes, including one that depicts lords and ladies milling in the garden in outlandishly fancy getup.

▶ 🚶 At the highest point of the Boboli Gardens. Just keep walking up. *i* Ticket 2.

Galleria d'Arte Moderna   MUSEUM

Palazzo Pitti Complex

☎055 23 88 616; www.uffizi.firenze.it/musei/artemoderna

Only in Florence could people define "modern art" as stuff that predates the French Revolution. This gallery begins in the 1780s when art was no longer just for dukes, but for nobles, too. Talk about progress! The focus then moves toward 19th-century Naturalism as the motifs shift to motion, countrysides, and social scenes. It's a good palette cleanser to keep you conscious through the gilded palace rooms full of gods and angels—and we promise, you won't see any Madonna and Child renditions here.

▶ *i* Ticket 1.

Other Sights

Museo di Storia Naturale: Zoologia La Specola   MUSEUM
V. Romana 17

☎055 23 46 760; www.msn.unifi.it

This natural history museum is not for the faint of heart. Preserved specimens of hundreds of species—from lions to walruses to stickbugs—leer audaciously at you from behind glass walls. If you had trouble stomaching giant pinned beetles and hairy spiders in the first rooms, close your eyes when you reach the snakes in vials and run through the rest of the museum. The last five rooms are filled with 17th-century wax models of human innards and nerves, including skinless people, severed legs, and twin fetuses curled up in the womb. There's also a gruesome but anatomically accurate diorama of people dying of the plague. Indulge your inner crow downstairs at the **crystal museum**—it's only a few rooms long, but you've never seen this many sparkly things. Over 500 rare crystals from the world over are assembled here while a video explains how crystals formed along Colorado fault lines and how miners used to swap silver for a pint at the bar.

▶ ⚲ Continue a few more min. on the multi-named street that runs in front of Palazzo Pitti. *i* Ticket office on 2nd fl. Advance booking required for groups of 10 or more. Ⓢ €10, ages 6-14 and over 65 €5, under 6 free. Crystal museum only €6/3/free. Ⓩ Open June-Sept Tu-Su 10:30am-5:30pm. Last entry 5pm.

EAST OLTRARNO

You haven't seen Florence until you've seen it from the **Piazzale Michelangelo.** You'll find an extensive network of designated jogging routes and a number of small, lesser-known churches and sights amid the area's greenery. Some less typical gems like the Bardini museum await the determined explorer of East Oltrarno's residential area.

🏛 **Piazzale Michelangelo**   PANORAMIC VIEWS
Piazzale Michelangelo

When you reach the top of your climb and find yourself facing Piazzale Michelangelo, you may wonder if you're in the right place. "I thought this was a famous sight, but all I see is a parking lot, some tourist stalls, and an oxidized *David* reproduction," you may say in disappointment. But then you'll turn around. Suddenly, you won't care how many cars are behind you sharing the same view, as Florence unfolds all around you in stunning clarity. If you stick around for the nighttime city lights, you may even begin to understand why the false *David* likes hanging out here so much.

▶ 🚶 From pretty much any bridge, bear east along the river until P. Guiseppe Poggi, where the base of the steps is located. If you're not wearing walking shoes, take bus #12 or 13. Ⓢ Free.

Museo Stefano Bardini   ANTIQUE MUSEUM
V. dei Renai 37
☎055 23 42 427

If you can't beat 'em, collect from 'em. When his painting career faltered, Stefano Bardini chose to channel his energies into collecting and dealing antiques. We know what you're thinking: "egad, antiques! The epitome of boring." But Bardini didn't buy 100-year-old desks—the man collected guns, spears, Donatellos, and suits of armor. He took frescoes from walls and ancient archways from buildings. The guy had taste. And when his business slowed toward the end of his life, he turned his loot into a permanent collection that was donated to the city of Florence. The rooms mix pieces from various time periods, and you may even recognize some of the artists, like the expressive faces of sculptor Nicola Pisano or the blue terra cotta of Luca della Robbia. Also, the endless Donatello Madonna and Child paintings are all placed in one room, so you can compare them, contrast them, or easily skip over all of them.

▶ 🚶 Cross over Ponte alle Grazie and continue 2 blocks. Ⓢ €5, ages 18-25 and over 65 €4, 4-17 €3, under 4 free. 🕐 Open M 11am-5pm, Th 11am-5pm, Sa-Sun 11am-5pm.

Sights

Food

Florence's cuisine is typical Tuscan fare: endless combinations of meat, olive oil, truffles, and (of course) pasta. Florence's signature dish is thin slices of extremely rare steak, known as *bistecca alla fiorentina*. Rustic trattorias are ubiquitous, and the good news is that you can't really go wrong with any of them. The only thing to note is the sneaky cover charge for table service, often tucked under a pushpin or typed in tiny font at the bottom of the menu. In casual joints, you can generally escape the cover by standing at the bar—hovering gets less awkward with practice. If predictable trattoria cuisine starts to lose its excitement, hole-in-the-wall panini places, pizzerias, or the international restaurants in Santa Croce provide delicious accents so you can attack your *tagliatelle al pomodoro* with renewed zeal. Food markets are also great for classic Tuscan prosciutto and cheese picnics to take down to the river. Breakfast is an adjustment: we hope you loaded up on bacon before you left home, because all you'll get here is a croissant and coffee. Get your cappuccino or latte macchiato fix before noon—coffee after noon is such a faux pas that some waiters may even refuse to serve it. Finally, as Florence claims to be the birthplace of gelato, it's totally acceptable to eat some every day that you're here, even if you're staying for the next five years.

Budget Food

Lucky for you, food is relatively cheap in Florence. In general, keep an eye out for breakfasts included in accommodations prices—a small breakfast at a hotel or hostel may get you through the morning while your weaker companions will be starving by the time they reach the Uffizi's Room of Niobe. ✎**Aperitivo buffets** are God's gift to budget travelers. Approach calmly and serve yourself a generous but socially acceptable portion. Repeat until the buffet runs out or closes, and feel delight in knowing that the elegant ladies munching two cocktail sausages and a sprig of mint are essentially paying for your multi-course pasta meal. When all else fails, you can always substitute gelato for a meal.

THE DUOMO

The places in **Piazza del Duomo** offer some great deals, making it a good spot for a bigger meal. If you want quick food, though, skip the square's overpriced snackbars and venture a few blocks further.

✎ Vestri Cioccolato d'Autore — GELATERIA $

Borgo degli Albizi 11r

☎055 23 40 374; www.vestri.it

While the masses descend upon (admittedly delicious) Grom, head a few blocks east for an artisanal gelato experience. This little shop is the kind of place that can tell you exactly what variety of pistachio they used for your gelato. The flavor list isn't extensive, but with top-notch combinations like the *cioccolato fondente* with mint, you'll neither notice nor care. Alongside the exceptional gelato, the shop also sells homemade chocolates and milkshakes.

▶ 🚏 From the Duomo, take V. Proconsolo south from the Duomo and turn left onto Borgo degli Albizi. [$] Gelato from €1.80. Cash only. ⏰ Open daily 10:30am-8pm.

✎ Mesopotamia — KEBAB $

P. Salvemini 14

☎055 24 37 05

For a cheap and delicious taste of something different, any student will tell you that simple, unobtrusive, and white-tiled Mesopotamia has the best kebabs in the city.

▶ ⇄ Follow V. dell'Oriuolo from the southeast corner of P. del Duomo. Mesopotamia is on the left when the street opens onto a *piazza.* $ Kebabs €4. ⏰ Open daily 11am-late.

Caffè Duomo

RISTORANTE $$

P. del Duomo 29/30r

☎055 21 13 48

This trattoria stands out among others under the Duomo for its specials: a light cheese and cold cut platter with a glass of Chianti for lunch (serves two people; €12), or a dinner of bruschetta, salad, spaghetti bolognese or lasagna, and a glass of wine. The young staff have also been known to dance to Justin Bieber when business is slow.

▶ ⇄ On the north side of P. del Duomo. $ Bruschetta, salad, entree, and wine €9. ⏰ Open daily noon-11pm.

Little David

RISTORANTE $

V. de' Martelli 14r

☎055 23 02 695

Little David's crowds are smaller than the big *David*'s, making it a great spot to drop by with your laptop, refuel, and connect to the free Wi-Fi. Be sure to ask about the student special (pizza or pasta and a soft drink; €6), as it's listed separately from the main menu.

▶ ⇄ Just north of the Duomo, on the right. $ *Primi* €4.90-9.40. Pizza €5.50-12. 0.5L wine €4.90. ⏰ Open daily noon-1am.

Pizzeria del Duomo

PIZZERIA $

P. di San Giovanni 21

☎055 21 07 19

For the fastest, cheapest option without leaving the *piazza,* Pizzeria del Duomo gets the job done. They cut a generous slab, so if you're not too hungry, don't feel shy asking for a smaller piece. Downstairs seating comes at no charge if you want to get out of the sun, but otherwise your slice can be taken to go.

▶ ⇄ Between where Borgo San Lorenzo and V. de' Martelli feed into the *piazza.* $ Pizza €1.50-3 per slice. ⏰ Open daily noon-11pm.

Buca Niccolini

RISTORANTE $

V. Ricasoli 5/7r

☎055 29 21 24; www.bucaniccolini.it

"Make food, not war" proclaim the placemats at this trattoria, and after a big lunch, it's hard to disagree. The restaurant is inches from P. del Duomo, but every inch is another penny saved. The interior features a panoramic picture of Florence, so you might as well skip the dome's stairs and spend that €8 on beer and pizza instead.

▶ Immediately north of the Duomo, on the left. $ Pizza and beer €8. Pasta and beer €9.50. ⏰ Open daily 11am-3pm and 5pm-midnight.

Trattoria La Madia

RISTORANTE $$

V. del Giglio 14

☎055 21 85 63

If you're tired of unsalted Tuscan bread, come here for a welcome dose of sodium. The bruschetta is especially good, as are the seafood specialties, and everything is pleasantly salty compared to the dishes in other identical trattorias.

▶ Off V. dei Banchi, toward P. Santa Maria Novella. $ Cover €2. *Primi* €7-9; *secondi* €10-18. ⏰ Open Tu-Su 1-10pm.

Grom

GELATERIA $

V. del Campanile

☎055 21 61 58; www.grom.it

Grom is a high-end *gelateria,* which means it has a posh location right off P. del Duomo, a branch in New York City and Tokyo, and slightly higher prices than the city's other top-notch *gelaterie.* Sure, you'll find it mentioned in every guidebook and, if you catch it at the wrong time, you'll be waiting in line for 15min., but at least your little cup is made with all-natural ingredients.

▶ Just south of the Duomo. $ Starting at €2. ⏰ Open daily Apr-Sept 10:30am-midnight; Oct-Mar 10:30am-11pm.

Le Botteghe di Donatello

RISTORANTE $$

P. del Duomo 27r

☎055 21 66 78

Le Botteghe di Donatello is one of many trattorias in P. del Duomo, but it can be a godsend for those in search of a gluten-free menu. The interior seating is surprisingly extensive, air-conditioned, and rustic, so it's a fine option no matter the weather.

▶ On the south side of the Duomo. $ Pizza and pasta €7-12. ⏰ Open daily 11am-11pm.

PIAZZA DELLA SIGNORIA

Considering that this area teems with tourists of the well-heeled variety, there are still a surprising number of diverse, budget-friendly eateries. Good rule of thumb: the farther north or east of the Uffizi, the better off you are. This is also the place to find the city's best panini.

🍴 Da Vinattieri — SANDWICHES $

V. Santa Margherita 4r

☎055 29 47 03

Nothing attests to quality quite like the willingness of customers to balance on disarrayed wooden stools under a damp archway. For only €3.50, you can watch your tripe or *lampredotto* panini made to order before your eyes. Step into the tiny shop or just nab a quick bite through the counter window. Choose from the long menu of sandwich suggestions or invent your own—they all cost the same.

▶ ⇄ Across the alley from Casa di Dante, so just follow the signs for that attraction. On V. del Corso, take a right just before Lush. $ Panini €3.50. Tripe €5. ⏰ Open daily 10am-8pm.

🍴 I Fratellini — SANDWICHES, VINERIA $

V. dei Cimatori 38r

☎055 23 96 096; www.iduefratellini.com

This open stall with an overhang and no seating dates to 1875. Yet it still manages to draw crowds thanks to the tantalizing smell of lunchmeat panini, local wines, and the crowd psychology of seeing everyone else outside.

▶ ⇄ Come to the junction of V. dei Cimatori and V. dei Calzaioli, and it will be on the left. $ Sandwiches €2.50. ⏰ Open Sept-June M-F 9am-8pm.

🍴 Festival del Gelato — GELATERIA $

V. del Corso 75r

☎055 29 43 86

Festival del Gelato is not what it sounds like (a festival) or what it looks like (an arcade). We had dismissed this tacky, neon-flooded *gelateria* as a certain tourist trap, but when a local recommended it, we caved and gave the disco gelato a try. At our first bite of *cioccolato fondente,* the garish fluorescence melted into warm candlelight and fireflies and a violinist in white tie began to... OK, no, the place still looked ridiculous, but hot damn, that be good gelato.

▶ ♯ V. del Corso is just east off P. della Repubblica. Look for the neon—you can't miss it. Ⓢ Gelato from €1.80. ⚅ Open daily noon-midnight.

O'Vesuvio   PIZZERIA $

V. dei Cimatori 21r

☎055 28 54 87

> If you gym, tan, laundry daily and have an "I heart Vinnie" tattoo on your neck, you might need a therapist. But you also won't want to miss the pizzeria where your favorite fist-bumpers worked during the Florence season. For those who couldn't care less about *Jersey Shore,* the place actually dishes up some really great pizza.

▶ ♯ 1 block west of the Baia on V. dei Cimatori, on the left. Ⓢ Pizza €3-9. Calzones €5.50. ⚅ Open daily noon-midnight.

Acqua al 2   RISTORANTE $$

V. della Vigna Vecchia 40r

☎055 28 41 70; www.acquaal2.it/Firenze.html

> Why restrict plates to live on tables? Acqua al 2 allows plates to follow their true passion: decorating walls. While otherwise a bit pricey, this cloth napkins kind of joint makes a dreamy 🔖blueberry steak.

▶ ♯ On the corner of V. della Vigna Vecchia and V. dell'Acqua. Ⓢ *Primi* €7-12; *secondi* €9-23. Cover charge 10%. ⚅ Open M-Sa noon-11pm.

Trattoria Gusto Leo   PIZZERIA $$

V. del Proconsolo 8-10r

☎055 28 52 17; www.gustoleo.com

> This yellow restaurant near the major sights should never have opted for the corny lion theme. But if you can't beat 'em, join 'em: at least the ext-roar-dinarily large calzones, pizzas, and salads provide a real lion's share!

▶ ♯ Coming from P. della Signoria, it will be on the right. Ⓢ Pizzas €5.40-8.90. Calzones €7.60-7.90. ⚅ Open daily 8am-1am.

Osteria del Porcellino   RISTORANTE $$$

V. Val di Lamona 7r

☎055 26 41 48; www.osteriadelporcellino.com

> Osteria del Porcellino's wrought-iron tables take up most of the alleyway under a yellow arch just off the Mercato Nuovo. This is the place to savor a glass of wine and a typical Italian meat or pasta dish once the area's tourist freight has calmed. We

have no reason to believe that the name is a jab at the owner's appearance.

▶ ⇆ Right off P. di Mercato Nuovo. $ Cover €2. *Primi* €7-11; *secondi* €15-26. ⏰ Open daily noon-3pm and 5-11pm.

SANTA MARIA NOVELLA

Pizzerias, cafes, and kebab shops abound near the train station and church. This is a good neighborhood to find a generic, cheap bite to eat, but look elsewhere for a sit-down meal.

Trattoria il Contadino — RISTORANTE $$

V. Palazzuolo 69/71r

☎055 23 82 673

Come check the chalkboard to fill up with a *prix-fixe* menu that includes *primo, secondo,* veggie, and wine. If you come at lunchtime, you can use the two euro you saved to go pack some gelato into what little stomach space may remain.

▶ ⇆ From P. Santa Maria Novella, take a right onto V. Palazzuolo. $ *Prix-fixe* menu €11-13. ⏰ Open M-F noon-9:40pm, Sa 11am-3pm and 7pm-midnight.

The Cold War

With hot food, hot weather, and hot residents, Florence is a hot place to be. You would think an ice cold drink is the perfect way to relax from all that humidity. But in Florence, this is simply not the case—Florentines have embarked on a cultural crusade against the cold. This doesn't mean that everything is warm (thank goodness for gelato), but be prepared for a few things, including milk, to be served slightly warmer than usual. Most of us have only heard of warm milk in the context of grandmothers and cats, but here it's common practice to leave milk out at room temperature or to give it a quick zap in the microwave.

Pizzeria Centopoveri — PIZZERIA $

V. Palazzuolo 31r

☎055 21 88 46

The two elegant Centopoveri restaurants that straddle punk bar Public House 27 (see **Nightlife**) make for quite the juxtaposition. Go to the right for the younger, cheaper sister: the pizzeria. True, the long dining rooms with curved ceilings may make you feel like you're eating in a tunnel, but the light at the end is the excellent pizza.

▶ Corner of V. della Porcellana, on either side of all the punks smoking outside Public House 27. $ No cover in the pizzeria. Pizza €4.50-9. *Primi* €7-10; *secondi* €9-15. ⏰ Open daily noon-3pm and 7pm-midnight.

Ristorante La Spada

RISTORANTE, ROAST MEATS $$

V. della Spada 62r

☎055 21 87 57; www.laspadaitalia.com

Roasting spits ooze an enticing scent at this to-go or sit-down locale. Meanwhile, slabs of meat and heaps of asparagus call your name from under a glass case.

▶ Near the corner of V. della Spada and V. del Moro. *i* Mention the "free website after-dinner treat." $ *Primi* €6.50-9. Roast meat from the spit €8.50-14. Grill menu €8-19. Vegetables €4-6.50. Desserts €3-5. ⏰ Open daily noon-3pm and 6-11pm.

50 Rosso

CAFE $

V. Panzani 50r

☎055 28 35 85

This is the kind of place you duck into to escape a rainstorm or buy chewing gum. Then you discover it offers a surprising selection. The tiny cafe's eclectic fare includes panini (€2.50), chickwiches (€3), and miniature Tic Tac boxes. And if you're not already a convert, the Nutella crepe (€3) will have you head over heels for the hazelnut spread.

▶ You'll find the start of V. Panzani in the northeast corner of P. Santa Maria Novella, nearer to the train station. $ Cappuccino €1.20. Cash only. ⏰ Open daily 6:30am-12:30am.

Caffè Giacosa

CAFE $

Inside Palazzo Strozzi

☎055 42 65 04 86

Backpacking is murder on your lower lumbar, and the curved wooden wall at Caffè Giacosa fits just right in the small of your back. Lean back with a cappuccino and it's as good as Ibuprofen. The prices triple for courtyard seating, but who cares? The nice wooden wall inside the self-serve area is the point of the visit. The pots of tea are made of fancy bagged stuff—a delight for tea-drinkers stranded in coffee country.

▶ Inside Palazzo Strozzi, which is west of P. della Repubblica. There is a 2nd location down the street at V. della Spada 10. $ Cappuccino €1.30. Pot of tea €2. ⏰ Open daily 10am-10pm.

La Grotta di Leo

TRATTORIA $

V. della Scala 41/43r

☎055 21 92 65

Far from the only lion-themed restaurant around, this brick-walled trattoria is bigger than it looks, with two grotto-esque dining rooms and a couple outdoor tables. It seems Italian lions really like pizza and pasta served in brick buildings, although some say the tiramisu (€4) is the *mane* attraction.

▶ ⯐ From P. Santa Maria Novella, take a right onto V. della Scala. $ Pizza €5-8. *Primi* €5.50-8; *secondi* €5-19. ⏰ Open daily 10am-1am.

SAN LORENZO

The **Mercato Centrale** contains a feast of lunch options, but venturing outside to nearby restaurants is no step down. For dinner, **Via Nazionale** is lined with standard-fare pasta and pizza that isn't the cheapest in the area, but it gets the job done.

🍴 Trattoria Mario

RISTORANTE $

V. Rosina 2r

☎055 21 85 50; www.trattoriamario.com

If you're starting to wonder where all the Italians are hiding, show up for a late lunch at Trattoria Mario. Diners are haphazardly packed into tables with strangers, wherever there's room, which makes for creative combinations. If you're lucky, your tablemates might share their wine with you as you dine on the day's pasta special.

▶ ⯐ Just off Mercato Centrale, on the right. $ Cover €0.50. Daily specials €6-9. ⏰ Open M-Sa noon-3:30pm, but try to show up a bit earlier to beat the lines.

🍴 Nerbone

RISTORANTE $

P. del Mercato Centrale

☎055 21 99 49

Nerbone is the love child of a garage and a picnic. It has stood in a corner of the Mercato Centrale for over 100 years. Crowd around the counter to order whatever happens to be on offer, take your tray, and squeeze in with some locals to remind yourself how fantastic your Italian isn't. A sign warns that tables are only for eating, so forget those autopsies you were planning on doing over lunch.

▶ ⯐ Enter Mercato Centrale from V. dell'Arte and go all the way to the right.

Ⓢ *Primi* and *secondi* €2.50-7. House wine €1. Cash only. ⏰ Open M-Sa 7am-2pm.

🏛 Il Pirata   RISTORANTE $
V. de' Ginori 56r
☎055 21 86 25

Buy homemade food (pasta, meats, or vegetables) priced by the kilogram from a glass case opposite a line of stools and a counter. Refuel your immune system with a plate of vegetables (€5.50) or fill up with a big plate of pasta and side of vegetables (€6.50), but be careful when attempting to pour the self-serve olive oil. If business is slow, the owner may try to guess your nationality.

▶ ♯ From P. San Lorenzo, walk north up V. de' Ginori for a few minutes. *i* Takeout available. Ⓢ Lunch specials €5.50-7.50. Buffet €7.50, with wine €10. ⏰ Open daily 11am-11pm.

🏛 Antica Gelateria Fiorentina   GELATERIA $
V. Faenza 2A
☎388 05 80 399; www.gelateriafiorentina.com

Antica's wide variety of cone sizes splay across the counter, starting at a one-flavor cone for just €1. Snack on classics or check the label stickers for the *gelati speciali*—flavors invented by the owner—such as Bianca (sweet coconut, honey, and yogurt), named after his young daughter.

▶ ♯ Toward the far end of V. Faenza, on the left. Ⓢ Cones from €1. €15.50 per kg. ⏰ Open daily noon-midnight.

Il Brincello   TUSCAN $
V. Nazionale 110r
☎055 28 26 45

The battle between convenience and quality is over at last. May we present: 🏛**takeout homemade pasta!** And for a reasonable price! The sit-down option is less exciting and more orange.

▶ ♯ Just down V. Nazionale from the train station on the right. Ⓢ *Primi* €3.50-10. Takeout pasta €5. ⏰ Open daily noon-3pm and 7-11pm.

Bar Cabras   CAFE $
V. Panzani 12r
☎055 21 20 32

Italy takes regional specialties seriously, so you'd usually be hard pressed to find decent cannoli outside its southern home turf. Yet these cylinders of desire glistening with creamy goodness pose seductively from behind glass until you just can't say no.

Food

▶ ✥ Just down the street from the train station. $ Cannoli €1.50-2.50. ⏰ Open daily 8am-8pm.

Osteria all'antico Mercato

RISTORANTE $$

V. Nazionale 78r

☎055 28 41 82; www.anticomercatofirenze.it

The €10 combo meals are the draw here—try the *bruschetta e spaghetti bolognese.* Those sick of carbs will be happy to find that "Big Salads" get their own section of the menu (oh hey, *Seinfeld*) and gluten-free lasagna and pasta are also available. You get the same view whether you dine inside or out: the dining room features a mural of the street outside, minus the noisy cars and mopeds.

▶ ✥ Slightly south of P. dell'Indipendenza. $ Combo meals €10. ⏰ Open daily noon-11pm.

Trattoria Zaza

RISTORANTE $$

P. del Mercato Centrale 26r

☎055 21 54 11; www.trattoriazaza.it

The alfresco seating is typical for a *piazza ristorante,* but the quirky logo on the menu—a naked child being stung on the buttocks by a bee—should give you a clue to the offbeat glamour of the dining rooms inside. Lurid frescoes coat the vaulted ceilings, while staid dead white men in gilded portraits watch you devour fresh pasta. For those not inclined toward the bloody *bistecca alla fiorentina* there are abundant creative salads—try Zaza's, with chicory lettuce, walnuts, brie, and Roquefort dressing.

▶ ✥ Exit behind the Mercato Centrale and go diagonally right, looking for tents. $ Cover €2.50. *Primi* €7-18. ⏰ Open daily 11am-11pm.

Ristorante le Fonticine

RISTORANTE $$

V. Nazionale 79r

☎055 28 21 06; www.lefonticine.com

This restaurant will call your name as you wander V. Nazionale looking for a place to eat. Standard pasta awaits you where the walls are packed full of paintings—don't look too closely at the humans with black holes for eyes, or they might try to steal yours. Also beware the exorbitant cover charge and spurious claims that their tap water comes from the river.

▶ ✥ To the right of the V. Nazionale fountain (hence the name). $ Cover €2.50. *Primi* €6-13; *secondi* €8-16. ⏰ Open daily noon-2:30pm and 7-10:30pm.

SAN MARCO

There are lots of self-evidently cheap places near the Accademia if you want to grab something for the botanical gardens. Venture a few blocks further for more pleasant sit-down options.

▨ Il Vegetariano   VEGETARIAN $

V. delle Ruote 30

☎055 47 50 30

This unobtrusive establishment will surprise you. Walk beyond the cool, shady front room for a bustling haven of custom salads, glistening cakes, and assorted teas. You won't rue the lack of meat in the lush, flavorful pasta dishes. Here's an itinerary to help you get food with the minimum amount of jostling: grab silverware on the right of the register, order and pay, then pick up a tray and give your order sheet to the guy behind the salad options. Seat yourself—we recommend the peaceful bamboo courtyard.

▶ 🚊 From V. Nazionale it's a subtle wooden sign on the left. *i* Gluten-free options. Ⓢ *Primi* €5.50-6.50; *secondi* €6.50-8.50. ⌚ Open Tu-Su 12:30-3pm and 7:30pm-midnight.

Ristorante Pizzeria da Zeus   PIZZERIA $

V. Santa Reparata 17r

☎328 86 44 704

The student special is as appealing as Zeus was promiscuous—only €5 for pizza and a soda. The large rear dining hall is air-conditioned, and the *prix-fixe* menu (drink, a salad or pizza or *primi,* dessert, and coffee) is one of the cheapest in town.

▶ 🚊 Off V. 27 Aprile. Ⓢ Cover €1. *Prix-fixe* menu €6.50. ⌚ Open daily noon-11pm.

Gran Caffè San Marco   CAFE $

P. di San Marco 11r

☎055 21 58 33; www.grancaffesanmarco.it

This chintzy but cheap cafe is the chameleon of eateries. Enter from the main *piazza* and it's a *gelateria.* Enter from the side street and it's a pizzeria. Walk further in, and it's a cafeteria meets coffee bar meets garden cafe. Don't be caught off guard by the charge for table service, or the fact that the enormous gooey bowls of lasagna (€4.50) are reheated. This food is good for a quick museum refueling rather than a lingering stay.

▶ 🧭 The south end of the *piazza.* [$] Panini €3. *Secondi* €7. ⏰ Open daily 8am-10pm.

Beef Up

Florence is known for its festivals, which usually include food, wine, and costumes. But there's one festival that's off the beaten track. The Sagra della Bistecca celebrates the region's most popular cuisines: steak. The festival is held in the Gardens of Parterre from August 14-16. Chefs line up to grill steaks *alla fiorentina,* and locals line up to get a taste. If you want some of the best beef around, head on down for some straight-off-the-cow chow.

Dioniso

GREEK $$

V. San Gallo 16r

☎055 21 78 82; www.ristorantegrecodioniso-firenze.com

Sick of typical Tuscan cuisine? Have a little baklava! It's your predictable Greek joint, in that predictable shade of blue that seems to be international code for "here be filo dough." The menu's in Italian and Greek only, but we are confident you can recognize the Greek for "souvlaki."

▶ 🧭 Just to the west of P. di San Marco. [$] Souvlaki and gyro plates €12. Baklava €3.50. Ouzo €3. ⏰ Open M-Sa noon-3pm and 7:30pm-midnight, Su 7:30pm-midnight.

Vin Olio

RISTORANTE $$

V. San Zanobi 126r

☎055 48 99 57; www.vinolio.com

Vin Olio is a quiet, grown-up sort of place, with subdued art and fans that slowly whir under the high beamed ceilings. The front room has a small bar serving cocktails (€3) and *grappa* (€1.80). Try the penne with duck meat, if the place is actually open when they claim to be.

▶ 🧭 From P. dell'Indipendenza, take V. 27 Aprile to V. San Zanobi. [$] *Antipasti* €5-9. *Primi* €8-9. ⏰ Open daily 11am-midnight.

SANTA CROCE

If you're craving something a little different, look no further than Santa Croce, where cheap and late-night food options abound. There are even a few upscale establishments huddled around the Basilica di Santa Croce. We almost don't want to spoil the fun you'll have discovering this quirky and diverse area on your own—in fact, we're tempted to just give you a world map and send you on a scavenger hunt to check off each country's cuisine. Then again, it never hurts to have some options handy; here are a few spots to get you started.

The Oil Shoppe SANDWICHES $

V. Sant'Egidio 22r

☎055 20 01 092; http://oilshoppe.blogspot.com

Whether it's the student-friendly prices, the warm and filling panini, the fresh salads, or the charm of friendly chef Alberto, something keeps every stool in The Oil Shoppe filled with study-abroaders. If the extensive menu overwhelms you, the meatball and the #24 are deservedly popular.

▶ From P. del Duomo, take V. dell'Oriuolo, turn right onto V. Folco Portiani then right onto V. Sant'Edigio. $ Sandwiches €3-4. Fries and drink €2. Cash only. ⏰ Open M-F 11am-6pm.

Cibréo Teatro del Sale RISTORANTE, PERFORMANCE VENUE $$$$

V. de' Macci 111r

☎055 20 01 492; www.cibreo.it

Normally we would never recommend a €30 meal. But this isn't a meal—it's the equivalent of buying infinite glasses of wine, ordering every dish on a fancy restaurant menu, and then buying theater tickets. You won't even need to eat lunch before this food marathon. The chef at Teatro del Sale is one of Italy's most renowned, and a meal at his restaurant across the street (served out of the same kitchen) goes for at least twice the price. Yet here, diners seat and serve themselves in the cozy interior and peer into the kitchen through a glass wall. We're pretty sure that this is the only place in the world where a famous Italian chef with a Santa Claus beard announces dish names in a town crier voice or merrily shouts things like "If I see anyone use a fork for these clams they will be thrown out on the spot!" Then, when you are full beyond your wildest dreams, the tables disappear and the focus shifts to the small stage for a live performance—young and upcoming theater performances, musical acts, dancers, film screenings, and lectures are all frequently on rotation. Membership may be private, but it's not exclusive—a one-year membership costs just €5 if you're foreign or under 26.

▶ # Just west of P. Sant'Ambrogio. *i* There's no stated dress code, but try not to look like a backpacker. Membership required. $ 1-year membership €10, foreign and under 26 €5. Breakfast €7. Lunch €20. Dinner buffet €30. A voucher from the previous Sunday's *La Repubblica* newspaper gets you a 30% discount. ⏰ Club open 9am-11pm. Dinner at 7pm. Performances begin around 9pm.

👍 Gelateria dei Neri — GELATERIA $

V. dei Neri 20/22r

☎055 21 00 34

Being a *Let's Go* researcher requires eating at a different *gelateria* each time in the quest of Florence's very best. So why can't we stop eating at this one? It might have something to do with the mousse-like *semifreddo*—try the tiramisu—or the insanely spicy Mexican chocolate, which we found too intense to finish.

▶ # From Ponte Grazie, head north on V. de' Benci and turn left onto V. dei Neri. $ Gelato from €1.50. Cash only. ⏰ Open daily 9am-midnight.

👍 La Ghiotta — CAFE $

V. Pietrapiana 7r

☎055 24 12 37

Take a number at this student-friendly rotisserie—the line is out the door during lunchtime. Patrons don't seem to mind waiting to pick their meals from platters behind the counter. Order one of the 20 varieties of pizza and cram into the seats in the back. It's even cheaper if you take it to go: you can get half a rotisserie chicken or a giant slab of eggplant *parmigiana* for just a few euro.

▶ # From Borgo Allegri, take a right onto V. Pietrapiana. $ *Primi* €5-6; *secondi* €5-7. Pizza and *calzoni* €5-7. Wine €6. ⏰ Open Tu-Su noon-5pm and 7-10pm.

Ruth's — KOSHER, VEGETARIAN $$

V. Luigi Carlo Farini 2A

☎055 24 80 888; www.kosheruth.com

This welcoming restaurant by the synagogue caters to Florence's Jewish community as well as local students. From the visitor drawings in the entryway to the bearded photos on walls, Ruth's has its own unique ambience.

▶ 🧭 To the right of the synagogue. $ *Primi* and *secondi* €7-10. Falafel platter €9. Entrees €9-18. W night student menu €10-15. ⏰ Open M-F 12:30-3pm and 7:30-10:30pm, Su 12:30-3pm and 7:30-10:30pm.

All'Antico Vinaio

CAFE $

V. dei Neri 65r

☎055 23 82 723

There's something endearing about the way this storefront trusts you to pour your own tiny glass of wine and pay for your self-serve coldcut sandwiches after eating them on the wooden seats out on the street. The prices don't hurt either.

▶ 🧭 2 blocks east of the Uffizi. $ Sandwiches from €1. Student special: sandwich and drink €4. Glass of wine €2. Cash only. ⏰ Open daily 8am-9pm.

Eby's Bar

MEXICAN $

V. dell'Oriuolo 5r

☎055 24 00 27

Heck yes, burrito joint! The food isn't exactly Mexican—it's more of a loose Italian variation—but hey, it's still a hot tortilla full of meat and cheese. This is a place that knows its clientele: a sign on the door proudly heralds the "Late Night Chicken Quesadilla." You can take your €4 burrito to go, munch it in the colorful interior, or head to the covered Volta di San Pietro alleyway. The alleyway also has a kebab place, so there are multiple options for the cheap, drunk, and hungry.

▶ 🧭 From the Duomo, head east on V. dell'Oriuolo. On the corner of V. dell'Oriuolo and V. dei Pucci. $ Nachos €3. Burrito €4. Sangria €3. ⏰ Open daily 10am-3am.

Trattoria Anita

RISTORANTE $$

V. Parlascio 2r

☎055 21 86 98

Anita is tucked off the major streets, protecting it from the largest tourist waves. Nestle into the homey interior for some home-cooked Tuscan specialties like *ravioli alla gorgonzola.*

▶ 🧭 Near the Uffizi, on the corner of V. Vinegia and V. Parlascio. $ *Primi* €7; *secondi* €7-12. ⏰ Open M-Sa noon-2:30pm and 7-10:15pm.

Caffè Pasticceria La Loggia degli Albizi

BAKERY $

Borgo degli Albizi 99r

☎055 24 79 574

If for some strange reason you don't feel like eating gelato, the baked goods here will satisfy your sweet tooth. The gorgeous pies are topped with nuts, the macaroons are as big as your face, and there are numerous Italian specialties like *biscotti* and *panforte*. You'll even be able to take your time over them, since, unlike gelato, they won't be melted by the hot summer.

▶ ⇆ From the Duomo, follow V. del Proconsolo south and turn right onto Borgo degli Albizi. [$] *Torrone* €4.50. *Panforte* €4.50. ⏰ Open daily 7am-8pm.

The Diner — DINER $

V. dell'Acqua 2

☎055 29 07 48; www.theflorencediner.com

Eating local food is one of the best parts of traveling, especially in Italy, but sometimes you just miss home. That's where The Diner comes in—you won't find a more American home-away-from-home in all of Florence. You might forget you're in Italy when you're munching on pancakes and burgers while chatting with friends back home via the free Wi-Fi.

▶ ⇆ From the Duomo, follow V. del Proconsolo south, turn right onto V. dell'Anguillara and left onto V. dell'Acqua. [$] American coffee free on W. ⏰ Open daily 8am-10:30pm.

WEST OLTRARNO

West Oltrarno is teeming with supermarkets and food machines, some of which even sell hot, fresh pasta. The restaurant scene is quirkier than across the river, but keep your eye out for sneaky cover charges.

👍 Dante — RISTORANTE $$

P. Nazario Sauro 12r

☎055 21 92 19; www.trattoriadante.net

Dante is an excellent choice for students—with any meal, students get a free bottle of wine. The pizza is the same as anywhere, but, dude, **free wine.** This place also displays lots of images of Dante on the wall, as you'd expect. Free wine!

▶ ⇆ A block south of Ponte alla Carraia, on the right. [$] €3 cover is hidden by pushpins on the outdoor menu. Fish €5-6. Pizza €6-9. Pasta €8-10. ⏰ Open daily noon-1am.

👍 Gustapanino — SANDWICHES $

V. de' Michelozzi 13r

☎333 92 02 673

Unlike other sandwich places around, this one makes your hot focaccia or *piadine* (wrap) to order, and you can see the ingredients prepared in front of you. The turkey, pesto, tomato, and mozzarella option is to die for. There's also a lewd pig in pink underwear on the counter, which can only be a plus. Gustapanino is perfect for a grab-and-go meal.

▶ ♯ In P. Santo Spirito; facing away from the Santo Spirito church, it's the 2nd building on the left. Ⓢ *Focacce* and *piadini* €3-4. ⏲ Open Tu-Su 11:30am-3pm and 7-11pm.

Gelateria La Carraia   GELATERIA $

P. Nazario Sauro 25r

☎055 28 06 95; www.lacarraiagroup.eu

An excellent gelato option right across the river, La Carraia serves cones starting at €1. Try the minty After Eight or Nutella yogurt. There's a lot of ambience in the shop, but go stand by the river—it's right outside.

▶ ♯ Right across Ponte alla Carraia. Ⓢ Gelato from €1. ⏲ Open daily 11am-11pm.

Test Your Gag Reflex

Italy is known for its pasta and wine, but there's another side of Italian cuisine that might make your stomach turn.

- **PORK BLOOD CAKE.** Florentines don't like to waste any part of the pig—they've even found a way to use the blood in this daring concoction, which is served warm.

- **CASU MARZU.** Not all the cheese you find in Florence will be palatable. This goat cheese, otherwise known as Maggot Cheese, is filled with fly larvae and must be eaten while the maggots are still alive.

- **CIECHE FRITTEN.** At the end of winter, baby eels born in the Saragasso Sea migrate and colonize the rivers of Italy. In Florence, these creatures are caught and served fried to those looking for a different seafood taste.

- **LAMPREDOTTO.** Give your stomach a taste of stomach with this local specialty. You'll see many stalls selling this gray, rubbery tripe, which comes from cow stomachs. It's usually served with tomato, onion, parsley, and celery on a panini.

Gusta Pizza

PIZZERIA $

V. Maggio 46r

☎055 28 50 68

Run by the same family as Gustapanino (see above), Gusta Pizza serves Neapolitan-style, thin-crust pizza. Eat on location for that personal service feel—if they really like you, they may even shape your pizza into a heart. Order to go if you want something warm and cheesy to eat by the river.

▶ ⇞ On the corner of V. de' Michelozzi and V. Maggio. Facing the Santo Spirito church, turn right. Look for it on the next corner, on the right. $ Pizza €4.50-8. ⏰ Open Tu-Su 11:30am-3pm and 7-11pm.

Osteria Santo Spirito

RISTORANTE $$

P. Santo Spirito 16r

☎055 23 82 383

Delightful wooden tables behind bamboo screens line the street in front of this *osteria,* while the inside has large round tables suffused with a flickering red light. Linger after your pasta for the crème brûlée (€6) and other posh desserts.

▶ ⇞ It's at the far end of P. Santo Spirito from the church, on the right. $ Pizza €6-9. *Primi* €7-12. Desserts €6. Wine by the bottle from €12. ⏰ Open daily noon-11:30pm.

EAST OLTRARNO

In **Piazza di Santa Felicita** there are a couple serviceable options for pit stops, including **Bibo, Ristorante Celestino,** and **Snack Le Delizie.** The eastern part of East Oltrarno is home to dinner gems frequented by locals, which means a lot less English on the menus.

L'Hosteria del Bricco

RISTORANTE $$

V. San Niccolò 8r

☎055 23 45 037; www.osteriadelbricco.it

Behind an unobtrusive entrance, this gorgeous space with brick arches, flowers, and stained glass over the door is well worth the cover. A suit of armor stands casually on the side as L'Hosteria's most steadfast patron. The smell will kick-start your appetite, and meat or pasta from the handwritten menu will indulge all your senses.

▶ ⇞ Cross Ponte alla Grazie and turn left onto Lungarno Serristori. After 3 blocks, turn right onto V. Lupo and then left onto V. San Niccolò. $ Cover €2.50. *Primi* €7; *secondi* €12-14. Desserts €4. ⏰ Open daily for lunch from noon and dinner 7:30pm-late.

Nightlife

Florence specializes in laid-back nightlife rather than the dance-until-dawn variety. We know this may be hard for under-21s recently unleashed in Europe and looking to booze-cruise, but if you come here with the go-hard-or-go-home mentality, you may end up sorely disappointed. Instead, drink wine and mingle by the river, fall in love with the concept of *aperitivo,* and chill in *piazze* that are full of students. Still, from the hilariously huge selection of Irish pubs to a number of chic venues that turn more club-like as the night goes on, you should be able to find an ambience that suits your intensity level. During major sporting events and festivals, the streets fill with people and spill with wine. If you're really serious about clubbing, you should think about taking a taxi to larger venues outside the city proper.

THE DUOMO

This isn't exactly a traditional nightlife area. You'll find a couple of bars right by the Duomo, but you'll be better of venturing into other neighborhoods. When the weather is beautiful and the town is particularly crowded, people hang out on the Duomo steps all night. Nearby shops like Mill Wine Shop (V. Camillo Cavour 32) offer student specials like 10 beers for €10, making an outdoor evening a highly affordable option.

Nightlife

Budget Nightlife

Florence's nightlife scene isn't one filled with lavish clubs and sky-high covers. This, of course, is good for the budget traveler, but may be a let down to those looking to rage. The cheapest option, and often most social, is to buy a bottle of wine or grab a beer and sit along the Arno or chill in a *piazza*. One of the local favorites is **Piazza Sant'Ambrogio** in Santa Croce. If you are shameless about both flirting and saving money, you can often get by in many a bar without having to pay—guys may think this doesn't apply to them, but clearly they just don't know how to chat up the right strangers. So, instead of planning your nights based on covers and clubs, go with the flow of Florence's scene. As they say, when in Florence... right?

Shot Cafe   BAR

V. dei Pucci 5
☎055 28 20 93

Umbrellas, lion paintings, and inner tubes beneath blue Christmas lights make up the aggressively quirky decor of this fun little bar. Those who haven't changed their money yet can pay for drinks in US dollars for the going exchange rate. The music is American "oldies," as long as you define oldies as anything recorded between 1920 and 2005. The TV is usually tuned to MTV—now that's retro.

▶ ✚ A block north of the Duomo. *i* Free Wi-Fi. Ⓢ Beer €3; pitchers €10. 10 shots for €19. More expensive in winter. Ⓩ Open daily 5pm-3am. Happy hour daily 5-9pm.

Astor Cafe   BAR

P. del Duomo 20r
☎055 23 99 318; www.astorcafe.com

Astor is a popular stop for locals and tourists just starting their night out. Hip hop and pop videos (and sometimes NFL) light up the walls of the interior, while the outside is a colorful candlelit scene looking up at the Duomo.

▶ ✚ On the northeast side of the *piazza*. Ⓢ Beer €5. Cocktails €7. 1L of whatever's on tap €10. Ⓩ Open daily 8am-3am.

PIAZZA DELLA SIGNORIA

At night, this area lights up with bars and fills with wandering groups of students. For a range of options in a short stretch, try **Via de' Benci** between P. Santa Croce and the river: Moyo is modern and trendy, the Red Gartello's karaoke entrance looks like the tunnel of love, and pubby Kikuya offers sandwiches and Dragoon Strong Ale. **Piazza della Signoria, Piazza della Repubblica,** and **Ponte Vecchio** are other excellent places to hang out with a beer—get one to go from a local bar for some DIY nightlife. It should also be noted that the Ponte Vecchio is a fine place for a snog and that *Let's Go* does not condone drunk-riding the P. della Repubblica carousel.

Moyo   BAR
V. de' Benci 23r
☎055 24 79 738; www.moyo.it

A sophisticated crowd lounges in Moyo's modern, two-pronged black chairs. Candles and green disco lights that shine through a chandelier give this place a surreal, smoky atmosphere with an undulating beat.

▶ ⚔ Just off P. de' Davanzati. Ⓢ Wine €6. ⏰ Open M-Th 8pm-2am, F-Sa 9pm-3am, Su 8pm-2am. *Aperitivo* sushi W 7-10:30pm.

Amadeus   PUB
V. dei Pescioni 3
☎055 28 17 09

Amadeus fosters a healthy young crowd that, as pubs go, is not too male-heavy. The genre changes nightly between "happy music," house, R and B, reggae, and hip hop.

▶ ⚔ Just off P. de' Davanzati. Ⓢ Beer €6. 3 drinks for €10. ⏰ Open daily 7pm-2:30am.

The Old Stove   IRISH PUB
V. Pellicceria 2r
☎055 29 52 32

Hey look, it's another Irish pub! Which, of course, actually means American, because Irish people know better than to go to Florence to drink. The dive-bar inside pales in comparison to the social outdoor seating. The soccer-match board indicates The Old Stove's rowdy fan days.

▶ ⚔ Walk to the side of P. della Repubblica that doesn't have the carousel and look down the street to the left. ⓘ Dollar Day on W—pay in US$ all day long. Another branch is located by the Duomo. Ⓢ Pints €6, happy hour

€4. Cocktails €7. ⏰ Open M-Th noon-2am, F-Sa noon-3am, Su noon-2am. Happy hour M-Th 5-9pm.

Twice

CLUB

V. Giuseppe Verdi 57r

☎055 24 76 356

Mostly sweaty guys, half-hearted dancing, and colored lights, Twice is the sort of place for clubbing when you don't feel like making a big production out of it. This cover-free club is a favorite of drunk students, people with no other club ideas, and Italian men on the prowl. (Unsurprisingly, this was a favorite *Jersey Shore* haunt while they were in Florence.) The weird mix of music should have you giggling every time some forgotten hit from eighth grade plays. There's also a booth in plain view where people get hot and heavy, and a fairly arbitrary VIP area—if you get waved in, just take the free drinks and roll with it.

▶ 🪧 From the Duomo, head east on V. dell'Oriuolo, then right onto V. Giuseppe Verdi. $ Beer €5. Cocktails €9. ⏰ Open daily 9pm-4am.

Slowly

BAR

V. Porta Rossa 63r

☎055 26 45 354; www.slowlycafe.com

Slowly will drain your bank account quickly. This blend of candlelight, flashing colors, thumping music, and well-dressed clientele leisurely sipping overpriced cocktails could have been imported from Manhattan.

▶ 🪧 Just off P. de' Davanzati. $ Beer €6. Cocktails €8. ⏰ Open daily 7pm-2:30am.

The Blob Club

CLUB

V. Vinegia 21r

☎055 21 12 09; www.blobclub.com

To visit this exclusive club, you have to submit for a membership card (€5) on the Blob website. Some travelers report that this is the choice haunt of bartenders after hours.

▶ 🪧 East of the Palazzo Vecchio, on V. Vinegia. $ Membership €5. ⏰ Live music Su.

Top 5 Smooch Spots

Florence is undeniably romantic, with movie-set side streets and constant streams of wine. If you're inspired to indulge in a Florentine romance, here are some options preferable to hostel bunk beds.

- **PONTE VECCHIO.** It's as cliché as the Eiffel Tower and not remotely private, but no one bats an eye at some smooching along the most famous bridge in town. Hope the constant stream of wedding parties isn't a turn-off though.

- **PONTE SANTA TRINITA.** Keeping along the Arno, score a little more isolation and an even better view on one of the broad stone triangles over the edge of this less trafficked bridge. Come early (or very late) to find one unoccupied, though—this is prime canoodling real estate.

- **THE DUOMO.** Want to tick blasphemous make-out session off your "Never Have I Ever" list? The steps in front of Florence's most recognizable church are scenic and quiet after midnight, but more daring couples could try climbing the dome or tower. Right before closing, the 300+ steps of winding stairwells will be mostly deserted, and your hearts will already be racing from the climb. If you make it to the top, the view ain't too shabby either.

- **PIAZZALE MICHELANGELO.** It might seem like an obvious choice, but it's a bit too parking lot to really set the mood. Try a corner along the hike up to the *piazzale* or keep going up the hill to find a small park that's far darker, deserted, and every bit as scenic.

- **LEAVE THE CITY.** Take your romance out under the Tuscan sun and head to the hills. Hostels in adjacent towns let you escape the crowds and perhaps snag a private room while staying within a backpacker's budget.

SANTA MARIA NOVELLA

In the evening, the streets of Santa Maria Novella are alive with youth. There are some stellar nightlife options, but in this area it's best to choose a destination and stick to it rather than bar hop due to cover fees, distance, difference of style, or some combination of the three. If you're trekking out to Central Park, be smart: pull a group together and set aside funds for a cab home.

Space Electronic Discotheque

CLUB

V. Palazzuolo 37

☎055 29 30 82; www.spaceelectronic.net

Do you wish you could go clubbing in Epcot? Then join the happy young crowd around the aquarium bar in this conveniently located space-age dance hall. Everyone joins in with whoever's blowing up the small karaoke stage. Meanwhile, the DJ upstairs rains techno down on you like a robot space god. If the bouncer waves you in, don't be fooled into thinking you got a free entrance—you'll pay the steep cover (€16) when you leave. Special events like guest bands and foam parties are extensively advertised on posters around town, so keep an eye out. The club's location means it's one of the few in the area that won't require you to take a cab home.

▶ ⇄ From the river, take V. Melegnano to V. Palazzuolo, and turn right. $ Cover €16. Shots €3. Cocktails €6.50. Fine for lost entry cards €50. ⏰ Open daily 10pm-4am.

The Joshua Tree Pub

PUB

V. della Scala 37r

www.thejoshuatreepub.com

There's something homey about the worn green paint on this pub's wooden walls. Smaller than similar places in town, the Joshua Tree feels cozier and less deserted in the early evening hours. Launch your evening itinerary here, or chill with the international regulars that often cluster on weeknights.

▶ ⇄ On corner of V. Benedetta. $ Pints €5. ⏰ Open daily 4pm-2am. Happy hour 4-9:30pm.

Public House 27

BAR

V. Palazzuolo 27r

☎339 30 22 330; www.publichouse27.com

This punk bar emits a sanguine glow and a cloud of smokers from early in the evening. If you aren't put off by the scary face stuck on the door, brave the red interior for a €3 pint.

▶ ⇄ On the corner of V. della Porcellana. $ Pints €3. ⏰ Open M-Sa 5pm-2am, Su 2:30pm-2am.

Central Park

CLUB

V. del Fosso Macinate 2

☎055 35 99 42; www.centralfirenze.it

This enormous, heavily staffed club in the middle of Parco delle Cascine is quite a schlep from the city center, but it's hard not to be at least a little impressed by the beautiful people and differently colored outdoor dance floors that undulate with house and hip hop astride chandelier-lined bars. They provide alcotesters, but save yourself the pocket change: you'll know you're drunk when you mistake the tree in the middle of the dance floor for a sexy lady.

▶ ✇ From the river, go to Ponte della Vittoria, the westernmost bridge of the city center. Follow Viale Fratelli Rosselli north (careful, it's busy), then turn left onto V. Fosso Macinante. *Let's Go* does not recommend walking through the area at night. Ⓢ Cover €20; international visitors before 12:30am €10, after 12:30am €13. Some travelers report negotiating entrance fees when in a large group. All drinks €10. ⓩ Open W 9:30pm-4am, F-Sa 9:30pm-4am. Often doesn't allow non-VIP guests in until at least 11pm.

SAN LORENZO

North American and Australian backpackers are common here due to the proximity of budget hostels. Nightlife is mostly pub-like places to chill and watch the game.

Mostodolce   BAR

V. Nazionale 114r

☎055 23 02 928; www.mostodolce.it

"In wine there is wisdom, in beer there is strength, in water there is bacteria." This is how the Mostodolce menu greets its patrons—in English, by the way, thanks to the influx of American tourists in the summer months. Come to watch a sporting event with big crowds, or just to drink artisanal beers brewed in Prato and ponder the random duck above the bar. Warning: pondering increases with alcohol consumption. If you're around for a while (or drink fast) there's a "10th beer free" punch-card.

▶ ✇ On the corner of V. Guelfa. Ⓢ 30cl beer €3.50; 50cl €5. ⓩ Open daily 11am-late. Happy hour from 10:30pm.

Dublin Pub   BAR

V. Faenza 27r

☎055 27 41 571; www.dublinpub.it

If men in their 20s and 30s are your calling, they're calling you from Dublin Pub. This little bar is great for some international mingling, but not so popular with women or those under 20 (though, if you're one of those, you can still have a good time). Also, the bar has purse hooks—score! Stick it out, because by the end of the night, an old Italian man could be teaching you how to curse in Italian.

▶ ♯ The far end of V. Faenza. Ⓢ Cider €4.40. Guinness €6. Pizza €5. ☼ Open daily 5pm-2am.

Kitsch the Pub   BAR
V. San Gallo 22r

☎328 90 39 289; www.kitsch-pub.com

What do you expect from a place called "kitsch" if not red velvet and stained glass? During the low season, try to nab some of the alfresco seating and mix with locals to avoid the TV that blares Gwen Stefani.

▶ ♯ Off V. Camillo Cavour. Ⓢ Shots €3.50-4.50. Small Fosters €3.60; medium €6.60. Cocktails €7. ☼ Open daily 5pm-3am. *Aperitivo* 6-9:30pm.

The Fish Pub   BAR
P. del Mercato Centrale 44r

☎055 26 82 90; www.thefishpub.com

While the ads for a "free crazy party" here every weekend night may seem slightly fishy, you might as well print the flier on the website for discounts and a free shot. While you're at it, capitalize on the free champagne glass for students on Thursdays and free champagne on Mondays for women. Once you've looted the area, grab a handy plastic cup from the exit and take your drink to go. As for the bar itself, downstairs is loud and lit up blue, while upstairs features a quieter lounge area, a license plate collection, and a distorted portrait of the queen of England.

▶ ♯ Right out of Mercato Centrale. *i* Rock music on Tu. Bring your own iPod on W. Latin music on Su. Ⓢ 5 shots for €5. Cocktails €7. ☼ Open daily from 3pm to "late night." Happy hour 3-9pm.

SAN MARCO

San Marco is not the liveliest neighborhood at night. The area north of P. di San Marco is particularly deserted, especially after the buses stop running, and the places that are open serve scattered crowds. But if you're looking for something relaxed or just want to meet a few locals, you might like it here.

The ClubHouse   BAR
V. de' Ginori 6r

☎055 21 14 27; www.theclubhouse.it

This sports bar serves alcohol from dresser drawers under a

chandelier—that is, except for the Absolut, which gets a special glowing shelf like it's the goblet of fire. Plasma TVs and martinis are at your disposal all day to coast toward a relaxed evening.

▶ ⚜ Off V. dei Pucci. *i* Wi-Fi. Ⓢ Shots €3. Beer €5.50. Cocktails €6. ⏲ Open daily noon-midnight. Kitchen open until 11pm.

Finnegan Irish Pub   IRISH PUB

V. San Gallo 123r

☎055 49 07 94; www.finneganpub.com

Another 🔲**Irish pub!** This one has outdoor seating, dedicated screenings of soccer and rugby, typical pub booths, and rugby paraphernalia on the walls. Finnegan boasts its international flair with an eclectic collection of currencies stuck behind the bar. You know the drill: good place for casually watching the game, whatever the game may be, and hanging with the regulars. They also advertise dartboard competitions, because sharp objects and alcohol are a fantastic mix.

▶ ⚜ North of P. di San Marco. Ⓢ Beer €4-5. Cocktails €6.50. ⏲ Open M-Th 1pm-12:30am, F-Sa 1pm-1am, Su 1pm-12:30am.

Wine Bar Nabucco   WINE BAR

V. 27 Aprile 28r

☎055 47 50 87; www.nabuccowine.com

You could live here from dawn to dusk. Nabucco starts the day

The Secret's Out

Ask any Florentine for late-night munchies and they may send you to a generic restaurant or simply shrug their shoulders. But ask them about the 🔲**secret bakeries**, and they'll suddenly lower their voice to a whisper and, if you're lucky, divulge the location of one of these glorious pastry speakeasies. If you find one, you'll probably just see a small cluster of locals huddled around a non-descript establishment. But the golden glow shining through the glass doors lets you know that something's going on inside. Working hard to supply the daytime pastry shops with fresh treats for when they open in the wee hours, these late-night pastry shops don't mind selling their delicious treats to those looking to chow down before hitting the sack. So, keep a nose out for chocolatey smells wafting from an alleyway, for even *Let's Go's* best researcher-writers had a hard time finding these places.

Nightlife

with an international breakfast (€1-4.20) followed by a coffee bar (coffee €1; lattes €1.10), lunch, and the *aperitivo* buffet. And of course, the wine bar. Try the frozen Bailey's (€4).

▶ ✠ On the corner of V. Santa Reparata. i Free Wi-Fi. h Open daily 8am-midnight. *Aperitivo* 6:30-9:30pm

SANTA CROCE

Santa Croce is the soul of Florence's nightlife. If the street you're on seems oddly quiet, just keep walking—the lively hotspots show up in unexpected pockets. Try **Via de' Benci** for a rich selection. On nice evenings, join the swarm of young people lounging and drinking in **Piazza Sant'Ambrogio** and **Piazza Lorenzo Ghiberti**.

◩ Las Palmas   PIAZZA
Largo Annigoni
☎347 27 60 033; www.laspalmasfirenze.it

What seems like a perfectly ordinary *piazza* by day tranforms into a rowdy beach-themed block party when evening rolls around. We're talking palm trees, seafood, and straw screens right in the middle of Florence's cobblestone streets. Performers grace the enormous stage with theater, dance, music, or some combination, setting the mood for a whole *piazza* of merriment. Groups of students, families, and older folk cram into the scores of tables and pile up on the generous *aperitivo* buffet, and children compete at foosball and table tennis. If you think the place is rowdy on a regular night, wait until you come when they're projecting sporting events on the big screen.

▶ ✠ Off of P. Lorenzo Ghiberti, in front of the La Nazione building. *i* Check website for performance and screening schedule. Ⓢ Beer €4. Pizza €5-8. *Primi* €7-10. ◨ Open May-Sept daily, hours vary. *Aperitivo* 8:30-9:30pm.

◩ Lochness Lounge   BAR
V. de' Benci 19r
☎055 24 14 64

"Get messy with Nessy" alongside a laid-back mix of young locals, students, and visitors. Art and photography exhibits frequently join Warhols on the red walls, while live music or dance hits set the mood for pool and foosball.

▶ ✠ From Ponte alle Grazie, follow V. de' Benci north. *i* Live acoustic music on Tu and Sa. 2-for-the-price-of-1 drinks during *aperitivo*. Ⓢ Beer €5. Cocktails €7. ◨ Open daily 6:30pm-2am. *Aperitivo* 7-11pm.

Nightlife

🖼 Caffè Sant'Ambrogio   BAR
P. Sant'Ambrogio 7r
☎055 24 77 277

Caffè Sant'Ambrogio's primary role is to seemingly single-handedly serve the young P. Sant'Ambrogio scene. Since everybody and their brother is out drinking in the *piazza,* that's saying something. The bar thinks it's being classy with its tasteful female nude, but it's the *piazza* that drives its business.

▶ ♯ The *piazza* is at the end of V. Pietrapiana. Ⓢ Wine €4-7. Cocktails €6-7. ⚃ Open M-Sa 8:30am-2am. *Aperitivo* 6-9pm.

Oibò   CAFE, LOUNGE
Borgo de' Greci 1
☎055 26 38 611; www.oibo.net

Florence's casual chic crowd comes here to sip drinks on the large outdoor patio and dance in the loud stone interior. As the night goes on, the DJ tends to break out the Italian hits, and you might witness a bar full of elegant Italians belting along. This is a great spot for an *aperitivo* on your way to the Teatro Verdi.

▶ ♯ On the corner across from the Basilica di Santa Croce. 𝒊 DJ parties on Th-Sa. Ⓢ Beer €6. Cocktails €7.50. ⚃ Open Apr-Nov Tu-Su 8am-2am. *Aperitivo* 6:30-9:30pm.

Naima   CAFE, BAR
V. dell'Anguillara 54
☎055 26 54 098; www.naimafirenze.it

The subtle violet-and-stone bar area of Naima is a great place to start the night, while the lounge has couches and candlelight for an intimate feel. Here you'll find lighthearted internationals and Euro-hipsters taking advantage of the affordable drinks.

▶ ♯ From southeast of the Duomo, follow V. del Proconsolo south and turn right onto V. dell'Anguillara. 𝒊 €1 vodka shots on M and W. €3 vodka lemon shots on Tu. Ⓢ Pizza and beer special €6. Cocktails from €7. *Aperitivo* €8. ⚃ Open daily 10pm-2am. *Aperitivo* 7-9pm.

Plaz   CAFE, BAR
V. Pietrapiana 36r
☎055 24 20 81

Plaz gets a lot of traffic. The 30-something crowd gathers inside, while the outdoor seating under the *piazza*'s ancient arches draws an equally ancient crowd. You'll find the youngest Plaz visitors standing around the street or under the tents just

Nightlife

outside the door, where you can make a pit-stop to watch the drunk university students stumble by.

▶ 🌡 On P. dei Ciompi at the end of V. Pietrapiana. Ⓢ Cover €1.50. *Aperitivo* from €8. Ⓩ Open daily 8am-3am.

Kitsch Bar
BAR, CONCERT VENUE

Viale Antonio Gramsci 1/3/5

☎055 23 43 890; www.kitsch-bar.com

If a summer evening's booze-fueled wanderings take you to this edge of the historic city center, a small outdoor stage that often features local musicians will probably lure you to Kitsch. The purple tablecloths, giant chandeliers, and zebra chairs live up to Kitsch's not-quite-ironic name. The bar's proximity to parking and the edge of the city center attracts locals driving from the parts of Florence they didn't include on your tourist map.

▶ 🌡 Follow Viale Giovine Italia up from the river, or take Borgo Croce east until you hit the traffic circle. It's on the northwestern corner. Ⓢ *Aperitivo* €8. Happy hour beer and cocktails €5. Ⓩ Open daily 6:30pm-2am. *Aperitivo* 6:30-10:30pm. Happy hour 10pm-1am.

Be Bop Music Club
CLUB, CONCERT VENUE

V. dei Servi 76r

☎055 29 52 30

This basement club attracts overheated foreigners with its gospel of air-conditioning. The grotto-like space doesn't have optimal acoustics, but for the price of a beer you can sit right by the stage and discover some pretty great cover bands.

▶ 🌡 Although the postcards hilariously provide a map all the way from the train station (clear on the other side of town), just walk up V. dei Servi from

GLBT Nightlife

A number of bars and clubs in this area cater to a ▼GLBT clientele—however, they would prefer not to be listed in guide-books. Many of these establishments are unmarked or tucked down alleys. If you can get yourself in the correct general vicinity, the staff at neighboring bars can usually direct you the rest of the way. For a list of gay-friendly nightlife options, contact the organization Arcigay (www.arcigay.it) or check out www.patroc.com/florence.

the Duomo and look for the "A/C" sign. Ⓢ Beer €5. Cocktails €6-8. 🕐 Open daily 11am-2am. Concerts start at 9pm.

Tartan Jock   PUB
Corso dei Tintori 41r
☎055 24 78 305

Don't worry, it's not another Irish pub... this one's Scottish! A lively young crowd kicks back in the bright wood interior, which is one of the most casual in the city. If too much Guinness gives you a sudden urge to be classy, cross the street to Gran Tintori. which beckons with an older crowd, occasional live music, black-and-white photographs, and leather seats.

▶ 🎯 On the right just off V. de' Benci near Ponte alle Grazie. Ⓢ Shots €3. Guinness €5. 🕐 Open daily 8pm-2am.

I Visacci Caffè   BAR
Borgo degli Albizi 80r
☎055 20 01 956

There are five-shots-for-€5 deals at a few places in town, but it's good to know which ones they are. This is an excellent joint for a pre-game—if you can convince yourself to leave the €5 cocktails and three beers for €10 behind.

▶ 🎯 From the Duomo, take a left off V. Proconsolo onto Borgo degli Albizi. 🕐 Open daily 10am-late.

The William   BAR, CONCERT VENUE
V. Antonio Magliabechi 9
☎055 26 38 357

An enormous railroad car of an English pub, The William features live music many nights and reasonably priced pub food. Belying the customer base, international flags line the comfy side room to the left of the bar.

▶ 🎯 To the right of the Basilica di Santa Croce. Ⓢ Pints from €5. 🕐 Open M-Th 11:30am-2am, F-Sa 11:30am-3am, Su 11:30am-2am.

WEST OLTRARNO

West Oltrarno has a good concentration of students, making it a lively and diverse evening locale, especially around the P. Santo Spirito. If you want to go dancing, you'll have to look somewhere else.

[thumbs-up] Volume

BAR

P. Santo Spirito 5r

☎055 23 81 460

There's a quirky atmosphere in this *"museo libreria caffè."* Busy and cluttered, Volume is decorated with woodworking tools, mismatched chairs, a jukebox, and a giant old printing press. The place is just as much about gelato and sweets as it is about cocktails, but the gelato is fancy, starting at €2.50.

▶ ⇆ To the right of the Santo Spirito church, sandwiched between 2 larger establishments. $ Cocktails €7. Crepes €4-7. ⏰ Open daily 11am-3am.

[thumbs-up] Dolce Vita

WINE BAR

P. del Carmine 6r

☎055 28 45 95; www.dolcevitaflorence.com

Trendy young adults with margarita glasses populate this happening, artsy bar. The bold interior hosts monthly photo shows as well as live Brazilian, jazz, or contemporary music every Wednesday and Thursday night. Travelers on a budget can break out that one nice outfit they brought, nab a spritz, and feast on the *aperitivo* buffet.

▶ ⇆ In P. del Carmine, by the Carmine church. ℹ Live music W-Th 7:30-9:30pm. $ Spritz €7. ⏰ Open M-Sa 5pm-2:30am. *Aperitivo* buffet 7:30-9:30pm.

Pop Cafe

BAR

P. Santo Spirito 18

☎055 21 38 52; www.popcafe.it

This funky, simple setup has a Pinocchio-nosed, one-eyed girl as its symbol, hinting at its draw to the artsy modern crowd. On the happening P. Santo Spirito, Pop Cafe is further enlivened by a DJ and cheap drinks. Carnivores take heed—the *aperitivo* buffet is vegetarian, as is the weekday lunch menu.

▶ ⇆ To the left of the Santo Spirito church. $ Beer, shots, and *prosecco* €3 at the bar, €4 at tables. Bagel sandwiches €5. ⏰ Open daily 11:30am-2am.

One-Eyed Jack

BAR

P. Nazario Sauro 2

☎055 62 88 040

You shouldn't have any trouble finding this Australian-run bar—a big painting of Jack in an eyepatch spans the front shutter. Live bands and international DJs often come by on weekends; other nights you can hit up the jukebox. This is a great spot for a pint and a bite.

▶ Across the street from Gelateria La Carraia and Dante. $ Pints €4.50. Cocktails €7. Sandwich €3.50-4. ⏰ Open daily 11am-2am. Happy hour daily until 11pm.

EAST OLTRARNO

Far east of any part of Florence you're likely to visit, East Oltrarno is where the locals go to party. Since they're real people with real jobs, things tend to be most happening here on weekends. Investigate **Piazza Giuseppe Poggi** (at the base of the hill up to Piazzale Michelangelo), **Via San Niccolò,** and **Via dei Renai** to get your game on. In late summer, bars alight along the southern banks of the Arno.

James Joyce Pub — BAR

Lungarno Benvenuto Cellini 1

☎055 65 80 856

This enormous, comfortable bar is filled with students for a reason, particularly on weekend evenings. You don't even have to step inside to order another round of drinks—a window in the bar opens onto the patio. There's foosball, literary kitsch on the walls, and a fun local vibe. Unusual offerings include crepes and staff favorite drinks such as the Mint Alexander with white chocolate, brandy, and mint liqueur.

▶ On the western side of the traffic circle after the Ponte San Niccolò. $ Shots €3-4. Wine from €4.50. Bottled beer €5. ⏰ Open daily until 3am.

Zoe — BAR

V. dei Renai 13

☎055 24 31 11; www.zoebar.it

The colorful outdoor seating and zebra decorations give this place an upbeat feel as it floods with 20- and 30-somethings for its renowned *aperitivo.* Take advantage of Zoe's extensive cocktail menu.

▶ Across the river from V. de' Benci. Cross Ponte alle Grazie, walk 1 block, and turn left onto V. dei Renai. $ Wine €7. ⏰ Open M-W 8pm-2am, F-Su 8pm-2am.

Rifrullo — BAR

V. San Niccolò 55r

☎055 23 42 621; www.ilrifrullo.com

This calm, classy restaurant-bar draws a mix of ages. Come for a subdued but busy weekday *aperitivo* in the garden or a weekend DJ dance set, especially on Sunday.

▶ Cross Ponte alle Grazie and continue 2 blocks. Turn left onto V. San Niccolò and continue walking. It's the place with a barely legible curlicue name. $ *Aperitivo* and drink €8. ⏰ Open May-Sept daily 7:30pm-2am.

Negroni

BAR

V. dei Renai 17r

☎055 24 36 47; www.negronibar.com

Negroni is the other big name on V. dei Renai, where patrons spill out of the official outdoor seating to populate the small green square and the banks of the Arno. The petite interior is hopping when there's a DJ or bad weather.

▶ Cross over Ponte alle Grazie and turn right onto Lungarno Serristori. The bar is on P. Giuseppe Poggi, to the right. $ *Grappa* €4. Beer €5.50. *Aperitivo* €7-11. ⏰ Open M-Sa 8am-2am, Su 6:30pm-2am. *Aperitivo* 7-11pm.

Arts and Culture

You may think that all the grand cultural events in Florence happened several hundred years ago during the Renaissance. In reality, those ancient frescoes and palaces now provide a great backdrop for modern culture. Florence's cultural scene is always changing, with lots of new and small venues. Follow the posters and brochures around town to be rewarded with the latest and greatest. Be on the lookout for festivals, which range from music to cinema to our personal favorite, gelato. Florence's lively bars and lounges tend to also be some of its best music and theater venues, and for some reason they don't charge extra for the entertainment. A good starting point on your cultural excursions is the Teatro Verdi, which sells tickets for theatrical, cultural, and sporting events all over the city. You can also check www.informacitta.net to see what shows are on during your stay.

LIBRARY CAFES

Florence's library cafes are the kind of place you could happily live in forever. Who knew nightlife, books, music, culture, and food could fuse so seamlessly into one?

◼ La Cité Libreria Cafe   WEST OLTRARNO
Borgo San Frediano 21
☎055 21 03 87; www.lacitelibreria.info
   Books, sandwiches, comfy couches, and affordable alcohol—

Budget Arts and Culture

Florentines love their festivals, and so does *Let's Go,* especially when great music, delicious food, and a first-person view into the Tuscan culture accompany them. And none of them cost a thing. See **Holidays and Festivals** or visit www.firenzeturismo.it to find out what bizarre tradition may be coming up soon. Be on the lookout for free musical recitals, like the ones at **Chiesa di Santa Maria de' Ricci.** You can also visit a library cafe for a budget-friendly mix of culture and nightlife.

this cozy three-room venue's got pretty much everything you need. And that's before you realize they've also got tango lessons, live music, dance, and theatrical performances.

► From Ponte alla Carraia, walk west on Borgo San Frediano. The library cafe spans 3 windows on the right. $ Beer €3.50. Cocktails €5-6. ⏰ Open M 3:30pm-midnight, Tu-Sa 11:30am-midnight, Su 3:30pm-midnight.

BRAC — SANTA CROCE

V. dei Vagellai 18r

☎055 09 44 877; www.libreriabrac.net/brac

This chameleon of a place is the perfect daytime escape. You can spend a whole afternoon with a book or laptop while sampling delicious pie in the glass-walled courtyard. In the evening, the back room full of books, glass tables, and artsy placemats becomes one of the few quality vegetarian dinner spots in Florence. The front room is also a fully operational bar.

► From Ponte alle Grazie, walk 2 blocks down V. de' Benci and turn left onto V. dei Vagellai. It's a small, discreet door on the right just before the *piazza.* *i* Free Wi-Fi; ask at bar for the code. $ Desserts €6. ⏰ Open M-Sa 11am-midnight, Su noon-5pm. Closed 2 weeks in Aug.

CLASSICAL MUSIC

Florence is typically a visual-arts city, but there's still plenty of music to be found in the world of frescoes. Operas are also sometimes hosted by **Saint Mark's Church** (V. Maggio 16).

Chiesa di Santa Maria de' Ricci — DUOMO

V. del Corso

☎055 21 50 44

An unassuming little church with a loud voice, this *chiesa* boasts

Festival Phobia

Florence spices up its streets with a number of festivals throughout the year. However, these apparently benign celebrations threaten the well-being of some sensitive travelers, so we've assembled a helpful calendar of events:

- **Don't like creepy-crawlies?** Steer clear of the Parco delle Cascine on Ascension Day (40 days after Easter). During the Festa del Grillo, thousands of "lucky crickets" are put up for sale in celebration of the arrival of spring. Actually, thanks to animal rights groups, none of the *grilli* are real—since 1999, Florentines have bought cages with electronic replicas instead.

- **Have pollen allergies?** Guess you won't see the P. della Signoria when it's carpeted in fragrant blossoms during the city's annual flower display (usually in late-spring or early summer).

- **Suffer from dodgeball-induced PTSD?** Save yourself from the testosterone frenzy of Calcio Storico, an annual tournament in which four teams compete in a 16th-century form of football. The tourney takes over P. Santa Croce in late June.

- **Pedophobic?** Some people find the procession of singing children who carry papier mâché lanterns through Florence's moonlit streets during the Festa della Rificolona charming. Others find it all too *Children of the Corn*. If you belong in the latter category, stay inside the evening of September 7th.

a pretty spectacular pipe organ. Fortunately for the music-starved traveler, it likes to show it off. The church doors are thrown open every evening for 7pm vespers and again at 9pm for an organ recital. The concert programs are crowd pleasers. If the only organ piece you know is Bach's *Toccata and Fugue,* you're still likely to be in luck, as it's performed frequently.

▶ ♯ From the Duomo, take V. dei Calzaioli south and turn left onto V. del Corso. Ⓢ Free. 🕐 Vespers daily 7pm. Organ recital daily 9pm.

Teatro Verdi   SANTA CROCE
V. Ghibellina 99r
☎055 21 23 20; www.teatroverdionline.it

Perhaps Florence's most famous music venue, this grand red-and-gold concert hall lined with box seats swells with concerts from symphonies to modern favorites.

▶ ♯ From P. Santa Croce, walk up V. Giovanni da Verazzano. *i* Credit card required for phone or online reservations. $ Prices vary depending on show and seat. ⏰ Box office open daily 4-7pm during the theater season. Alternative box office at V. delle Vecchie Carceri 1 open M-F 9:30am-7pm, Sa 9:30am-2pm.

ROCK AND JAZZ

The rock and jazz venues in Florence attract lively crowds and tend to cost no more than the price of a drink—and any drink tastes sweeter when sipped to the sound of a sweet serenade. Many of the places we list in **Nightlife** regularly host live music, including West Oltrarno's **Dolce Vita** and **Volume.** Big-name artists have been known to show up anywhere from the **Teatro Verdi** to small cafes, so keep your eyes peeled for posters.

✓ Sei Divino — SANTA MARIA NOVELLA

Borgo Ognissanti 42r

☎055 21 77 91

Live music fills this *aperitivo* destination every Thursday. On all the other days, you can still count on a strict diet of rock and roll to go with your cocktails and wine. For some reason, the tourist crowds haven't discovered this gem yet, so, for your sake, please don't tell them.

► ✣ Go northwest on Borgo Ognissanti from Ponte alla Carraia. It's on the right. ℹ Live music on Th. $ Cocktails from €7. ⏰ Open M-Sa noon-2am, Su 3pm-2am.

Jazz Club — SANTA CROCE

V. Nuova de' Caccini 3

☎055 24 79 700; www.jazzclubfirenze.com

Contrary to what you might expect, Jazz Club isn't just about jazz: they also play blues, rock and roll, rock, funk, soul, swing, and world music. Whatever the genre, their live music guarantees a relaxing night out.

► ✣ Going north on Borgo Pinti, turn left just before V. degli Alfani. Jazz Club is on the left. ℹ Rock and blues on Tu. Jazz on W. $ Cover €5. ⏰ Open Tu-Sa 9pm-late. Concerts 10:15pm.

THEATER

Don't be scared off because you assume performances will be in Italian; theaters are some of the best evening experiences in Florence, and the fact that they're often free is the icing on an already awesome cake. Florentine theater turns up in the most unexpected places, like restaurants and museums. In the summer, the **Bargello** sometimes hosts site-specific productions in its courtyard, while temporary stages in the **Piazza della Signoria** host music and dance acts. If you're here a bit longer, there are some worthy venues just outside town like the **Teatro Puccini,** the **Teatro Sotteraneo,** and the **Saschall.**

Teatro della Pergola   SAN MARCO

V. della Pergola 18

☎055 22 641; www.teatrodellapergola.com

Nowadays, the only opera you hear in this 1656 opera house happens during the *Maggio Musicale Fiorentino* festival. The rest of the time, you can enjoy a selection of about 250 drama productions each year from its plush red seats and gilded galleries.

▶ ⚘ At the intersection of V. della Colonna and V. Nuova de' Caccini. Ⓢ Prices vary by performance. ⏰ Box office open M-F 9:30am-6:45pm, Sa 10am-12:30pm.

CINEMA

Check listings for VO *(versione originale)* to find films that have not been dubbed over in Italian. There's also a trend among Italian cinemas to have 3D screenings of concerts or theater performances happening elsewhere in Italy.

Cinema Teatro Odeon   PIAZZA DELLA SIGNORIA

P. degli Strozzi 1r

☎055 21 40 68; www.odeon.intoscana.it

The grand cinema itself will probably outshine whatever film you intend to watch here. Beyond the massive stones and imposing wooden doors, the interior is so ornate that the ticket booth is decked with Doric columns, the columns are decked with golden orbs, and the orbs are decked with golden elephants and **dragons.** The month's schedule of English-language features is posted outside, but you may want to stop in anyway for the fresh, air-conditioned interior.

▶ ⚘ From P. della Repubblica, walk up V. degli Strozzi. *i* A/C. Bistro and bar inside. $ Tickets €7.50, students M-F €6. ⏰ Screenings begin in early evening.

SPECTATOR SPORTS

Stadio Artemio Franchi

OUTSKIRTS

Viale Manfredo Fanti 4A

☎055 55 32 803; http://en.violachannel.tv

As is true for most Italian cities, Florence has a soccer team, and that soccer team is one of the primary obsessions of the city's residents. Purple-clad Fiorentina waver on the brink of success but never quite seem to achieve it, making them a great team to support if you're more into roller-coaster rides than easy victories. Catch the games here on Sunday during most of the year. The stadium is largely uncovered, though, so pick a day when it's not raining.

▶ 🚏 Take bus #7, 17, or 20, or the train from Santa Maria Novella to Firenze Campo di Marte. The bus takes you directly to the stadium; it's a short walk from the train. $ Tickets €14-80. ⏰ Box office open M-F 9:30am-12:30pm and 2:30-6:30pm. Most matches Sept-May Su afternoons.

Shopping

Florence may not be Paris or Milan, but it sure has some snazzy window displays—you'll be tempted to stop at nearly every store you pass. For upscale designer shopping, look to Piazza della Signoria, while San Lorenzo and Santa Croce tend to be home to the boutiques. Florence is also brimming with open-air markets where you can find just about anything—if you know where to go. Whatever you do, steer clear of fake merchandise, like knock-off handbags. They're cheap (and for a reason), but they're illegal to buy as well as to sell, and you could face a hefty fine if caught with one.

Budget Shopping

The best month for shopping in Florence is July. As retailers prepare for the August slump, when the locals empty out and head for the seashore, they chop prices drastically. By the end of the first week in July, signs are springing up all over the city for sales and discounts, with some things 50% or more off. Mid-July is also the season of scorching temperatures, so you'll have more than one reason to stay inside the air-conditioned stores. The rest of the year, hit up Florence's top-notch markets for some bargains.

OPEN-AIR MARKETS

Open-air markets are some of the most authentic experiences Florence has to offer. Of course, you'll have to break through the natural assumption that foreigners are too stupid to bargain. If you need further venues to hone your negotiation techniques, you can also try the enormous food and clothing market in **Parco delle Cascine** (P. Vittorio Veneto ✚ Off Viale Fratelli Rosselli on the western edge of the city. ☒ Open Tu 7am-1pm.), the flower market in **Piazza della Repubblica** (☒ Open Th 10am-7pm.), or the antique market at **Giardini Fortezza Firenze.** (✚ Follow V. Faenza north as it becomes V. Dionisi. ☒ Open Sept-June every 3rd Su of the month.)

▨ Mercato Centrale   SAN LORENZO
P. del Mercato Centrale

This technically isn't an outdoor market, but it's chaotic enough to feel like one. At Mercato Centrale you can find just about anything within the realm of food, from cheeses to spices to singing butchers. To stand out, stalls tack up random items (like a pair of striped purple and white balloon shorts) to their roofs or counters. You can also find unusually shaped pasta casually mixed in with the standard shapes: tortellini, spaghetti, penises, ravioli, striped farfalle... Wait—striped farfale? If all this food ogling is making you hungry, some stalls in the center sell pizza and sandwiches by weight.

▶ ✚ It's the huge green-and-red building in the middle of all those sidewalk vendors. ☒ Open spring-fall M-Sa 7am-2pm; winter Sa 7am-2pm.

▨ San Lorenzo   SAN LORENZO
V. dell'Ariento

San Lorenzo's market spans the entire length of V. dell'Ariento. Vendors actively try to sell you hats, scarves, journals, or souvenirs as you pass, regardless of your apparent interest level. If you've got an eye for quality, this is the place to buy some of that famous Florentine leather. Just walking past, this researcher was offered a 90% discount on anything in an entire leather stall, so don't feel guilty working that price down. Vendors are used to ignorant tourists paying full price, so don't expect to shave more than a few euro off the price except through some hard-line bargaining. Since so many stalls have similar wares, you can always move on to the next one (or pretend you're going to) to get better prices.

▶ ⚡ Walking away from the station on V. Nazionale, V. dell'Ariento is on your right just across from the fountain. ⏰ Open daily 9am-7pm.

Santo Spirito   WEST OLTRARNO
P. Santo Spirito

This *piazza* across the Arno offers a smaller, more local flea market. Shoes, clothes, cosmetics, and plants await every day of the week (particularly on Saturday), but the best time to go is on the second and third Sunday of each month. Artisans and antique vendors flood the square on the second Sunday, while the third Sunday hosts the Fierucola organic foods market. Be careful cutting through the tree-adorned center of the market—locals have been known to convert this fountain space into a neighborhood water fight.

▶ ⚡ From Ponte Santa Trinita, walk past the bridge, turn right onto V. di Santo Spirito, and turn left onto V. del Presto di San Martino. It's in the *piazza* at the end of the street. ⏰ Open M-Sa 8am-1pm. 2nd and 3rd Su of the month open 9am-7pm.

CLOTHING

The true traveler is a clothing chameleon; here are some shops that can help you blend in. **Piazza della Signoria** and **Santa Maria Novella** are home to department stores and fun display windows, which become increasingly expensive toward the river. For cheap boutiques, hit up **San Lorenzo,** especially along V. Faenza and around the outdoor market, and **Santa Croce,** notably along V. Giuseppe Verdi.

Promod   SAN LORENZO
V. de' Cerretani 46-48r
☎055 21 78 44; www.promod.eu

Akin to H&M or Forever 21, Promod sells relatively disposable women's fashions at bargain prices. When we visited, the "in" thing was bold color motifs and revamped granny flower patterns.

▶ ⚡ Take V. de' Cerretani west from the Duomo. *i* Women's clothing only. ⏰ Open daily 10am-8pm.

Goldenpoint   SAN LORENZO
V. de' Cerretani 40r
☎055 28 42 19; www.goldenpointonline.com

Goldenpoint deals in women's swimsuits and lingerie. It offers

Shopping

few bargains, but there's a bigger selection of swimsuit sizes and styles than elsewhere. Curvy women take note: Italian swimsuits offer far better support than American styles.

▶ ⚑ Take V. de' Cerretani west from the Duomo. *i* Other locations at V. Panzani 33 (☎055 21 42 96) and V. dei Calzaioli 6 (☎055 27 76 224). ⏲ Open daily 10am-7pm.

ARTISAN GOODS

Florence has numerous artisan goods for which it is justly famous. It is particularly renowned for its soft, quality leather. The cheapest place to find it is the **San Lorenzo** market (see above). If you want to learn about the actual craft of leatherworking, stop by the **Scuola del Cuoio** within the Basilica di Santa Croce. Founded by Franciscan friars in the 1930s, this leather school continues to offer courses that last from one day to six months. Classes don't come cheap, though. Visit www.scuoladelcuoio.com for information, or enter their storefront in the basilica via the apse entrance at V. di San Giuseppe 5r. If you're looking for gold, the **Ponte Vecchio,** lined with numerous goldsmiths and jewelers as well as shady street sellers, is the place for you. There is also a smattering of gold stores around the city, misleadingly called *"Oreficerie. "* Finally, though masks are a bigger deal in Venice, you can still get a sense for the *commedia dell'arte* tradition at Alice Atelier. With any luxury good, we recommend you do background research before making any serious purchases. The listings below are included more because of how fascinating they are to browse than for the likelihood of you actually buying anything from them.

Shopping

▨ **Farmaceutica di Santa Maria Novella**   SANTA MARIA NOVELLA

V. della Scala 16
☎055 21 62 76; www.smnovella.com

You can smell the talcum and perfume before setting foot in this time capsule of a perfumery. The Santa Maria Novella monks have been bottling medicines in this museum-worthy space since the 13th century, but the "modern" pharmacy is straight from the Victorian age. Elixirs, perfumes, juleps, salts, spirits, waters, and protective oils are all available, displayed on shelving and sold in packaging that's been updated little over the course of the past century. As you browse through colored bottles of essence of myrrh under a chandelier, imagine your life as a Victorian aristocrat.

▶ ⚔ At the corner of V. della Porcellana. Coming from P. Santa Maria Novella, turn right onto V. della Scala. Ⓢ Candles €10-50. 500ml liqueurs
€50. Dog collars from €30. 🕐 Open daily 10:30am-7:30pm. In Aug, closes
on Sa at 1pm.

🖼 Alice Atelier: The Masks of
Prof. Agostino Dessì
SAN LORENZO

V. Faenza 72r
☎055 28 73 70; www.alicemasks.com

Masks aren't just quick and easy Halloween costumes—at Pro-
fessor Agostino's Dessì's studio, they are a true art form. Here
you can find the perfect two-faced mask to express your split
personality, or to give to a friend as an elaborate insulting pun
set-up. Handmade masks of things you never imagined, from
bionic metal-faced creatures to puzzle people, are as good as
a museum visit. Highly involved in Florence's art scene, Dessì
has been making masks for world exhibitions since the '70s and
brought his daughter, Alice, into the family business in 1997.
The shop offers mask-making courses and will happily direct
you to nearby exhibitions.

▶ ⚔ From P. della Stazione, take V. Nazionale and turn left onto V. Faenza.
i Application form for mask-making courses can be found on the website.
Ⓢ Masks from €50. 5-session course €500. 🕐 Open M-Sa 9am-1pm and
3:30-7:30pm.

Galleria Michelangelo
SANTA CROCE

P. Santa Croce 8
☎055 24 16 21

This vast, Japanese-run leather emporium is a frequent stop for
cruise-ship shore excursions. They often have whole rooms full
of items at a 50% discount.

▶ ⚔ On the left side of the *piazza,* facing the basilica. Ⓢ Bags from €80. 🕐
Open daily 9am-2pm and 2:30-8pm.

BOOKS AND JOURNALS

Florentine leather isn't just to drape on your own body—albums
and notebooks can wear it too. Marbelized and leather journals
are a big thing in this city. Follow our lead (and check the street
markets) to avoid paying €60 for a journal you'll start and probably never finish.

📓 Alberto Cozzi

SANTA MARIA NOVELLA

V. del Parione 35r
☎055 29 49 68

You can see right into the workshop of this artisanal paper-goods shop, which has been passed down through four generations. They sell items like glasses cases and bracelets in addition to the standard albums and notebooks. You can get your leather photo album customized with gold etching right before your eyes for no additional cost, and they have demos on Saturday afternoons. A word of warning: if you pet the sweet spaniel, she'll insistently follow you around for the rest of your visit.

▶ 🍴 From P. Carlo Goldoni, head right onto V. del Parione. Ⓢ 5 handmade pens €12. Marbleized leather-bound journals from €18. Refillable leather

How They Stack Up

Paul Newman or Robert Redford? Chocolate or vanilla? Dante or Boccaccio? OK, people may not debate Italian authors the way they do ice cream or attractive cinema stars, but they should. Both writers grew up and spent important parts of their life in Florence, revolutionized literature by writing in vernacular Italian, and are famous for sprawling allegorical works (*The Divine Comedy* and *The Decameron,* respectively). If you're spending any amount of time in Florence, you may find the rich cultural history infecting you with a desire to pick up one of these masterpieces. To help you decide which one, here's a quick summary of how they stack up:

* **Artistic influence:** Both are hugely influential, but we've got to give this one to Dante. His work paved the way for Boccaccio and popularized a new conception of heaven and hell. Boccaccio gets points for inspiring Hugh Hefner's attempt to adapt the bawdier stories of *The Decameron* into highfalutin porn.

* **Originality:** A tie. Using established biblical and classical themes, Dante crafted an original tale of spiritual discovery. Boccaccio drew on international folktales to fashion his patchwork of plots.

* **Piety:** Definitely Dante. In the *Inferno,* he depicts heretics punished in flaming tombs. In one of Boccaccio's tales, an abbess has her way with a gardener. Did we mention the porn connection?

Shopping

journals from €35. 🕐 Open daily 9am-1pm and 3-7pm. Workshop demonstrations on Sa afternoons.

Made in Tuscany   SAN MARCO
V. degli Alfani 120r

This is the way to have the artisan experience on a budget. For the same price as the options on the shelf, the owner will make you one with your own selection of leather and cover stamp.

▶ ✠ Just south of the Accademia, off V. Ricasoli. *i* Custom journals usually take overnight to make. Ⓢ Custom leather journals from €10. 🕐 Open M 2:30-7pm, Tu-Su 9:30am-2pm and 2:30-7pm.

Excursions

Tuscany is one of the most romantic destinations in the world. Maybe it's the wine, the rolling hills, the narrow medieval streets, or the panoramic views in every direction. It's all a bit swoon-inducing. Don't worry, though: Tuscany is more than just a region-sized honeymoon suite. Full of incredible architecture and intense local pride, the towns and cities that dot the area boast unique and often gory histories. (Many of these towns were locked in battles to the death for centuries.) Some features are shared by all—a soaring *duomo,* the occasional Etruscan ruin, a unifying resentment of Florence—but these cities are not interchangeable. Siena has centuries-old neighborhood rivalries that explode in the semiannual Palio. Famous Pisa has a lot more to its name than a certain tilty tower. Lucca is green and slow-paced, with the sound of Puccini spilling nightly through its streets and onto its incredible walls. The vertical streets of San Gimignano catch the heels of ritzy tourists by the millions. There's no need to squash every central Italian city into a single trip, and an attempt to hit four in one week will make them seem a scenic blur. Take your time. After all, these hills and stones have been here for millennia—they're not going anywhere.

Budget Excursions

Most of the excursions from Florence cost about the same, making it difficult to choose based on price. Opt for taking the train, as it's just as cheap—and sometimes cheaper than—taking the bus, and infinitely more comfortable. Note that many of Tuscany's best sights, like Siena's Il Campo and Lucca's walls, are free, so an excursion need not cost much more than your train fare. If you're worried about food, hit up **Mercato Centrale** and make yourself a picnic before leaving.

SIENA

Thanks to the semiannual Palio, Siena shares a reputation with Spain's Pamplona for being crazy two days of the year and asleep the other 363. That's really not a fair rep, though, because the Sienese provide plenty to see even when they aren't racing bareback around Il Campo. Take the steep pedestrian-only streets of Siena's *centro,* for example. The completely befuddling medieval layout is Tuscany taken to its illogical—and charming—extreme. Amid the frozen-in-time Gothic architecture, Siena is also a respectable university town with a campus indistinguishable from the city around it; you'll only realize you're at the university when you poke into a church and discover it's actually the Linguistics Department. With quirky nightlife, relative freedom from the overwhelming Florentine tourist crowds, and a maze of streets hiding secrets you could spend months trying to unlock, Siena is worth an extended stay.

Orientation

The first thing you should know is that the train station is down a steep hill fairly far north of the town center. Exit the station and follow the signs to the bottom of the parking garage, where you can catch a bus to the *centro*—look at the digital display board to see which bus is on its way and whether it's going where you need it to. That being said, try to arrive in Siena by bus instead of by rail. Almost all intercity buses arrive in **Piazza Gramsci,** in the northwest of the *centro.* The upper part of this *piazza* opens up onto **Luna Park** and then onto the **Fortezza Medicea.** Walk away from the park to head deeper into the *centro,* where you will soon see many **Il Campo** and **Duomo** signs, which are the best tools for navigating Siena's labyrinth of curling dead ends and steep alleyways. Learn your way home from the Campo and these signs will be your best friends. Meanwhile, Siena's many churches form a sort of holy compass: **San Francesco** is northeast, the **Pinacoteca** is south, and **San Domenica** is west.

Accommodations

We are sad to report that there are exactly eight dormitory beds in the entirety of Siena. Solo travelers had better nab one in advance or prepare for a lengthy commute. If you have a friend with whom to share a bed-and-breakfast double, you're in luck. No matter what you're looking for, plan ahead for visits in July or August, when every room in the city is booked (and has been for months in advance) and prices double for the Palio. The period in August between the two races is pretty quiet, though, and rooms will rent at mid-season rates.

👍 Casa di Antonella — B AND B $$$

V. delle Terme 72

☎0577 48 436

This hands-off B and B feels like a student apartment, from the hairdryer in the shared bathroom to the guitar resting on the couch. Well, except that most student apartment bedrooms tend to lack ceiling frescoes. The owner only comes around to prepare breakfast—it's kind of like having a personal chef—so don't expect to waltz in and book a room. You'll need to call in advance to have the door key with a Post-it with your name on it waiting for you.

▸ 🪧 From P. Giacomo Matteotti, take V. dei Termini and then turn onto the parallel V. delle Terme. ℹ Breakfast included. $ Doubles €50-60.

Piccolo Hotel Etruria — HOTEL $$$

V. delle Donzelle 3

☎0577 28 80 88; www.hoteletruria.com

Look for an ivy-covered entryway to find this unobtrusive little hotel. Your room may look like the bed, sink, and dresser are all awkwardly standing in a too-small elevator, but these are the lowest prices anywhere near the *centro*. At least the proximity means you're less likely to spend the night locked outside after the 1am curfew.

▸ 🪧 North of V. Banchi di Sotto. Follow the signs in the area north of Il Campo. ℹ Breakfast €6. Small pets allowed. $ Singles €40-50, with bath €45-55;

doubles as singles €60-70; doubles with bath €80-110; triples €90-138. Extra bed €10-28. ⏰ Reception 7am-1am. Curfew 1am.

YHA Ostello di Siena

HOSTEL $

V. Fiorentina 89

☎0577 52 212; www.ostellosiena.com

Sadly, Siena's one hostel barely counts as a hostel, and it's barely in Siena. The YHA is a 15min. bus ride from the *centro,* and offers mostly doubles and one eight-bed dormitory. What it lacks in location it also lacks in character—it's a standard-issue hostel, with shared bathrooms at each end of the rather institutional halls. If you're schlepping outside the *centro,* you'd like to be getting a little more than this. Pity it's the only game in town. Attention aspiring entrepreneurs: move to Siena and open a hostel. You'd make a fortune.

▶ 🚏 From the train station take bus #4 or 77. From the *centro* take #10, 15, or 77. Ask the driver to let you off at the *ostello.* *i* Breakfast included. Wi-Fi €1.50 per 30min. $ Dorms €20; doubles €40. Cash only. ⏰ Reception until midnight.

Camping Siena Colleverde

CAMPING $$$

Strada di Scacciapensieri 47

☎0577 33 40 80; www.sienacamping.com

It's neither near the *centro* nor is it rustic, but if you're here for a while and really pinching pennies, this campground may do the trick. The mobile home accommodations are private, which is good, because you're in rather close quarters. On the bright side, the grounds are spacious and include a big swimming pool, a bar, and a market; plus the RVs have private baths with surprisingly good heat and water pressure. To really take it up a notch, you can get one with a kitchenette. Be warned that you are not within easy walking distance of the *centro,* and the last bus leaves before midnight. Camping Siena Colleverde is best if you have your own transportation or no interest in hitting the town after hours.

▶ 🚏 By bus, take bus #3 or 8 from P. Gramsci to Scacciapensieri 2, or anywhere up in the hills after you've passed the train station. Follow the camping signs. If on foot, walk to the nearby bridge over the train tracks and cross it. There's a big intersection—take the right-hand fork, Strada di Malizia, where you will be walking against the traffic. The street twists around in the beginning, but otherwise it's a straight 1km to the campground. *i* You can pay for Colleverde Wi-Fi, if it happens to be working. $ Tents €5.70-6.70; campers €13-14 per person; 2- to 5-person RV €45, with kitchenette €65-115. ⏰ Reception 24hr.

Siena in Centro

B AND B $$$

V. di Stalloreggi 14-16

☎0577 43 041, for English 331 26 10 136; www.bbsienaincentro.com

One family runs all three B and B properties bundled together as Siena in Centro, providing a range of options from garden singles to apartments. Casa del Giglio, with ornate headboards and fancy curtains, is the poshest, but Casa del Conte still boasts wood-beamed ceilings, fancy mirrors, and flowerboxes in the windows. Stairs-only access makes B and B dei Rossi the cheapest choice.

▶ ⇄ For reception, follow signs from the Duomo to the Pinacoteca but bear right onto V. di Stalloreggi. ℹ Breakfast included. Laundry service available. Internet access only at reception. $ Singles €40-80; doubles €65-120; triples €90-150. Bike rental €3 per ½-day. ⏰ Reception 9am-1:30pm and 3-7pm; otherwise ring the bell.

Sights

There are a wealth of things to see in Siena, but the biggest attractions are **Il Campo** and the area around the **Duomo.** The six sights of the Duomo complex—the Duomo, the Baptistery, the Crypt, Museo dell'Opera, Santa Maria della Scala, and Museo Diocesano—can be visited with a single ticket, which is available at the ticket booth to the right of the cathedral (last ticket sold 30min. before close). The ticket is valid for 48hr., so you don't have to cram all the sights into one day; plus, with the exception of the Museo Diocesano, they are all conveniently clustered in the same *piazza.* At only €12 (students €5), this is one of the best deals in Tuscany. Unfortunately, Santa Maria della Scala is under renovation until 2013.

Piazza del Campo

PIAZZA

Piazza del Campo, simply called Il Campo by locals, is Siena's humming, tower-crowned, restaurant-laden beating heart. During the semiannual Palio, this shell-shaped *piazza* is crammed with as many bodies as possible while the hooved beasts beat around the *piazza*'s edge. During the rest of the year, lovers lounge and children scamper on the sun-warmed stone. We're talking prime real estate for picnicking, people-watching, and eerie Hitchcock bird swarms. It's also a student nightlife haunt into the early hours.

▶ ⇄ Follow the ubiquitous signs that point to Il Campo.

Duomo CHURCH

P. Duomo 8

☎0577 28 30 48; www.operaduomo.siena.it

Siena's Duomo will impress you, no matter how many (or few) Tuscan cathedrals you've visited. This colossal zebra-columned cathedral is decked in graffiti—and we don't mean dirty words written in spray paint. *Graffito* is actually a 14th-century technique of chiseling thin grooves out of slabs of white marble to be filled in with black *stucco*. The resulting marble cartoons on the floor are blocked off by metal posts to stop distracted tourists from trampling them. The later examples also use marble inlay to create richly colored designs that look like they're painted. The small, richly adorned **Piccolomini Library** displays the massive pages of books from the days when pages were hand-decorated with fancy script and gold.

▶ Follow the dozens of signs. The ticket booth is to the right of the cathedral. $ €3. Combined ticket with other Duomo sights €12, students €5. ⏰ Open June-Aug M-Sa 10:30am-8pm, Su 1:30-6pm; Sept-Oct M-Sa

In-Siena-ty

Pretty much everywhere in the world thinks it has the best sports fans. People worship their own sports god. They follow your team "religiously," and consider themselves part of the be-jerseyed devout. They think they're better than the people on the other side of the stadium. Well, they're all wrong, because they aren't from Siena.

Twice a year, Siena plays host to the Palio di Siena, a horse race so epic that it blurs the line between enthusiasm and clinical insanity. In these events, reason is suspended in favor of uncensored fanatic fervor, with each neighborhood racing its own horse through an incredibly dangerous course in Il Campo, where the horse that finishes first, with or without a jockey, is declared the victor. And though these races attract tourists from around the world, don't doubt that the Palio remains a largely local affair. Indeed, over the centuries, rivalries between neighborhoods have only become stronger, and the fans only more devout. How many towns, we ask you, baptize their children in fountains that represent their equine loyalties? In Siena they do, and if you want to see real fanatical fandom, this is the place to be in late July or early August.

10:30am-7:30pm, Su 1:30-5:30pm; Nov-Feb M-Sa 10:30am-6:30pm, Su 1:30-5:30pm; Mar-May M-Sa 10:30am-7:30pm, Su 1:30-5:30pm.

Fortezza Medicea   FORTRESS
P. della Libertà

This imposing fortress remains from the days when Siena fended off Rome and Florence with a rain of cannon fire. Today, the wide walls create the feel of an elevated park with some stellar city views, especially at sunset. Student crowds come here to picnic and joggers come to, well, jog. In the summer, the amphitheater seating in the courtyard hosts movie screenings, and the interior sometimes houses an amusement park. If you're around on a Wednesday, peruse the clothes, shoes, and flowers of the market along the fortress walls.

▶ ⚔ From P. Giacomo Matteotti, take Viale Tozzi and Viale Maccari north around the stadium. Ⓢ Free. ⏰ Street market W 7am-1pm.

Palazzo Pubblico and Torre del Mangia   MUSEUM, PALAZZO
P. del Campo 1
☎0577 29 26 14

Who says churches and rich families get to have all the fun (and by fun, we mean grandiose buildings)? This 1297 town hall, built to show up hotshot Florence, has a tower slightly taller than that of its rival's Palazzo Vecchio. Proving that size doesn't matter, Siena was decimated by the Black Death shortly after the tower's completion, while Florence went on to become the birthplace of the Renaissance. Insecure in more ways than one, the civic government then passed ordinances preventing citizens from building anything that would rival the *palazzo* in size, which nowadays ensure the tower has an unbeatable view of Siena and the surrounding countryside. The *palazzo*'s **Museo Civico** is most remarkable for what they've done with the swaths of wall space created by the high ceilings—Ambrogio Lorenzetti's full-wall frescoes of "good government" and "bad government" could bear the alternate titles of "aren't we awesome" and "land of the sadistic vampire king." In one interpretation of Adam and Eve, the serpent has a human head and a sketchy ponytail.

▶ ⚔ It's the big building at the bottom of P. del Campo. Ⓢ Museum €7.50, students €4. Tower €8. Museum and tower €13. Cash only. ⏰ Museum open Mar 16-Oct 10am-7pm; Nov-Mar 15 10am-6pm. Tower open Mar-Oct 15 10am-6:15pm; Oct 16-Feb 10am-3:15pm. Last entry 45min. before close.

Museo dell'Opera   MUSEUM

P. Duomo

☎0577 28 30 48; www.operaduomo.siena.it

The Duomo's museum houses all kinds of sculptures. Either time has not been kind or they host a statue fight club after hours, because many sculptures have lost fingers, chunks of limbs, or parts of noses, giving them that signature Voldemort face. Among the more intact are de Nicolo's fantastically expressive wood sculptures and a stone set of apostles that reveals which follower didn't get the memo to grow a beard. Upstairs, beyond the jumble of reliquaries, you'll find the **Facciatone** at the end of the Hall of Vestments. The waiting crowd is led up a winding staircase that opens to the roof. The unpleasant climb is worthwhile for the breathtaking countryside and city view, provided you're not claustrophobic or planning to climb the Torre del Mangia.

▶ ⚤ Opposite the Duomo, on the left. Ⓢ €6. Combined ticket with other Duomo sights €12, students €5. ⏰ Open daily June-Aug 9am-8pm; Sept-Oct 9:30am-7pm; Nov-Feb 10am-5pm; Mar-May 9:30am-7pm.

Crypt   CHURCH

P. Duomo

☎0577 28 30 48; www.operaduomo.siena.it

Sick of faded frescoes? Experience the brightness of original blues preserved by centuries of being forgotten about. The crypt is not actually a crypt—they just thought it was when they discovered the space while digging along the outer edge of a cathedral to lay some pipes in 1999. Stroll bravely onto the transparent false floor several feet above the real one to see the brickwork of the cavern as it was found. This space is worth visiting if you bought the combined ticket, but alone the sparse three rooms may not meet the expectations of the €6 entry fee.

▶ ⚤ Just past the ticket booth, on the left. Ⓢ €6. Combined ticket with other Duomo sights €12, students €5. ⏰ Open daily June-Aug 9am-8pm; Sept-Oct 9:30am-7pm; Nov-Feb 10am-5pm; Mar-May 9:30am-7pm.

Baptistery   CHURCH

P. San Giovanni

☎0577 28 30 48; www.operaduomo.siena.it

For centuries, Sienese children were baptized in this small, sumptuously decorated building. Intelligent visitors take a seat on wooden benches before letting themselves be absorbed by the ceiling fresco, which illustrates the Apostles' Creed. Less

Excursions

intelligent visitors crane their necks upward and trip up the altar steps. If you're not going in, at least check out the building's decorated marble exterior.

▶ ✣ From the ticket booth, it's straight ahead and down the stairs. Ⓢ €3. Combined ticket with other Duomo sights €12, students €5. Ⓩ Open daily June-Aug 9am-8pm; Sept-Oct 9:30am-7pm; Nov-Feb 10am-5pm; Mar-May 9:30am-7pm.

Fontebranda   FOUNTAIN

V. di Fontebranda

This ancient fountain made its neighborhood the center of Siena's social life in medieval times and managed to score a mention in Dante's *Inferno*. First constructed in 1081 and then rebuilt in 1246, Fontebranda was originally divided into three basins. The spillover from each filled the next, with the first for drinking water, the second for watering animals, and the third for mills and other industrial uses. Nowadays the calm neighborhood may not boast anything more ornate than this shady water grotto, but they've taken home more Palio victories than anyone else in Siena. Although the water in the fountain is not potable, it's still fresh—the air around the water's surface is cool on a hot summer day.

▶ ✣ Follow signs to Santuario di Santa Caterina, then continue downhill to the left. The fountain is on the right, down a few stairs. To avoid scaling the hill back toward the *centro,* walk behind the pink house at the end of the street for an escalator. Ⓢ Free.

Food

Thanks to Siena's slightly higher population of homegrown residents than other Tuscan cities, the town has a large number of groceries and delis—great news for cheapskates. Avoid the restaurants that border Il Campo unless you get off on €9 bowls of pasta, and look north for €1 pizza slices on **Via Montanini.** Stop by a bakery to try some *panforte.*

▨ La Pizzeria di Nonno Mede   PIZZERIA $

V. Camporeggio 21

☎0577 24 79 66

It takes a little bit of effort to find this pizzeria, but that's because it's saving itself for the locals. There's a bunch of spacious patio seating overlooking the town skyline, and on clear summer evenings, every inch of it will be packed, so make a reservation or expect to wait. You'll have a better chance at scoring a walk-in meal if you opt for an early lunch. This is the place to try adventurous pizza toppings—the apple and gorgonzola white pizza is particularly impressive.

▶ ⚡ Take the stairs behind Fontebranda uphill and to the right; they lead directly to the pizzeria. Alternatively, from Casa di Santa Caterina, take the street on the right and follow it until it opens onto the *piazza*. Ⓢ Cover €1.60. Pizza €5-7.50. *Primi* €6-7.50. 🕐 Open daily noon-3:30pm and 7pm-1am.

Pizzicheria di Miccoli   DELICATESSEN $
V. di Città 93-95
☎0577 28 91 84

Duck through the fuzzy door strings and past the wild boar head into this busy meat and cheese shop that brings all your prosciutto, cheese, and roasted pork dreams to life. You'll know you're close when you see a bunch of people huddled on stoops devouring sandwiches (€5). They slice the meat before your eyes, making the perfect portable lunch so you can get back to sightseeing. The prosciutto and cheese *torta rustica* is also worth a taste.

▶ ⚡ Walking south on V. di Città, it's the place with the boar head and fuzzy red garland. Ⓢ Sandwiches €5. Meat €35 per kg. 🕐 Hours vary.

La Compagnia dei Vinattieri   ENOTECA $$
V. delle Terme 79
☎0577 23 65 68; www.vinattieri.net

This *enoteca* is literally a wine cellar. Walk down a flight of stairs to reach the stone-walled dining room that is lined with over 100 wines from around the world. The layout is welcoming, with couch seating, large tables, and a piano. Dinner includes pasta and *secondi* as gourmet as "leg of rabbit stuffed with pecorino cheese and savory cabbage." This is also a great spot for an odd-hours hunger pang; they serve cheese, cold meat, and lasagna all day. Jazz and other music groups occasionally perform as well.

▶ ⚡ At the corner with V. dei Pittori. Ⓢ Wine from €3. Pasta €9-12; *secondi* €12-16. 🕐 Open daily noon-midnight.

La Fontana della Frutta   GROCERY STORE $
V. delle Terme 65-67
☎0577 40 422

For a budget lunch, you can't beat the takeout counter at this corner grocery. The packaged goods and produce are reasonably

Excursions

priced, but the counter is the real draw with selections like cold pasta, stuffed tomatoes, and vegetable dishes sold by the kilogram. Split several quarter-kilos of different cold pastas, grab a couple of table-wine juice boxes, ask for some plastic utensils, and have a lovely picnic on Il Campo while laughing at the fools wasting money in real restaurants.

▶ 🍴 At the corner of V. Santa Caterina. Ⓢ Cold pasta €11 per kg. ⏰ Open daily 8am-8pm.

Sale e Pepe   RISTORANTE $$

V. Garibaldi 23

☎0577 60 00 89; www.ristorantesalepepe.it

Wander a bit farther north of the *centro* for the reward of affordability: pasta, 0.5L of water, and a coffee for only €5.50. The place also has a nice bread list and may be the only restaurant in Italy that charges supermarket prices for bottled water.

▶ 🍴 Off P. del Sale. Ⓢ Breads €3.50. 1L of wine €4.50. ⏰ Open daily 11am-11pm.

Savini   BAKERY $

V. dei Montanini 9

☎0577 40 949; www.dolcezzesavini.com

Since 1959, this chain bakery has been producing delicious Sienese specialties like *panforte,* a sort of trail mix from the Crusades now sold by the block, and *ricciarelli,* sugary almond cookies. Savini will give you a taste of Tuscan pastries—which will never be French pastries, but are a valid substitute on a quick snack stop. There's no seating, but the clothing shop across the street has a beanbag out front.

▶ 🍴 From P. Gramsci take V. Cavallerizzo, then turn right onto V. dei Montanini. Ⓢ Pastries €1-2.50; also sold by the kg. Cash only. ⏰ Open M-Sa 7:30am-7:30pm, Su 8am-1pm.

Nightlife

There are a handful of nice bars in Siena, but the lively student population has brought about a constantly changing nightlife scene. Keep your ears open and you may find a neighborhood festival or one-night hole-in-the-wall dance spot. Otherwise, you can always go the BYOB route—pick up a couple of bottles and head to Il Campo for the nightly block party. The tourist-trap restaurants surrounding the *piazza* become tourist-trap bars at night, so load up elsewhere to avoid €8 pints.

▨ San Paolo Pub   PUB

Vicolo San Paolo 2

☎0577 22 66 22; www.sanpaolopub.com

For access to Il Campo without the tourist prices, this alleyway
pub is your best bet. The outdoor seating tends to draw a slightly
older crowd than the glowing green space draped with rugby jer-
seys beyond the open doorways. The drunk and hungry may be
especially happy with San Paolo's 40 sandwich options (€3.50).

▶ ⚔ In a little covered alley just off Il Campo—it's one of the streets directly opposite the *palazzo*. Ⓢ Beer €4.20. Cocktails €5. Hot and cold sandwiches
€3.50. Cash only. 🕐 Open daily noon-2am. *Aperitivo* buffet 6-8pm.

▨ Antica Enoteca Italiana   ENOTECA

P. della Libertà 1

☎0577 22 88 11; www.enoteca-italiana.it

This *enoteca* offers the truly Italian experience of sipping wine
inside the high-walled courtyard of a fortress. When the fortress
also houses an amusement park, the rides' music rolls down over
the old brick walls. Early in the day, Antica is simply a small
wine museum. At night, the rotating tasting menu (€11) springs
from their collection of over 1600 different wines, so if you
want to taste them all, you may need to move to Siena.

▶ ⚔ From P. Gramsci, walk through Luna Park. It's inside the Fortezza Medicea, on the left. Ⓢ Tasting menu with 2 glasses of wine €11. 🕐 Open M-Sa
noon-1am. Museum open 1-7pm.

Caffè del Corso   BAR

V. Banchi di Sopra 25

☎0577 22 66 56

If you've been mystified by Italian distinctions between different types of cocktails, then Caffè del Corso is here to help! One
wall of this corner pub is covered with the drink list which is
divided into *aperitivi,* after-dinners, and long drinks. An evening of "studying" will have you fluent in Italian booze. Inside
you can get pizza, but sidewalk seating feels more like a night
out than the restaurant-style interior.

▶ ⚔ V. Banchi di Sopra is 2 blocks up from Il Campo, on the right. Ⓢ Cocktails €5. Pizza €5-7. 🕐 Open Tu-Su 8am-3am. Kitchen closes at midnight.

Dublin Post   IRISH PUB

P. Gramsci 20/21

☎0577 28 90 89; www.dublinpost.it

Dublin Post is yet another Irish pub in Italy. You know the drill.

This one has a lot of outdoor seating. It's outdoor seating on the bus-stop *piazza*, to be sure, but at least you can watch people leaving town—perhaps they're en route to the real Dublin, where Guinness isn't a ridiculous €6.

▶ ⚑ Directly across from the end of the bus lines. *i* Frequent live music. Free W-Fi. Ⓢ Beer €5. Cash only. 🕑 Open M-Sa noon-1am, Su 3pm-1am. Happy hour 6-9pm.

Essentials

Practicalities

- **TOURIST OFFICES: APT Siena** provides maps for a small fee. It also has brochures and a bookstore. (P. del Campo 56 ☎0577 28 05 51; www.terresiena.it ⚑ Facing the tower in P. del Campo, it's on the left side of the *piazza*. 🕑 Open daily 9am-7pm.)

- **CURRENCY EXCHANGE: Maccorp Italiana Spa.** (V. di Città 78)

- **ATMS: Banca Toscana** in P. Gramsci.

- **LUGGAGE STORAGE:** The underground **bus station** in P. Gramsci.

- **LAUNDROMATS: OndaBlu** is self-service. (V. Casato di Sotto 17 ☎516 25 68 98; www.ondablu.com ⚑ Just off P. del Campo. Ⓢ €3 per 7kg. 🕑 Open daily 8am-9pm.)

- **INTERNET: Dublin Post** has free Wi-Fi. (P. Gramsci 20/21)

- **POST OFFICES: Poste Italiane.** (P. Giacomo Matteotti 37 ☎0577 21 42 95 ⚑ Just past the main bus stops.)

Emergency

- **POLICE:** The police station is at V. del Castoro 1. (⚑ Near the Duomo.)

- **LATE-NIGHT PHARMACIES:** Several pharmacies in the *centro* share a late-night rotation. Visit any one of them to check the schedule outside and get the number of the pharmacy on duty. The easiest to find is **Farmacia del Campo.** (P. del Campo 1 ☎0577 28 02 34 ⚕ Facing the tower, it's on the right, nestled between the restaurants.)

- **HOSPITALS/MEDICAL SERVICES: Santa Maria alle Scotte.** (Viale Mario Bracci 16 ☎0577 58 51 11 ⚕ Take bus #3 or 77 from P. Gramsci. ⏰ Open 24hr.)

Getting There

Siena is surprisingly difficult to reach. Coming from Florence is easy, but if you're arriving from elsewhere, you're almost certainly going to have to transfer trains or buses at least once.

By Bus

Although Siena does have a train station, it's much farther from the city center than the bus stop. The **TRA-IN/SITA** (}0577 42 46; www. trainspa.it) bus is also faster and goes directly from Florence to Siena's P. Gramsci, about 5min. north of P. del Campo (the second to last stop is P. San Domenica). Facing the trains in the Santa Maria Novella train station, exit from your left, walk straight until your first left, and follow the long driveway on your left with all the buses. Take the #131 bus *extraurbano* toward P. Gramsci, Siena. The Corsa Rapida bus takes you directly. (💲 €6.80. ⏰ 1½hr., at least 1 per hr. Ticket office open daily 7am-7pm.)

By Train

If bumpy roads make you feel like you're trapped in a popcorn bag, the train may be a better option for you. However, be prepared for a long uphill trek or an awkwardly crowded bus ride from the station. You can buy a train ticket at Santa Maria Novella station. The Siena train station is in P. Rosselli, 15min. outside Siena town by bus #3, 4, 7, 8, 10, 17, or 77. (⏰ Ticket office open daily 6:30am-1:10pm and 1:40-8:10pm.) Trains arrive from Florence (💲 €6.30. ⏰ 1½hr., every hr. 8am-8pm.) and Poggibonsi. (💲 €2.40. ⏰ 30min., 2 per hr.)

Excursions

Getting Around

Siena's extensive but hardly necessary **bus** system may be useful to those staying far outside the *centro*. (Ⓢ Tickets €1.) Nearly all buses finish their routes at P. Gramsci in the northwest of the *centro,* and the underground station sells tickets for bus trips to other towns. **Cars** are useful primarily for visiting surrounding towns, but have little wiggle room within Siena's walls. Steep hills make cycling somewhat of a nuisance, while **scooters** are a slightly more popular choice for those confident in their tourist-dodging abilities. For bike, scooter, or car rental call **Perozzi Automotoci-cli** (☎0577 28 83 87; www.perozzi.it). For a taxi, call **RadioTaxi** (☎0577 49 222) or head to the cab stands in P. Giacomo Matteotti and P. Independenza.

PISA

This is what Pisa has to offer: one tower, leaning; one budget airline hub, useful; and three universities, sweet. If Florentine nightlife left you doubting the Tuscan party scene, come to Pisa, where the cheap sangria will have you leaning at a 3.99° angle too. Pisa's wide streets make it feel more like a city than other Tuscan towns. If you've forgotten how to live with the heat after so many shady alleyways, a 20min. bus ride will get you to Pisa's shoreline, where the proliferation of swimmers belies the fact that you're not actually allowed to swim.

Orientation

Whether you arrive in Pisa by train or plane, you will enter the *centro* from the **train station.** The city knows why people visit, so street signs bearing the image of a leaning tower and an arrow are everywhere. When you leave the station, you'll be in the southern end of the city. Take shop-lined **Corso Italia** straight ahead to reach the river, which is central to city life. **Via Santa Maria** will take you straight from the river to **Piazza dei Miracoli.**

Accommodations

Those staying overnight in Pisa are likely in transit; therefore, our picks weigh access to the train station and airport over proximity to the tower.

▧ Walking Street Hostel   HOSTEL $

Corso Italia 58

☎393 06 48 737

Dorms in this hostel are your standard small-locker-and-bunk combo, except for some reason they've been lavished with Chinese-themed decor, and some rooms even have floor-to-ceiling stained glass. Two red lounges have a pool table, TV, and dartboard for you and your soon-to-be hostel friends, and guests can help themselves to the laundry and kitchen. Security is unusually strong with three keys necessary to access the hostel—the staff will only laugh at you a little if you can't figure out which one goes where.

▶ ⚑ On Corso Italia, halfway from the train station to the river. *i* Free Wi-Fi. Complimentary coffee and tea. Ⓢ Dorms €22. Cash only. ⌚ Reception until 3am.

Hotel Pisa   HOTEL, HOSTEL $

V. Giuseppe Sainati 8

☎347 77 30 237

If you get the sense that some dude just decided to turn his house into a hostel and called it Hotel Pisa, then you're absolutely correct. Carlo is a backpacker himself, but the sort who cares more about community than security. If you're the same, you'll love it here. The bathrooms are knees-touching-the-wall tiny, the Ikea-furnished dorms are rather warm, and no one bats an eye at the door that is left open pretty much all the time. Nevertheless, the neighborhood is quiet, and the hostel's side yard contains a little bar and TV where you can usually find Carlo and his friends. These digs are a bit far from the *centro,* but that's why bicycles are available for rent. You won't need to borrow one when it's time to skip town, though: the proximity to the train station couldn't be better.

▶ ⚑ Leave the train station at track 14, take a right onto V. Quarantola, and turn left onto V. Giuseppe Sainati after 5min. *i* Free Wi-Fi. Complimentary coffee and tea. Free bike rental. Ⓢ Dorms €20. Cash only.

Hotel Helvetia   HOTEL $$

V. Don Gaetano Boschi 31

☎050 55 30 84; http://pensionehelvetiapisa.com

Looking to be right near the sights, but off noisy V. Santa Maria? We suggest this bargain hotel. Four floors of private rooms have brick trim, ceiling fans, green wooden shutters,

Excursions

and iron bedstands. Navigating to the tower couldn't be easier, and the front hall bears a painted map of Pisa and the full Pisa Centrale train schedule in case you need to get anywhere else. The breakfast room's Keith Haring-style mural gives the place some character—as does the well-kept garden, which is home to Pisa's tallest (and potentially only) cactus.

▶ ⚡ V. Don Gaetano Boschi begins in the southeast corner of P. dei Miracoli. *i* Free Wi-Fi. Ⓢ Singles €35; doubles €45, with bath €62; quad suite €100. Extra bed €20. ⚡ Reception 8am-midnight.

Relais Under The Tower   HOTEL, HOSTEL $

V. Santa Maria 165

☎050 520 0231; www.relaisunderthetower.it

Almost literally under the threat of being crushed by that perilous leaning tower, this hotel-hostel has rooms that can be private or shared depending on demand. Guests may use the kitchen and tiny breakfast nook. Simple and tiny with widely fluctuating prices, Relais is best for those who prioritize location above everything else.

▶ ⚡ Just south of the tower. It may be slightly hidden if the market stalls are present. Look for Trattoria Pizzeria Toscana—Relais is next door on the right. *i* Free Wi-Fi. Complimentary toast and coffee. Ⓢ Dorms €20-25; doubles €45-50, with bath €65-100.

Sights

Walled in and covered with trim green grass, Pisa's **Piazza dei Miracoli** is an island unto itself. True, the eager tourist crowds and relentless sun are free to barrage the square; even so, the clean-lined monuments maintain a sense of quiet grace—well, apart from that tall one in the back who can't seem to stop falling over. Entrance to the *piazza* itself is free, and possibly the best part of Pisa is hanging out in the shadow of the tower, watching tourists direct one another in how to take the perfect photo. Meanwhile, if you're intent on scouring for sights beyond the square, Pisa offers the usual selection of grand old Italian churches, and everyday Pisa is at its prettiest along the Arno. The **Opera della Primaziale Pisana** sells tickets for all the monuments in the *piazza*. (☎050 83 50 11; www.opapisa.it Ⓢ Tower €15. Joint admission for non-leaning monuments: 2 monuments €5, 3 monuments €6, all 5 €10. Disabled visitors and 1 guest free. ⚡ All monuments open daily June-Sept 8am-11pm; Oct 9am-7pm; Nov-Feb 10am-5pm; Mar 9am-6pm; Apr-May 8am-8pm. Last entry 30min. before close. Ticket office closes at 7:30pm.)

Piazza dei Miracoli

◪ Leaning Tower of Pisa   TOWER

Jaded travelers that we are, we expected Pisa's famous tower to be
something of a tourist trap, on par with a leaning Big Block of
Cheese. We were very wrong. Turns out the postcards, placemats,
and neckties simply cannot do justice to the ridiculous slant of
this tipsy structure. If you're getting sick of the sense of wonder
inspired by most great European monuments (we told you we
were jaded), get stoked for the tower. Your first reaction will be
less OMG and more LOL. LMAO, even. It really is hilariously
tilted. You probably haven't noticed, but the tower's construction
involved a few minor hiccups, leaving it only fully reconstructed
and climbable in 2010, after 800 years of work. Climbing the
tower is much like any other slanted, narrow, slippery tower climb
in Tuscany, except more slanty, narrow, and slippery. Oh—and
it's expensive, too. Maybe that's why even 17-year-olds need Mom
or Dad with them if they want to scale this bad boy.

▶ *i* Make reservations in the Museo del Duomo, online, or next to the tourist
info office. Visitors under 18 must be accompanied by an adult. Tickets are
for a specific time; be prompt. The climb consists of over 300 narrow, twisty,
and very slippery stairs; consider your health and tendency to experience
vertigo before attempting it. ⏱ Guided visits last 30min.

Battistero   CHURCH

Constructed in 1152, Diotisalvi's marble baptistery is lit by
slit-like stained glass and arcs symbolically upward toward the
heavens. Its uniquely elongated shape leads to its most intrigu-
ing feature—to see what we mean, stick around for the guards'
"acoustical demonstration" every 30min. The Battistero is so
resonant that a choir singing inside can supposedly be heard from
2km away. Don't get too excited, though—for some reason, this
remarkable space isn't used for performances. Instead, the demo
consists of a staff member repeating some simple notes a few times,
looking blasé but sounding like a choir of angels. Unfortunately,
the Battistero is always crowded and guarded, so conducting your
own "acoustical demonstration" is frowned upon.

Camposanto   CEMETERY

A rectangular hall's thin archways open onto a central green
courtyard in this cemetery, which is surprisingly peaceful for
a major tourist attraction. The various tombs show that you
can still get lucky after death: some very worn ones are stuck

Excursions

Tuscan Tower Climbers

Tuscany has a thing for towers. Coincidentally, tourists have a thing for scaling these towers. Here are the types of people you'll find scaling those slippery heights:

- **THE BRAVADO JOES:** These guys just started climbing and still have confidence in their physical fitness. Just wait, the tower will reduce them to quietly moaning scufflers, desperate to mask their ragged breath. Typical moves: an overly bouncy step, wasting precious oxygen by talking, or even laughing—they will regret this.

- **THE SLOW AND STEADY:** These people haven't worked out in months. Their plodding speed would make a tortoise cry. Best of all, they are somehow always right in front of you. Typical moves: stopping frequently to catch their breath, letting you pass so you'll stop obnoxiously breathing down their necks.

- **THE FAMILIES:** Why are parents forcing their tiny children to scale hundreds of steps? Is this some kind of extreme family fitness regime? Do they really think the child is going to remember and benefit from that minute of peering at the roofs of tiny villas? You can't even get annoyed at slow climbing kids—their limbs are literally half the size of yours. Typical moves: complaining, holding hands, excessive rest breaks.

- **THE RUB-IT-IN-YOUR-FACES:** These travelers have already been there, done that, and got the T-shirt. They're coming back down now, strolling easily like, "Oh, are you struggling? This was no challenge at all for me. I do a climb like this every morning as a light warm-up." Typical moves: the if-I-hold-my-breath-I'll-somehow-be-skinny-enough-for-you-to-pass and the classic awkward corner straddle.

directly underfoot, other guys enjoy prime wall real estate, and the luckiest are adorned with topless lady sculptures (then again, that kind of lucky is more enjoyable alive than dead). The fragmented frescoes aren't just due to age or a bad choice of paint—the damage was inflicted by the Nazis.

Duomo CHURCH

For once, a church in great condition! Maybe it's cheating that it was heavily refurbished after a 1595 fire, but oh well. Pisa's

Duomo skipped the sparse decor trend and went for huge, vivid Renaissance-style paintings, an enormous mosaic Jesus, and an intensely gold-flowered ceiling. Be sure to check out Adam, Eve, and an androgynous human-faced serpent in the left alcove.

▸ $ €2. Free during mass. ⏰ Mass Su 8am-1pm.

Museo delle Sinopie MUSEUM

Restoration work on the Camposanto's frescoes, which were severely damaged by Nazi shelling, revealed enormous preparatory drawings hidden underneath. The Museo delle Sinopie once housed the poor and orphaned, but now it houses these poor fragments. If you were a connect-the-dots master as a kid, maybe there's hope for you in these faded bits and pieces. The explanation panels are especially helpful and feature minute pictures of what the complete images would have looked like. Upstairs, there are historical clothes based on a study of these and other frescoes, including costumes from the 1954 *Romeo and Juliet* film. You have to wonder if our clothing will look this outlandish in a couple hundred years. If you are stuck in the mercilessly unshaded *piazza* on a hot summer day, step inside for some air-conditioning.

Museo dell'Opera del Duomo MUSEUM

The Duomo's museum contains even more information on the construction, reconstruction, and preservation of the cathedral and its surrounding buildings. If you ever happen to travel back in time to Pisa in 1064, you'll be able to tell them exactly how they can keep their buildings from getting all tilty. Then again, what's the fun in that? In other news, the museum holds a surprising number of pudgy-faced, nondescript stone men as well as some Roman, Etruscan, and Egyptian art and artifacts. If you're not buying the five-sight ticket, we wouldn't recommend prioritizing this spot, though the courtyard view of the tower is not too shabby.

Other Sights

Giardino Scotto PARK

Lungarno Leonardo Fibonacci

☎050 23 044

For a change of scene and a breath of fresh air, Giardino Scotto is the place to be. Its main draws are the ruins and love-note-covered walkable portion of the Roman walls, but local students flock here on sunny weekends for the desk-like benches. There's also a permanent outdoor movie theater where films are screened every night of the summer. The playground will take you back to your childhood, provided you grew up in space and had a spinning gazebo. You probably won't be able to kick the happy children off the little in-ground trampoline; it's probably more socially acceptable to hang around on the swings.

▶ 🪧 At the bend in the river, east of the *centro.* [$] Free. ⏰ Open daily July-Aug 9am-8:30pm; Sept 9am-8pm; Oct 9am-6pm; Nov-Jan 9:30am-4:30pm; Feb-Mar 9am-6pm; Apr 9am-7pm; May-June 9am-8pm.

Food

This port city brims with seafood to spice up your carb-only diet. Unlike in Florence, you can get pizza with actual toppings in the €5-6 range—you'll find about half a dozen similar but viable pizzerias along **Via Santa Maria,** just south of the monuments. Meanwhile, a number of Pisa's restaurants double as bars that offer cheap and delicious *aperitivi.* People tend to dine earlier than in Florence, though, so don't roll up at 1pm and expect a closing restaurant to cook you *tagliatelle.*

👍 Argini e Margini — SEAFOOD $

Lungarno Galilei

☎329 88 81 972; www.arginiemargini.com

For a quick fix of beach-style escapism, look no further than this sandy bank of the Arno's southern shore. Argini e Margini's floating dock comes to life in the summer with fresh seafood and live jazz. They also serve *aperitivi* and cocktails along the pier under orange umbrellas and palm trees. Sounds pricey, right? Hardly—you won't need to shell out anything extravagant for fresh fish.

▶ 🪧 Look over the wall at the edge of the river down near Ponte della Fortezza. [$] Cover €1. Seafood priced by the kg. *Aperitivi* and cocktails €3.50-5. ⏰ Open high season M-Th 6-11pm, F-Sa 6pm-midnight, Su 6-11pm.

La Bottega del Gelato — GELATERIA $

P. Giuseppe Garibaldi 11

☎050 57 54 67; www.labottegadelgelato.it

Even Florentines wouldn't turn up their noses at these generous servings of super smooth gelato. A word of warning, though—for a walk along the sunny and windy river, opt for a cup if you don't want to end up with more melty gelato in your hair than in your mouth.

▶ ⚑ North of Ponte di Mezzo on P. Giuseppe Garibaldi. Ⓢ Gelato from €1.50. ⓣ Open daily high season 11am-1am; low season 11am-10pm.

Dolce Pisa   CAFE $
V. Santa Maria 83
☎050 56 31 81

Pastas, salads, and smoothies galore! Most things on the menu cost €6, so for once, we cheapskates actually have options. Also, there's no cover charge at the tea salon tables, so no need to chomp pastries while awkwardly hovering by the bar.

▶ ⚑ From the monuments, it's a 5min. walk down V. Santa Maria; it's on the right on the corner with V. Luca Ghini. Ⓢ Pastries €0.90. Most entrees €6. Cappuccino €1.20. ⓣ Open M-Tu 7:30am-11pm, Th-Su 7:30am-11pm.

Osteria i Santi   RISTORANTE $$
V. Santa Maria 71
☎050 28 081; www.osteria-isanti.com

With a real canopy, tall green plants, and twinkling Christmas lights, Osteria i Santi offers nicer outdoor seating than most places in the area. Dishes are affordable, with lasagna and spaghetti on the low end and seafood risotto and baby octopus on the high. Dine indoors only if you can stomach garish portraits of saints judging you for your sinfully delicious meal.

▶ ⚑ From the monuments, walk down V. Santa Maria; it's on the right. Ⓢ Cover €1.50. Entrees €6.50-9. ⓣ Open daily noon-3pm and 7-10:30pm.

Il Baronetto   RISTORANTE $
V. Domenica Cavalca 62
☎050 97 01 78; www.ilbaronetto.com

Il Baronetto's quiet side street awaits you with self-service pizzas in 45 varieties as well as specialty Pisan soup (€5).

▶ ⚑ Off V. Curatone. From the river, turn right. Ⓢ *Primi* €4-5; *secondi* €4.50-6. ⓣ Open daily 8am-4pm.

Nightlife

You really don't need our help with this one. Pisa is jam-packed with bars and pubs, most of which are quite cheap. Basically, if you're paying more than €3 for a bottle of beer, then you'd better really like the atmosphere. Florentine *piazza*-based nightlife is less popular here, mainly because the *piazze* aren't as pretty and

Excursions

the pubs are more plentiful. The main gathering spot, **Piazza delle Vettogaglie,** is a near-hidden square lined with small pubs, picnic tables, and cheap late-night food. For slightly more upscale options, try **Borgo Stretto.** Like restaurants, bars tend to close a bit earlier in Pisa (around 1am). Also, if you can make it here in June, Pisa takes to the streets for a line-up of large-scale nighttime festivals. The most happening spots change frequently, so your best bet is to explore. Here are a few scenic options on the water to get you started.

Sunset Cafe — BAR

V. Litoranea 40, Marina di Pisa

☎050 36 857

Spend your entire beach day at this bar—you won't regret it. With its own cove along Marina di Pisa's long string of private beaches, Sunset Cafe has the whole seaside ambience thing down. During the day, the beach is full of lounge chairs. At night, Sunset replaces them with wicker mats, enormous cushions, and big candles. Up near the bar, seating for large groups and cozy couples is shaded by thatched umbrellas and bamboo screens. Around 7pm, the *aperitivo* buffet comes out, an extravagant affair with enough options to easily serve as dinner. Plus, the sunset is really marvelous.

▶ From under the west archway in P. Vittorio Emanuele II, follow as it veers left to find the buses. Tickets (you want Corsi 2) are €4 and can be bought inside on the right. Get off at New Camping Internazionale on the left; the entrance for Sunset Cafe is directly opposite. $ Beer €4-6. Cocktails €6. ⏰ Open daily noon-2am.

Bazeel — BAR

Lungarno Pacinotti 1

☎340 28 81 113; www.bazeel.it

This upbeat corner bar on a major *piazza* dominates the scene around the Ponte di Mezzo, the most central of the *centro* bridges. The frozen cocktails make this a refreshing destination after a hot day. When it's cold, hang out on the catwalk above the cavernous indoor seating.

▶ Just over the north side of Ponte di Mezzo. $ Beer €3-4.50. Frozen cocktails €6.50. ⏰ Open daily 2pm-2am.

Bulldog   PUB

V. Mazzini 320

☎330 91 15 28

Cheap beer, live music, and an international vibe right by the Arno—what more could you want?

▶ ☂ On the north bank of the river. Ⓢ Beer €3-4. ⏰ Open Th-Su 6pm-2am. Beer garden open May-Sept.

Amaltea   BAR

Lungarno Mediceo 49

☎050 58 11 29

Bumping riverside Amaltea draws a mixed crowd of students and adults. The generous *aperitivo* makes it a great starting point for your night out on the town.

▶ ☂ In P. Cairoli, on the river. Ⓢ Cocktails €4.50-6. ⏰ Open daily 5pm-2am.

Essentials

Practicalities

- **TOURIST OFFICES:** The office at **Piazza Vittorio Emanuele II 13** provides maps, an events calendar, and other assistance. (☎050 42 291; www.pisaunicaterra.it ⏰ Open daily 9:30am-7:30pm.) Second office on **Piazza del Duomo.** (☎050 56 04 64 ☂ In Museo dell'Opera. ⏰ Open daily high season 9:30am-7:30pm; low season 10am-5pm.) **Airport office.** (☎050 50 25 18 ⏰ Open daily 11am-11pm.)

- **ATMS: Deutsche Bank** is on the corner of V. Giosuè Carducci and V. San Lorenzo. (☂ Between P. Cavalieri and P. Martiri della Libertà. ⏰ Open 24hr.)

- **LUGGAGE STORAGE:** In the **train station.** (☂ At the left end of Binario 1. Ⓢ €3 per 12hr., €5 per 24hr., €9 per 48hr. ⏰ Open daily 6am-9pm.)

- **LAUNDROMATS: Lavanderia** provides washers, dryers, and detergent. (V. Carmine 20 Ⓢ Wash or dry €4. ⏰ Open daily 7am-11pm.)

- **INTERNET: Internet Surf** has computers and Wi-Fi. (V.

Giosuè Carducci 5 🪧 Off V. San Lorenzo. $ €2.50 per hr., students €2 per hr. ⏰ Open daily 9am-10pm.)

- **POST OFFICES:** Office at P. Vittorio Emanuele II 7/9 (☎050 51 95 14 🪧 On the right of the *piazza.* ⏰ Open M-F 8:15am-7pm, Sa 8:15am-1:30pm.)
- **POSTAL CODES:** 56100.

Emergency

- **POLICE: Polizia Municipale.** (V. Cesare Battisti 71/72 ☎050 91 08 11)
- **LATE-NIGHT PHARMACIES: Lungarno Mediceo 51.** (☎050 54 40 02 🪧 On the north shore of the river, to the east. ⏰ Open 24hr.)
- **HOSPITALS/MEDICAL SERVICES: Santa Chiara.** (V. Bonanno Pisano ☎050 99 21 11 🪧 Near P. del Duomo.)

Getting There

By Plane

Galileo Galilei Airport (☎050 84 93 00; www.pisa-airport.com) is practically within walking distance of the city, but the train shuttle (€1.10) takes only 5min. The shuttle arrives at platform 14, Pisa Centrale. The airport is a major **budget airline** hub for all of Tuscany, including Florence. No intercontinental flights serve Galileo Galilei, but you can fly directly to Pisa from most European cities.

By Train

Pisa Centrale is the main port of entry from other Italian destinations. (P. della Stazione }050 41 385 🪧 South of P. Vittorio Emanuele II. ⏰ Ticket office open 6am-9pm, but there is always a long line; check out the 24hr. self-service machines.) Trains run to and from Florence ($ €5.80. ⏰ 1-1¼hr.; 6 trains daily to Florence 4:15am-1:12am, from Florence 7am-10:25pm), Rome ($ €18. ⏰ 4hr., approximately every hr. 5:45am-7:56pm), and Lucca. ($ To Lucca €5.10, from Lucca €2.40. ⏰ 30min.;

approximately every hr. 6am-8pm.) If leaving from San Rossore, Pisa's secondary station is in the northwest of town; buy tickets from *tabaccherie*.

By Bus

SITA (☎043 62 28 048; www.sitabus.it) and **Terravision** (☎44 68 94 239; www.terravision.eu/florence_pisa.html) run buses between Pisa's airport and Florence, while **Lazzi** (}058 35 84 876; www.lazzi.it) and **CPT** (}050 50 55 11; www.cpt.pisa) buses arrive in P. Sant'Antonio. (Ⓩ Ticket office open daily 7am-8:15pm.) Buses leave from Florence's Santa Maria Novella bus station. (⚐ From the train station, take a left onto V. Alamanni; the station is on the left by a long driveway. Ⓢ €6.10. Ⓩ 1¼hr., 1 per hr.) Buses to Lucca leave from Pisa Airport and run to and from P. Giuseppe Verdi in Lucca. (Ⓢ €4. Ⓩ 40min., 1 per hr.) You can also easily take a bus to Marina di Pisa. (⚐ From under the west side of the archway in P. Vittorio Emanuele II, follow as it veers left to find the buses. Ⓢ €2. Ⓩ 25min., every 20min.)

Getting Around

On Foot

There's little need for anything but your feet while you're in Pisa. The walk from the train station to P. dei Miracoli—the longest diameter of the city and also the route you're most likely to take—takes about 20-25min., depending on the route.

By Bus

LAM ROSSA runs a loop between the airport, train station, tower, and several other points in Pisa every 20min. (€1.10). Most buses stop at P. Sant'Antonio, just west of P. Vittorio Emanuele II. You can purchase bus tickets at *tabaccherie* or at ticket machines at Pisa Centrale and Galileo Galilei Airport.

By Taxi

RadioTaxi (☎050 54 16 00) has taxi stands at the airport, Pisa Centrale, and P. del Duomo.

By Bike

Pisa is somewhat less bike-friendly than other Tuscan cities, with lanes that tend to disappear right when you actually need them.

Excursions

Rentals are available at **Eco Voyager.** (V. Uguccione della Faggiola 41 ☎050 56 18 39; www.ecovoyager.it Ⓢ €4 per hr., €12 per day, €50 per week. ⌚ Open daily 9am-noon.)

LUCCA

Ask a native of Lucca to compare Florence to his beloved hometown, and he is likely to mutter dismissively about canine excrement. The fiercely proud Lucchesi have every reason to be protective of their little fortified Brigadoon, as it's everything Florence is not: musical, uncrowded, green, and slow-paced. You can throw away your map here and get lost—the walls will keep you safe as you wander labyrinthine alleys, distinctive *piazze,* and streets full of bicycling Lucchesi balancing cappuccinos. Those amazingly intact 16th-century walls that hug the city not only provide a gorgeous 4km stroll, but also keep out most cars and two-days-per-country Round-the-Worlders. As the birthplace of Puccini, Lucca is an extremely musical city, with at least one concert every day of the year—your first stop might be at one of the ubiquitous poster kiosks to find out which university choir is touring through town that day. *Let's Go* recommends staying at least a night or two in Lucca—you don't want to miss the walls at sunset.

Orientation

Your first step is to put down this book. But wait! Finish reading this section before you toss us to the wayside. Lucca is not a place for checklist tourism. Whether you are here for an afternoon or a week, the best thing to do is to get lost. Put a map in your pocket in case of an emergency, resist the temptation to follow the stops of the carefully signposted Tourist Route, and have at it. In any event, sooner or later you'll always hit the city wall, but you'll probably find that despite hidden *piazze* and winding alleys, these medieval streets are so distinctive that you'll know your way around in a day.

When you do look at a map, you'll see a big square-shaped area inside the ellipse of Lucca's walls. This square marks the original Roman city boundaries, and the streets within it form a surprisingly reliable grid. If they suddenly begin to spiral in on themselves, you're probably nearing the **Piazza Anfiteatro** in the north. Coming from the station you will most likely enter from the south, passing Lucca's **Duomo.** A little west from there is

Piazza Napoleone, the heart of community life. The other major gateway to the town is **Piazzale Verdi**—if you're here, it means you're in the westernmost point of the city. **Via Fillungo,** lined with posh shops and department stores, runs roughly north to south until it starts veering east in that wacky Anfiteatro zone. East of the canal on **Via del Fosso** you'll find the city's "new" section, a 16th-century extension. The walls, of course, are all around you.

Accommodations

There's just one hostel in town, but it's big enough to accommodate everyone. Otherwise, you can find a cozy room in one of Lucca's 54 (and counting) bed and breakfasts for what you'd spend on a hostel in Florence.

🏨 La Gemma di Elena   B AND B $$

V. della Zecca 33

☎0583 49 66 65; www.virtualica.it/gemma

Most bed and breakfasts feel like they were decorated by your kooky aunt. This one feels like it was designed by that awesome guy from college who lived in Tibet and now writes an antiquing blog. It's spacious yet cluttered in an utterly lived-in way, with colorful sarongs on the wall and a wind chime hanging from the chandelier. Each room has a distinct character and name—Zelda, for example, has a crystal ball. Since Italian breakfast generally consists of one croissant, the B and B's buffet of bread, Nutella, jam, pastries, lunch meat, and cheese is a great incentive to get out of bed.

▶ ✿ Off of V. del Fosso. *i* Guests receive a key to the front door. Parking available. Free Wi-Fi. Ⓢ High-season singles €35; doubles €55, with bath €65. Low-season singles €25-30; doubles €45-50, with bath €55-60. Ⓞ Reception open until the last guest arrives. Breakfast 8:30-10am.

Ostello San Frediano (HI)   HOSTEL $

V. della Cavallerizza 12

☎0583 46 99 57; www.ostellolucca.it

Goodness knows why someone thought Lucca needed an enormous HI hostel, but that means all the more space for you! This former monastery has wooden bunk beds, impossibly high ceilings, and cavernous common spaces. If only there were more people to fill them. There's also a huge breakfast room with seating for about nine billion and a courtyard facing the historic wall.

The semi-private bathrooms aren't attached to the dorms, but each room has its own bathroom on the same hall. Travelers report both extremely welcoming and rude experiences with reception.

▶ Just past V. San Frediano. It's the only hostel in town, so you can safely follow the *Ostello* signs. *i* Lockers included. Free Wi-Fi in the lobby. $ Dorms €19, with bath €21; doubles €60. ⏰ Lockout 9:45am-3:30pm.

B and B La Torre

B AND B $$$

V. del Carmine 11

☎0583 95 70 44; www.roomslatorre.com

La Torre, Lucca's oldest bed and breakfast, consists of two locations several blocks apart. This means that if you're in La Torre 2, you'll have to actually get dressed (gasp!) to walk to La Torre 1 for breakfast and the Wi-Fi in the reception. It's worth the walk, though, because breakfast involves pastries, jam, and prosciutto with melon. La Torre 1 has small rooms with brass beds and wicker furniture, and its hallway is lined with a *New York Times* photo essay of the most classic Italian grandmother ever—the proprietor's own *nonna*. La Torre 2 has spacious rooms with double beds, lots of drawers, and Lucca posters on the walls. The real deal in La Torre is the one-bedroom apartment on P. Anfiteatro, equipped with a full modern kitchen (€80). In other news, ye lovelorn travelers are in good hands! La Torre's proprietor met his girlfriend when she stayed at La Torre... on *Let's Go*'s recommendation. (Send your LG-enabled love stories to us at feedback@letsgo.com.)

▶ Across from the Mercato. *i* Free Wi-Fi. Parking available. $ Doubles used as singles €40-50, doubles with bath €50-80; quads €120. €20 per additional person. ⏰ Reception 8am-8pm.

Guesthouse San Frediano

B AND B $$$

V. degli Angeli 19

☎0583 46 96 30; www.sanfrediano.com

There's nothing generic about this family-run bed and breakfast, although its nine rooms all seem to feature the same color palette: rusty orange. The pointed exposed-beam ceilings and skylights make it feel rather like an alpine lodge. Bathrooms have a tub, are shared by three rooms, and are (you guessed it) rusty orange. You might start wondering if they accidentally bought too much of that wallpaper. At least there's nothing orange in the common room, which houses a mannequin proudly bearing the military uniform of the guesthouse chef's grandfather.

▶ Off V. Cesare Battisti. *i* Guests receive key to front door. Wi-Fi €4 per hr. Ⓢ Singles €40-50, with bath €60-70; doubles €50-70/70-95. Extra bed €20-25. Cash preferred. 🕐 Reception 8:30am-12:30pm and 3-6pm.

Sights

The main sight in Lucca is the town itself. While you wander, there are several places of interest to run across. The **Basilica di San Frediano,** with its splendid Byzantine Jesus mosaic, displays the desiccated corpse of St. Zita in a glass case like a gruesome Snow White. The elliptical **Piazza Anfiteatro** was once the site of a Roman amphitheater. The **Torre dell'Ore** has been rented to clock-runners since 1390 and allows you to climb past the clock's inner workings, while the **Torre Guinigi** has tiny trees on top. We suggest you enjoy the towers from the ground, though, as they aren't Tuscany's most spectacular views. (Ⓢ 1 tower €3, students and over 65 €2. 2 towers €5/4. 🕐 Torre dell'Ore open daily June-Sept 9:30am-7:30pm; Oct-May 9:30am-6:30pm. Torre Guinigi open daily May-Sept 9am-midnight; Oct-Feb 9am-5pm; Mar-Apr 9am-7:30pm.)

🏛 The Walls
WALLS

Some cities have a park. This park has a city. Lucca's walls were built as fortification in the second half of the 16th century, expanding previous Roman and medieval walls. Despite all their ramparts, sally ports, and cavaliers, though, they never had to face an enemy worse than the 1812 flood. Today, the 4.2km of walls are mossy and tree-covered, and the old army quarters now serve as public facilities, cafeterias, and study centers. At any time of the day or evening, the town's residents can be found jogging or hanging out on their beautiful fortifications. Metaphorically, the walls continue to be a defense—they guard this Tuscan Atlantis from the outside world, protecting the tiny city's rhythm from being disrupted by the frantic tick-tock of modernity. "Once it was a place for military protection," says the city's official guide to the walls, "and now it protects memories."

▶ 🚶 Walk away from the town center and you're certain to hit them. 𝒊 For more info, visit the Opera delle Mura at Castello Porta San Donato Nuova (☎0583 58 23 20; www.operadellemura.it) or just pick up the guide to the walls from the tourist office.

🏛 Piazza Napoleone
PIAZZA

If you need more evidence that Lucca is the best small town ever, look no further than its green, bustling town square postered with ads for upcoming concerts. Along one side of the L-shaped *piazza* you'll find a carousel, kids playing soccer, and an enormous inflatable screen that lights up during major sporting events. Around the bend, in front of Teatro Verdi, candles in brown paper bags occasionally cordon off a section of pavement for community tango sessions.

▶ ✢ Just above the southern center walls. ⓢ Free.

Duomo di San Martino   CHURCH
P. di San Martino
☎0583 49 05 30; www.museocattedralelucca.it

The Duomo di San Martino is an excellent example of Lucca's distinctive church style, in which a long, rectangular sanctuary is divided into three aisles by arches. Inside, you can visit the **Tomb of Illyria** and the oldest surviving marble carving of Renaissance artist Jacopo della Quercia. Next door in P. Antelminelli, the **Museo della Cattedrale** displays graduals and other sparkly things from the Middle Ages to the 15th century. Yet even the bold purples of the interior's stained glass pale in comparison to the beauty of the facade. Dozens of columns, each unique, adorn the church's face, as though the beholder is the judge of some ancient marble-column-design competition.

▶ ✢ From P. Napoleone, take V. del Duomo. ⓢ Duomo free. Audio tour €1. Tomb of Ilyria €2. Baptistery €2.50. Museum €4. All 3 €6. ⓧ Open M-F 9:30am-5:45pm, Sa 9:30am-6:30pm, Su 9:30-10:45am and noon-6pm. No tourist visits to the cathedral during mass.

Puccini Opera   MUSEUM
V. Santa Giustina 16
☎0583 95 58 24; www.puccciniopera.it

Though the information panels are rather dry, this free museum will help you understand why Puccini is important to Lucca and to opera in general. Peruse vintage poster art, costume design sketches, and souvenir schlock from the original runs of masterpieces like *Turandot, La Bohème, Madame Butterfly,* and *Tosca;* hear numbers from Gallone's cinematic interpretations of the operas; and read (but not understand, unless you speak Italian) letters to and from the maestro himself. To extend the Puccini pilgrimage, grab one of the red postcards that bears his signature bowler hat and mustache for directions to his childhood home, which is not open to the public. The postcards also indicate the birthplace of legendary cellist Boccherini, in the hope that someone cares.

▶ ✢ Off P. San Salvatore. ⓢ Free. ⓧ Open M 10am-7pm, W-Su 10am-7pm.

Lu.C.C.A.

MUSEUM

V. della Fratta 36

☎0583 57 17 12; www.luccamuseum.com

The full name of Lu.C.C.A is Lucca Center of Contemporary Art, showing that Lucca is as good at acronyms as it is at everything else. Those who like white-on-white designs and signs that say things like "this is the narrative plot of a peripheral network that harks back to the omnivorous particles of a tentacular research" will adore this museum. For everyone else, it's still a fascinating stage for the latest avant-garde and experimental modern art, particularly in the realms of material and technique.

▶ ⯐ At the intersection of V. Santa Gemma Galgani, V. della Zecca, and V. dei Fossi. $ Prices vary, but exhibits run from free to €10, sometimes with student discounts. ⏰ Open Tu-Su 10am-7pm. Last entry 6pm.

Palazzo Pfanner

MUSEUM

V. degli Asili 33

☎0583 95 40 29; www.palazzopfanner.it

What do beer-brewing tools, vaginal irrigators, lemon trees, and Jesus sculptures have in common? Well, we're not sure either, but you can find all of them at Palazzo Pfanner. You see, in the 19th century, *nouveau riche* Felix Pfanner made his fortune turning this 1660 five-room palace into a brewery. Felix's son Pietro was a surgeon, explaining all the WWI-era medical instruments, as well as a war hero and mayor of Lucca. Visiting here is like entering a time warp where centuries stand side by side. The visit is quick, but certainly unique.

▶ ⯐ Near the San Frediano gate in the walls. $ Palazzo €4. Garden €4. Combined ticket €5.50; students, ages 12-16, and over 65 €4.50. In Apr and Oct €0.50 less. ⏰ Open daily Apr-Oct 10am-6pm.

Food

Many of Lucca's loveliest dining spots are tucked into alleyways and hidden courtyards, but follow lines of candles or paper lanterns and they're easy to find. During the day, fresh produce, meat, and fish are available in **Piazza del Mercato** (open M-Sa 8am-1:30pm). Lucchese specialties tend to be pasta, such as the meat-filled *tortelli alla lucchese*. You should also be aware that if you're coming from Florence, the gelato in Lucca is nothing to get excited about, so take a break from your regular treat and gorge on Nutella crepes, baked goods, or fruit-filled yogurt instead.

🍴 San Colombano

RISTORANTE, CAFETERIA $$

Baluardo di San Colombano

☎0583 46 46 41; www.caffetteriasancolombano.it

The conversion of the walls' old bulwarks into public spaces brought about the creation of San Colombano, the walls' only restaurant, which was carved out of an enormous battlement. There's a pretty seamless transition between indoor and outdoor seating in San Colombano's E-shaped space. The interior lies to the left, the outdoor tables sit in the center, and there's a more casual cafeteria on the right. Dinner patrons are hit with a €2 cover, but the staff refills the bread basket frequently. The Lucchese specialties are excellent—try the macaroni with gorgonzola and pear sauce. Bottles of wine run from €12 to €200, but there are several nice local wines at the bottom end of the price range.

▶ ⇄ Atop the wall, in the southeast at San Colombano. $ Cover €2. Crepes €3-4. *Primi* €7-9. Pizza €6-9. Cocktails €6. ⏰ Open Tu-F 8am-1am, Sa 8am-2am.

🍴 Pizzeria Bella Mariana

PIZZERIA $

V. della Cavallerizza 29

☎0583 49 55 65

Pizzeria Bella Mariana has the best pizza around, hands down. You're expected to order at the desk and clean up after yourself, but this just means a lower price for the fire-oven pizza. Try the eggplant Pizza Siciliana. This is a great place to pick up some to-go pizza for watching the sunset from the city walls.

▶ ⇄ Across from the Ostello San Frediano. $ Pizza €5-8. ⏰ Open M 12:30-2:30pm and 6:30-11:30pm, W-F 12:30-2:30pm and 6:30-11:30pm.

Antico Sigillo

RISTORANTE $$

V. degli Angeli 13

☎0583 91 042; www.anticosigillo.it

A handful of alley seats make Antico Sigillo a great place to set up in the fresh air with a friend or book. You should err on the early side of Italian dinnertime if you want to nab a table, though. Antico Sigillo serves excellent chef specials, delicious fresh bread, and local specialties like *tortelli alla lucchese.*

▶ ⇄ Courtyard entrance off V. Fillungo. $ Cover €1.50. *Primi* €7-12. Chef's specials €8-15. ⏰ Open M-Tu noon-10:30pm, Th-Su noon-10:30pm.

Mara Méo

PIZZERIA $

P. San Francesco 17

☎0583 46 70 84; www.mara-meo.it

Mara Méo's thin-crust, made-to-order pizza is served by tired girls in orange visors and T-shirts. They're tired for good reason though—the place is hopping and they get your food to you at record speeds (for Italy). Pizza comes in small and large: small is a personal pizza, and you'll probably want to share a large unless you're Michael Phelps. (Michael Phelps, if you're reading this, go for the large. You have our blessing.)

▶ ⚷ Just off Piazzale Verdi. $ Small pizza €4.50-6.50. ⏰ Open daily 10am-11pm.

Basion Contrario

RISTORANTE $$

V. San Paolino 69

☎0583 53 403

Truffles are the specialty here, with an entire menu of truffle *antipasti,* truffle *primi,* and truffle *secondi,* all for around €17-19. For a somewhat less pricey but no less gourmet meal, stick to the truffle-free menu, where *primi* are a more reasonable €7.50-13. The extensive dessert menu—featuring, you guessed it, more truffles, and not of the chocolate variety—will leave you drooling.

▶ ⚷ At the intersection of V. San Paolino and V. Galli Tossi. $ *Primi* from €7.50. Desserts €4-5. ⏰ Open daily noon-3pm and 7pm-midnight.

Spaghetti Lasagne Pizza

RISTORANTE $

P. San Salvatore

The immense creativity of this restaurant's name extends to its decor and menu. Although the tablecloths are plastic and the bread is nonexistent, the outdoor seating in the *piazza* is pleasant, service is quick, and no one looks at you funny if you're eating alone. The waitresses recruit passersby like military officers in a high school. Lasagna here is the cheapest in town (€4.30) although it's served a bit too quick for comfort.

▶ ⚷ Just off P. Napoleone. $ Cover €1. Lasagna €4.30. Pizza margherita €4.80. ⏰ Open daily 11am-11pm.

Nightlife

Nice bars and *enoteche* dot the old city, but **Piazza San Michele, Piazza San Frediano,** and the intersection of V. Vittorio Veneto and Corso Garibaldi are your best bet. Lucca is not the place to get your pre-game on and dance until dawn, but it's a welcoming place for laid-back drinking and mingling. If there's a warrant for celebration, you'll find the whole town out and about in **Piazza Napoleone.**

👍 Elemento — ENOTECA

V. Carrara 16

☎0583 14 52 21

There are a half dozen bars, pubs, and *enoteche* around the intersection of V. Vittorio Veneto and Corso Garibaldi, but super-mod Elemento is *Let's Go*'s favorite. This *enoteca* fancies itself an old movie. The chic interior is entirely black and white, and equally chic clientele perch on the metal seats. Elemento is a good stop at *aperitivo* time for one of the nicest buffets in town.

▶ 🪧 Across from Baluardo Santa Maria. $ Bottled beer €4. Cocktails €5. ⏰ Open M-Tu 7am-1am, Th-F 7am-1am, Sa 7am-2am, Su 7am-1am.

Betty Blue Cafe — BAR

V. del Gonfalone 16/18

☎0583 49 21 66; www.bettybluelucca.it

At night, the red stools of this internet cafe fill with young locals who come to enjoy beer and guacamole. It's not the cheapest joint, but it has the most laid-back ambience of anywhere in the northeastern part of town.

▶ 🪧 Between V. della Zecca and Porte dei Borghi, just behind the fountain. $ Bottled beer €5. Cocktails €8. Wi-Fi €2 per 15min., €4.50 per hr. ⏰ Open daily 11am-1am.

Gelateria Veneta — GELATERIA

V. Vittorio Veneto 74

☎0583 46 70 37; www.gelateriaveneta.net

While it may seem odd to picture a *gelateria* as a nighttime destination, visit adorable Veneta in the evening and you'll understand. The locals have made it an after-dinner hotspot in the manner of a 1950s ice cream parlor full of bobby-soxers and drugstore Romeos. In the early evening, it's full of teenagers smooching over sundaes. In the later evening, the long benches outside fill with groups making a gelato pit stop on their way from one bar to the next. It may not be Florentine gelato, but this Lucchese staple since 1927 is worth sampling just for the experience.

▶ 🪧 At the intersection of V. Vittorio Veneto and Corso Garibaldi. ℹ Other locations at V. Beccheria 10 (☎0583 49 68 56) and Chiasso Barletti (☎0583 49 37 27). Ⓢ Cover €1. Yogurt and gelato cones from €2. Sundaes €4.50-7. ☒ Open daily 10:30am-1am.

Arts and Culture

Lucca is an extremely musical town. The **Puccini Festival** ensures at least one performance every day of the year, and summertime sees an explosion of concerts and musical events. Additionally, it's a popular destination for university choirs and orchestras on tour, so stop by the box office at **Teatro Verdi,** visit www.comune.lucca. it, or take a look at one of the many poster kiosks to see what's happening during your visit. If you're here on a Friday summer night, you should also stop by the **Orto Botanico** (V. del Giardino Botanica 14) for free candlelit musical performances.

▩ Puccini e la sua Lucca   OPERA

Chiesa di San Giovanni

☎0583 32 70 41; www.puccinielasualucca.com

Hometown hero **Giacomo Puccini** is celebrated every single night of the year in Lucca with recitals of his arias and art songs, which are often paired with works by Mozart and Verdi. That makes this the only permanent ▨**festival** in the world and suggests that these folks don't really understand the concept behind festivals. We certainly aren't complaining, though, even if the church where performances are held is a bit too resonant to be an ideal recital hall. The program is different every single night, not a daily march through the greatest hits. Christmas and Easter's extra batches of concerts are especially festive, and a full Puccini opera is produced in the fall.

▶ ✠ Off V. del Duomo; coming from P. Napoleone, it's the church on the left before the Duomo. Ⓢ Concerts €17, students €12. Galas and staged opera performances €15-40. Discount on following night's recital with ticket stub from previous night. ☒ All performances at 7pm. Tickets sold at Chiesa di San Giovanni daily 10am-6pm. Advance sales online or at authorized festival sales points.

▩ Music of the Trees   CLASSICAL MUSIC

Giardino Botanico

www.comune.lucca.it

If you're lucky enough to be in Lucca on a Friday night in June, July, or August, you should be here at *Il canto degli alberi*. The city's botanical garden hosts chamber music concerts on summer Fridays at 9pm, and they are free and open to the public. Better still, the whole garden is open and illuminated with candles along the pathway.

▶ ✣ In the botanical garden in the southeast corner of the city. $ Free. ⏰ Performances in summer F 9pm.

Summer Festival
FESTIVAL

P. Anfiteatro

☎0584 46 477; www.summer-festival.com

In July, P. Napoleone becomes a mass concert stage for the latest names in music. This festival recruits a number of big names: previous line-ups have included Arcade Fire, Amy Winehouse, and James Blunt. Some of the concerts are free, so check out who's playing while you're in town.

▶ ✣ Gates and seating vary by concert, but all are based out of P. Anfiteatro. $ Prices vary, but generally €30-50, with a couple free concerts each year. ⏰ Concerts every few days in July.

Essentials

Practicalities

- **TOURIST OFFICES: Centro Accoglienza Turistica,** the main branch of Lucca's primary tourist office, schedules guided tours and provides audio tours, information about events, and internet access. (Piazzale Verdi ☎0583 58 31 50; www.luccaitinera.it ✣ Look for "i" sign on the left. ⏰ Open daily 9am-7pm.) **Ufficio Regionale** includes internet access, currency exchange, accommodations-booking assistance, and a tourist bus checkpoint. (P. Santa Maria 35 ☎0583 46 99 64 ✣ Look for the "i" sign on the right. ⏰ Open Apr-Oct 9am-7:30pm; Nov-Mar 9am-12:30pm and 3-6:30pm.) **Ufficio Provinciale** provides general tourist assistance. (Corile Carrara ☎0583 91 99 41 ✣ Beside P. Napoleone. ⏰ Open daily 10am-1pm and 2-6pm.)

- **CURRENCY EXCHANGE:** Available at the **Ufficio Regionale** tourist office.

- **ATMS: UniCredit Banca.** (Corner of Vle. Agostino Marti and V. San Paolino ✣ 50m from bank, off Piazzele Verdi. ⏰

Open 24hr.) **Deutschebank.** (Corner of V. Fillungo and V. Mordini ⏰ Open 24hr.)

- **LAUNDROMATS: Lavanderia Niagara.** (V. Michele Rosi 26 ☎349 16 45 084 ⇄ Off P. San Michele. $ Wash and dry €4 per 7kg. ⏰ Open daily 7am-11pm.)

- **INTERNET: Tourist Offices** all provide computers with internet. The office at P. Verdi has Wi-Fi (when it's working). **Betty Blue** internet cafe has both computers and Wi-Fi and keeps the longest hours. (V. del Gonfalone 16/18 ☎0583 49 21 66; www.bettybluelucca.it ⇄ Between V. della Zecca and Porte dei Borghi. $ €2 per 15min., €4.50 per hr. ⏰ Open daily 11am-1am.) Wi-Fi is also available at the **train station** in Piazzale Ricasoli. ($ €1.50 per 20min.)

Emergency

- **POLICE: Polizia Municipale.** (Piazzale San Donato 12 ☎0583 44 27 27 ⇄ In the westernmost point inside the walls.) **Carabinieri.** (Cortile degli Svizzeri 4 ☎0583 46 78 21 ⇄ In the southwest of the *centro*.)

- **LATE-NIGHT PHARMACIES: Farmacia Comunale.** (P. Curatone 7 ⇄ Outside the city walls, opposite Baluardo San Colombano. ⏰ Open 24hr.)

- **HOSPITALS/MEDICALSERVICES: CampodiMarte.**(V.dell'Ospedale ☎0583 95 57 91 ⇄ Outside the city walls, northeast of the city. ⏰ Open 24hr.)

Getting There

By Train

To get to Lucca from Florence, the train is your most reliable option. Take the Viareggio train—Lucca's the third to last stop before Viareggio. You can order your ticket (€5.20) from the self-service kiosk or window. Validate your ticket before boarding by stamping it in the yellow machine by your train. You will arrive in Piazzale Ricasoli, just south of the city walls. (⏰ Station open M-F 4:30am-12:30am, Sa-Su 5:30am-12:30am. Ticket office open daily 6:30am-8:10pm.) Direct trains run back to Florence ($ €5.10. ⏰ 80min., 2 per hr. 5:05am-10:32pm.) and Pisa. ($ €2.40. ⏰ 30min., 2 per hr. 7am-9:42pm.)

By Bus

Take the **Blue Lazzi** bus (☎0583 58 78 97; www.valibus.it) from the Florence bus terminal to Piazzale Verdi. (🧭 From the left side of the train station facing the trains, take the 1st left and walk up the block. The terminal is on the left. $ €4.60. ⏰ 1½hr., 1-2 per hr.)

Getting Around

By Taxi

RadioTaxi. (☎0583 33 34 34) Taxi stands (marked with codes identifying the pick-up point) can be found at the train station, P. Napoleone, P. Santa Maria, and Piazzale Verdi.

By Bus

Lucca offers both suburban buses and seven town buses around the city, run by the company **CLAP** (☎0583 54 11; www.clapspa.it). You can catch pretty much any bus at Piazzale Verdi, just inside the west side of the city walls. Buses stop running around 8pm.

By Bike

You'll find the same rates and hours at each of the major rental places around town. ($ Street bikes €2.50 per hr., €13 per day; mountain bikes €3.50/18; tandem bikes €5.50 per hr. ⏰ Open daily 9am-7:30pm.) Here are some options: **Poll Antonio Biciclette** (P. Santa Maria 42 ☎0583 49 37 87), **Promo Tourist** (Porta San Pietro ☎348 38 00 126), and the **tourist office** in Piazzale Verdi.

SAN GIMIGNANO

Both picturesque and formidable, the 14 towers of San Gimignano loom over the city's small *piazze* and meandering walls. The towers date back to a period when prosperous families used the town square as their personal battlefield. During sieges, they were a handy vantage point for dumping boiling oil on neighbors. Nowadays there's very little need for scalding fluids, as

San Gimignano's impressive skyline and the region's dry white Vernaccia wine draw nothing more dangerous than tourists by the busload—30 buses a day from Poggibonsi, to be precise.

You will never see so many older folk chugging their way up steep hills as you will in this town. V. San Giovanni is congested with tourists and tourist schlock, and you can hardly move for fear of stepping into a photograph or onto a Pinocchio doll. Luckily, San Gimignano's infernal verticality means that the crowds rarely wander off the *very* beaten path—you need only walk a few meters down (more likely up) a side street to be completely alone. Strap your feet into some walking shoes and explore the towers of San Gimignano from the outside in.

Orientation

The bus from Poggibonsi will let you off right outside the city's main entrance. Through that gate you'll enter onto **Via San Giovanni,** the main tourist drag. Follow that uphill to reach **Piazza Duomo** and the adjacent **Piazza della Cisterna,** which you can identify by the big well *(cisterna)* in the center. This is the path on which you'll find most of San Gimignano's activity, and therefore the most tourists. Past P. Duomo is **Via San Matteo,** which leads you through to **Porta San Matteo** on the other side of the city. There are signs pointing the way to most sights and many restaurants as well. If you intend to stray off this main artery, **Rocca di Montestaffoli** and **Via dei Artisti** to the left are good places to explore, as is the path around the city's walls.

Accommodations

San Gimignano's size and quiet nightlife make it more of a daytrip destination than an overnight stop. This means accommodations are mostly geared toward well-off older visitors, so ask at the tourist office for a list of places in the greater San Gimignano area for some more affordable options. Sticking around for the night may appeal to those who enjoy romantic empty streets and forested paths.

🏠 Foresteria Monastero di San Girolamo   CONVENT $$
V. Folgore 30/32

☎0577 94 05 73; www.monasterosangirolamo.it

There are no hostels in all of San Gimignano, so if you're on a budget and absolutely must spend the night in town, we hope you don't have spheniscíphobia (that's the fear of nuns). You might have to ring a few times and knock at several doors to find a sister to check you in, but you'll be led to a small, simple room with a private bath and a discreet cross above the doorway. Guests are given a key and left to their own devices for the remainder of their stay, unless they dare wander beyond the "private" doors into the fully operational convent, which guests should know is strictly nunacceptable.

▶ ⛪ From Porta San Matteo, walk 2 blocks uphill, then turn left onto V. XX Settembre, which becomes V. Folgore. *i* Breakfast €3. Parking €2. Men and women welcome. Reserve ahead by emailing monasterosangimignano@ gmail.com. Ⓢ Dorms €27. Cash only. 🕐 Reception 11am-1pm and 4-6pm.

Ostello in Chianti (HI)   HOSTEL $
V. Roma 137

☎055 80 50 265; www.ostellodelchianti.it

This hostel is actually nowhere near San Gimignano, but by kilometers and travel minutes, it *is* the nearest hostel—and it's quite a nice one at that. Buses to Florence, Siena, and San Gimignano (via Poggibonsi) are a bit spotty, so this is a better base for those with their own vehicle. The rooms have wooden bunks with big lockers, while the large common space features a couch, some picnic chairs, and a ping-pong table as well as a dining area. If you catch them when they're actually in, the incredibly friendly hostel staff greet guests by name, offer coffee or tea, navigate bus schedules, and may even allow guests to use their washing machine or borrow a bicycle.

▶ ⛪ From San Gimignano, buy a ticket in the cafe just before the main gate and head to the bus stop beyond the walls on the right. Take the bus to Poggibonsi station. There, ask inside the station at the bar on the left for a ticket to Tavernelle Val di Pesa and ask the driver to stop when you get to the unmarked town. *i* Breakfast €1.80. Free Wi-Fi. Computer in reception. Parking available. Ⓢ Dorms €15; private rooms with bath €17-23 per person. 🕐 Reception 8:30-11am and after 4pm.

Locando Il Pino   B AND B $$$
V. Cellolese 6

☎0577 94 04 15; www.ristoranteilpino.it

No nuns, no long commute—some people want it all. Well, you'll have to step up your going price. Just inside the city walls, Locando Il Pino features spacious rooms, exposed beams, and large wooden armoires. The bed and breakfast is run by the same couple who manage the adjacent restaurant. The husband's English is minimal, so be prepared to pantomime that you want a bed rather than a table, or you might end up with very uncomfortable and board-like sleeping quarters.

▶ ⚑ Turn left just after entering the walls at Porta San Matteo. *i* Breakfast €5. Ⓢ Doubles used as singles €45; doubles €55; triples €70.

Sights

The best sight in San Gimignano is the beautiful city itself. Your typical indoor sights are all within the central *piazze,* but a walk along the city walls can be just as charming. If you're in town on Thursday, check out the market in P. della Cisterna.

▣ Rocca di Montestaffoli and Museo del Vino   FORTRESS, MUSEUM
Villa della Rocca
☎0577 94 12 69

The ruins of this ancient fort are now an overgrown Eden of silver-green leaves. Along the walls, the stunning view of the city and countryside may erase any other plans you had for the day. Unusual buskers such as Bible reciters and harp players frequent this space, and you may even encounter a wild hedgehog meandering across your path. In summer, movies are shown on a small outdoor screen. The adjacent Museo di Vino is unimpressive, but its wine tastings are affordable.

▶ ⚑ Follow the signs from P. Duomo. Ⓢ Fortress and museum free. Taste 4 wines for €6. 🕐 Fortress open daily dawn to dusk. Museum open Mar-Oct daily 11:30am-6:30pm.

Palazzo Comunale and Torre Grossa   MUSEUM
P. Duomo
☎0577 99 03 48

If you're planning on scaling the tower, avoid your loose skirt and neon underwear combo because the gridded stairs up the tower happen to be quite see-through. You may find them unusually wide for a panorama climb, but don't you worry—the final stretch features a steep, awkward ladder that will punish you for the comfort you may have enjoyed earlier. Tourists come here to scale the tower and take pictures that will never truly capture the phenomenal panorama. Meanwhile, the only remarkable part of the palace area is the **Sala di Dante** on the first floor, which supposedly hosted a visit from the great bard himself.

Excursions

▶ Facing the Duomo, the entrance is on the left. $ €5; students, under 18, and over 65 €4. Entry to all civic museums €7.50/5.50. ⏰ Open daily Mar-Oct 9:30am-7pm; Nov-Feb 10am-5:30pm.

Duomo and Museo di Arte Sacra — CHURCH, MUSEUM

P. Duomo and V. Costarella 1

☎0577 94 22 26

Lacking the frames, chapels, and side altars that break up the frescoes of most big cathedrals, the San Gimignano Duomo is a huge expanse of color. The floor-to-ceiling, brightly colored frescoes create one continuous panel of decoration depicting the New Testament. The funky perspective in some of them creates a house-of-mirrors effect, while the rear wall features a stained-glass window design that may have been based on a plate of rainbow spaghetti. The Museo di Arte Sacra houses spillover from the church's collection, including monstrances (crowns), reliquaries (holy relics), chasubles (robes), and other unexciting objects with misleadingly fancy names. Try as you might, you probably won't spend more than 15min. here.

▶ Enter the Duomo on the left side. The museum is on the opposite side of the courtyard. $ Duomo €3.50, students and under 18 €1.50. Museo €3/1.50. Combined entry €5.50/2.50. ⏰ Duomo open Apr-Oct M-F 10am-7pm, Sa 10am-5:30pm, Su 12:30-5:30pm; Nov-Mar M-Sa 10am-5pm, Su 12:30-5pm.

Food

Bargains are rare in a town as tourist-ridden as San Gimignano. Likewise, since hardly anyone makes San Gimignano his or her actual home, you'll be hard-pressed to find a real grocery store, but there is a **Co-op Supermarket** in the parking lot off Porto San Giovanni (open M-Sa 8:30am-8:00pm). Bring a sandwich for lunch and splurge on a nice restaurant for dinner. Market days are Thursdays until 1pm in the main *piazza*.

👍 Gelateria di Piazza — GELATERIA $

P. della Cisterna 4

☎0577 94 22 44; www.gelateriadipiazza.com

It's easy to tell which *gelateria* in San Gimignano is considered the best—the door to this centrally located artisanal shop is plastered with awards and recommendation stickers. All those critics were likely won over by Gelateria di Piazza's rich

Museums Are Torture

Ask the staff at any of San Gimignano's three (that's right, three) torture museums which one was first, and they'll all have the same answer: "We were." Sadly, *Let's Go* has failed to determine the lineage of these storefront exhibits, or why someone thought little San Gimignano would draw the torture-hungry hoards. But if you are psyched at the idea of seeing plastic mannequins in spiked collars and iron maidens (you sick freak), then these are the "museums" for you. You can find the Museo Pena di Morte at V. San Giovanni 16, the Museo della Tortura at Porta San Giovanni 123, and the other Museo della Tortura at V. del Castello 1/3.

chocolates and creative flavors like gorgonzola cheese and walnuts—that's right, savory gelato—and a Vernaccia flavor based on San Gimignano's specialty wine.

▶ ⇄ In the north side of the *piazza*. *i* Lactose-free options available. $ Small cone €1.80. Chocolate-dipped cone with 3 flavors €2.80. ⏰ Open daily 9am-11pm.

Trattoria Chiribiri — TRATTORIA $

P. della Madonna 1

☎0577 94 19 48

As you pass the open door to the busy kitchen, the smell of daily dishes such as thin strips of pasta in wild boar sauce will drown out any questions you had about where you're eating tonight. The dining room may be slightly underground, but the street scene wall mural is like dining alfresco *sans* mosquitoes.

▶ ⇄ Walking in through the main city entrance on V. San Giovanni, it's upstairs to the left. Enter through the alley on the left side. $ Cover €1.60. *Primi* €5.50-7.50; *secondi* €7-15. ⏰ Open daily 11am-11pm.

Ristorante Enoteca il Castello — RISTORANTE, ENOTECA $

V. del Castello 20

☎0577 94 08 78; www.enotecailcastello.it

Ristorante Enoteca il Castello is named after a 12th-century Gonfiatini palace and has the clip-art knights on the menu to prove it. There's more than enough seating between the glass-enclosed courtyard with palm trees, balcony with a view of the valley, dining room with a suit of armor and picnic benches, and wine bar excavated out of the hill's limestone. Il Castello serves Tuscan classics like *ribollita* and wild boar *tagliatelle*.

▶ ✦ Take a right off P. della Cisterna. Ⓢ Pizza €6.50-7.50. Soups and pasta €7-13. *Secondi* €12-13. ⌚ Open daily M-Th Apr-Oct noon-2:45pm and 7-9:45pm; Nov-Mar noon-2pm and 7-9pm.

Caffè delle Erbe   CAFE $

V. Diacceto 1

☎0577 90 70 83

This quick and handy snack bar on somewhat quieter P. delle Erbe offers fancy panini, cold plates like *caprese* and *bresaola* (salted beef, beets, arugula, parmesan, tomato, and oil), and a short stock of *primi*.

▶ ✦ On P. delle Erbe, just north of P. Duomo. Ⓢ Panini €4.50-6.50. *Primi* €6-8. Cold plates €6.50-9. ⌚ Open M-W 8:30am-11pm, F-Su 8:30am-11pm.

Nightlife

Nothing stays hopping too late in San Gimignano, but you can always make it a do-it-yourself night in P. della Cisterna by picking up a bottle of crisp local Vernaccia (€4.50) from **La Buca**. (V. San Giovanni 16 ☎0577 94 04 07)

Caffè Combattenti   BAR

V. San Giovanni 124/127

☎0577 94 03 91; www.sangimignano.com/aco008e.htm

This isn't exactly your typical night haunt: a crowd of wine and olive oil bottles on one side, a cute little bar huddled next to gum, pastries, and cigarette boxes on the other. Caffè Combattenti sells everything from gelato to bus tickets and closes at 11pm. It's a great place to sip a cocktail while watching the masses meander toward the gate, but don't miss the last Poggibonsi bus.

▶ ✦ It's the 1st thing after entering the main gate into the city. Ⓢ Wine from €3. Cocktails €4. Beer €5. Crepes €4-5.50. ⌚ Open M-Tu 8am-11pm, Th-Su 8am-11pm.

Bar Piazzetta   BAR

Piazzetta Buonaccorsi 5

☎0577 94 03 21

This rather empty neighborhood bar, somewhat off the main tourist path, has been providing adult beverages to locals and wanderers since 1927. This history hasn't bestowed Bar Piazzetta

with much character, but at least there are plenty of seats—just
know that table service costs a euro or two more.

▶ ⚔ Just before Porta San Matteo. Ⓢ Wine from €2; bottles from €12. Beer
€2.50-3.50. Cocktails from €4. 🕙 Open in summer daily 6am-midnight; in
fall, winter, and spring M-Tu 6am-11pm, Th-Su 6am-11pm.

Essentials

Practicalities

- **TOURIST OFFICES: Ufficio Informazioni Turistiche** provides
  free maps, bus tickets, and lists of internet points. It also runs
  daily walking tours. (P. Duomo 1 ☎0577 94 00 08; www.
  sangimignano.com ⚔ Right in P. Duomo; look for the "i"
  sign. *i* 2hr. winery tours with tastings; reserve at office. Ⓢ
  Winery tour €20. 🕙 Open daily in summer 9am-1pm and
  3-7pm; in fall, winter, and spring 9am-1pm and 2-6pm.)

- **CURRENCY EXCHANGE: Protur** has a 24hr. number for
  emergency currency exchange. They charge no commission
  except 5% on traveler's checks. (P. della Cisterna 6 ☎0577
  94 06 61 🕙 Open daily 10am-1pm and 3-6pm.)

- **LAUNDROMATS: Wash and Dry.** (V. del Pozzuolo 8 ⚔ Left
  of V. San Giovanni. *i* Full service. Ⓢ Wash and dry for up
  to 5kg €13. 🕙 Open M-Sa 9am-1pm and 3-7pm. Can take
  a full day.)

- **INTERNET: Libreria La Francigena** provides internet access
  on one computer. (V. Mainardi 12 ☎0577 94 01 44 ⚔
  Enter at Porta San Matteo and take the 2nd right. Ⓢ €0.10
  per minute, €2.50 per 30min., €4 per hr. 🕙 Open M-Sa
  10:30am-1pm and 2:30-7:30pm.)

- **POST OFFICES:** (P. delle Erbe 8 ⚔ Behind the Duomo. 🕙
  Open M-F 8:15am-1:30pm, Sa 8:15am-12:30pm.)

- **POSTAL CODES:** 53037.

Excursions

Emergency

- **POLICE: Polizia Municipale** is the town police station. (V. Santo Stefano ☎0577 94 03 46 ⇄ From P. della Cisterna, take V. del Castello and then turn left onto V. Santo Stefano.) **Carabinieri.** (Piazzale M. Montemaggio ☎0577 94 13 12 ⇄ Outside Porta San Giovanni, the main gate of the Old City. Another station is located at P. Duomo 1.)

- **LATE-NIGHT PHARMACIES: Farmacia** has a 24hr. help line. (P. della Cisterna 8 ☎3480 02 17 10 ⏰ Open daily 9am-1pm and 4:30-8pm.)

- **HOSPITALS/MEDICAL SERVICES: Ospedale Alta Valdelsa** provides emergency room and hospital care. It's in Poggibonsi, so try not to get sick. If you do, call an ambulance. (Localita Campostaggia 8, Poggibonsi ☎0577 99 41. Call ☎118 for an ambulance; they'll know the way to the hospital. Or take a shuttle down to Poggibonsi. ⏰ Open 24hr.)

Getting There

Other than driving, biking a really long way, or taking the occasional direct bus (for example, one runs from Siena's P. Gramsci), the **shuttle bus** from Poggibonsi is the sole option for getting to San Gimignano. Poggibonsi is an active train station, reachable from Empoli, Florence, or Siena by hourly trains. Take either the train from Santa Maria Novella or the Florence-Poggibonsi-Siena bus (€6) from the bus station. To find the Florence bus station, starting on the left side of the train station facing the trains, take the first left, and walk up the block a little ways. The station is on the left where you see a long driveway. Buses leave every hour, and the trip takes 1-2hr. Get off at Poggibonsi. Exit the station and look at the departures board outside to see when the next shuttle to San Gimignano arrives. The shuttle leaves from Area 2, up a little bit and on the right. ($ €1.80. ⏰ 20min., runs every 15-30min.) From Siena, the bus takes about 1¼hr. and costs about €5.20, depending on where you buy your ticket.

Getting Around

Although San Gimignano is tiny and pretty much walkable, its hills are a bit of a nuisance. Two **buses** run a loop through the city for €0.50 (daily ticket €1), mostly providing transport between the parking lots, the Co-op Supermarket, and the Duomo. Cars are not an option within the city walls. If you're truly interested in alternative transportation options, **Bellini Bruno** bike, scooter, motorcycles, and car rental may be worth investigating. (V. Roma 41 }0577 94 02 01; www.bellinibruno.com ✚ Downhill and to the right from Porta San Giovanni. *i* Provides delivery and pickup of vehicles at your accommodation.)

Essentials

You don't have to be a rocket scientist to plan a good trip. (It might help, but it's not required.) You do, however, need to be well prepared, and that's what we can do for you. Essentials is the chapter that gives you all the nitty-gritty you need to know for your trip: the hard information gleaned from 50 years of collective wisdom and several months of furious fact-checking. Planning your trip? Check. Where to find Wi-Fi? Check. The dirt on public transportation? Check. We've also thrown in communications info, safety tips, and a phrasebook, just for good measure. Plus, for overall trip-planning advice from what to pack (money and as little underwear as possible) to how to take a good passport photo (it's physically impossible; consider airbrushing), you can also check out the Essentials section of www.letsgo.com.

So, flick through this chapter before you leave so you know what documents to bring, while you're on the plane so you know how you'll be getting from the airport to your accommodation, and when you're on the ground so you can find a laundromat to solve all your 3am stain-removal needs. This chapter may not always be the most scintillating read, but it just might save your life.

Entrance Requirements

- **PASSPORT:** Required for citizens of all countries.
- **VISA:** Required of non-EU citizens staying longer than 90 days.
- **WORK PERMIT:** Required of all non-EU citizens planning to work in Italy.

RED TAPE

Documents and Formalities

We're going to fill you in on visas and work permits, but don't forget the most important one of all: your passport. **Don't forget your passport!**

Visas

Those lucky enough to be EU citizens do not need a visa to globetrot through Italy. You citizens of Australia, Canada, New Zealand, the US, and other non-EU countries do not need a visa for stays of up to 90 days, but this three-month period begins upon entry into any of the countries that belong to the EU's **freedom of movement** zone. For more information, see **One Europe** (below). Those staying longer than 90 days may apply for a longer-term visa; consult an embassy or consulate for more information.

Double-check entrance requirements at the nearest embassy or consulate of Italy (listed below) for up-to-date information before departure. US citizens can also consult http://travel.state.gov.

Non-EU citizens planning to study in Italy must apply for a special visa. For more information, see the **Beyond Tourism** chapter.

Work Permits

Admittance to a country as a traveler does not include the right to work, which is authorized only by a work permit. For more information, see the **Beyond Tourism** chapter.

One Europe

The EU's policy of freedom of movement means that most border controls have been abolished and visa policies harmonized. Under this treaty, formally known as the Schengen Agreement, you're still required to carry a passport (or government-issued ID card for EU citizens) when crossing an internal border, but, once you've been admitted into one country, you're free to travel to other participating states. Most EU states (the UK is a notable exception) are already members of Schengen, as are Iceland and Norway. In recent times, fears over immigration have led to calls for suspension of this freedom of movement. Border controls are being strengthened, but the policy isn't really targeted against casual travelers, so unless you've been traveling so long that you look like an illegal immigrant, you should still be fine to travel with ease throughout Europe.

Embassies and Consulates

- **ITALIAN CONSULAR SERVICES IN AUSTRALIA: Embassy.** (12 Grey St., Deakin, Canberra, ACT 2600 ☎02 6273 3333; www.ambcanberra.esteri.it ✆ Open M-Tu 9am-noon, W 9am-noon and 1-3pm, Th-F 9am-noon.)

- **ITALIAN CONSULAR SERVICES IN CANADA: Embassy.** (275 Slater St., 21st fl., Ottawa, ON K1P 5H9 ☎613-232-2401; www.ambottawa.esteri.it ✆ Open M-Tu 9am-noon, W 9am-noon and 2-4pm, Th-F 9am-noon.)

- **ITALIAN CONSULAR SERVICES IN IRELAND: Embassy.** (63/65 Northumberland Rd., Dublin 4 ☎01 660 1744; www.ambdublino.esteri.it ✆ Open M-W 10am-noon, Th 1:30-3:30pm, F 10am-noon.)

- **ITALIAN CONSULAR SERVICES IN NEW ZEALAND: Embassy.** (34-38 Grant Rd., Thorndon, Wellington ☎04 473 5339; www.ambwellington.esteri.it ✆ Open M-Tu 9am-1pm, W 9am-1pm and 3-4:45pm, Th-F 9am-1pm.)

- **ITALIAN CONSULAR SERVICES IN THE UK: Embassy.** (38 Eaton Pl., London, SW1X 8AN ☎020 7235 9371; www.conslondra.esteri.it ✆ Open M-F 9am-noon.)

- **ITALIAN CONSULAR SERVICES IN THE USA: Embassy.** (3000 Whitehaven St. NW, Washington, DC 20008 ☎202-612-4400; www.ambwashingtondc.esteri.it ⏰ Open M 10am-12:30pm, W 10am-12:30pm, F 10am-12:30pm.)

Embassies in Italy are situated in Rome. The UK and the US have consulates in Florence.

- **AUSTRALIAN CONSULAR SERVICES IN ROME: Embassy.** (V. Antonio Bosio 5 ☎06 85 27 21, emergency 800 87 77 90; www.italy.embassy.gov.au ⏰ Open M-F 9am-5pm.)

- **CANADIAN CONSULAR SERVICES IN ROME: Embassy.** (V. Zara 30 ☎06 85 44 41; www.canada.it ⏰ General Services available by appointment M-F 9am-noon. Emergency services available M-F 9am-4pm.)

- **IRISH CONSULAR SERVICES IN ROME: Embassy.** (P. di Campitelli 3 ☎06 69 79 121; www.ambasciata-irlanda.it ⏰ Open M-F 10am-12:30pm and 3-4:30pm.)

- **NEW ZEALAND CONSULAR SERVICES IN ROME: Embassy.** (V. Clitunno 44 ☎06 85 37 501; www.nzembassy.com/italy ⏰ Open M-F 8:30am-12:30pm and 1:30-5pm.)

- **UNITED KINGDOM CONSULAR SERVICES IN FLORENCE: Consulate.** (Lungarno Corsini 2, 50213 Florence ☎055 28 41 33; www.britain.it ⏰ Open M-F 9:30am-12:30pm and 2:30-4:30pm.)

- **UNITED STATES CONSULAR SERVICES IN FLORENCE: Consulate.** (Lungarno Vespucci 38, 50123 Florence ☎055 26 69 51; http://florence.usconsulate.gov ⏰ Open M-F 8:30am-12:30pm.)

MONEY

Getting Money from Home

Stuff happens. When stuff happens, you might need some money. When you need some money, the easiest and cheapest solution is to have someone back home make a deposit to your bank account.

Essentials

Otherwise, consider one of the following options.

Wiring Money

Arranging a **bank money transfer** means asking a bank back home to wire money to a bank in Florence. This is the cheapest way to transfer cash, but it's also the slowest and most agonizing, usually taking several days or more. Note that some banks may only release your funds in local currency, potentially sticking you with a poor exchange rate; inquire about this in advance.

Money transfer services like **Western Union** are faster and more convenient than bank transfers—but also much pricier. Western Union has many locations worldwide. To find one, visit www.westernunion.com or call the appropriate number: in Australia }1800 173 833, in Canada 800-235-0000, in the UK 0808 234 9168, in the US 800-325-6000, or in Italy 800 788 935. Money transfer services are also available to **American Express** cardholders and at selected **Thomas Cook** offices.

US State Department (US Citizens Only)

In serious emergencies only, the US State Department will help your family or friends forward money within hours to the nearest consular office, which will then disburse it according to instructions for a US$30 fee. If you wish to use this service, you must contact the Overseas Citizens Services division of the US State Department. (☎+1-202-501-4444, from US 888-407-4747)

Withdrawing Money

To use a debit or credit card to withdraw money from an ATM (*Bancomat* in Italian), you must have a four-digit Personal Identification Number (PIN). If your PIN is longer than four digits, ask your bank whether you can just use the first four or if you'll need a new one. If you intend to hit up ATMs in Europe with a credit card, which doesn't come with a PIN, call your credit card company before your departure to request one.

The use of ATM cards is widespread in Italy. The two major international money networks are MasterCard/Maestro/Cirrus and Visa/PLUS. Most ATMs charge a transaction fee, but some Italian banks have relationships with international banks and waive the withdrawal surcharge. Check with your domestic bank to see before traveling if it has one of these relationships.

Tipping and Bargaining

In Italy, a 5% tip is customary, particularly in restaurants (10% if you particularly liked the service). Italian waiters won't cry if you don't leave a tip; just be ready to ignore the pangs of your conscience later. Taxi drivers expect tips as well, but lucky for alcohol lovers, it is unusual to tip in bars. Bargaining is appropriate in markets and other informal settings, though in regular shops it is inappropriate. Hotels will often offer lower prices to people looking for a room that night, so you will often be able to find a bed cheaper than what is officially quoted.

The Euro

Despite what many dollar-possessing Americans might want to hear, the official currency of 16 members of the European Union—Austria, Belgium, Cyprus, Finland, France, Germany, Greece, Ireland, Italy, Luxembourg, Malta, the Netherlands, Portugal, Slovakia, Slovenia, and Spain—is the euro.

Still, the currency has some important—and positive—consequences for travelers hitting more than one eurozone country. For one thing, money-changers across the eurozone are obliged to exchange money at the official, fixed rate and at no commission (though they may still charge a small service fee). Second, euro-denominated traveler's checks allow you to pay for goods and services across the eurozone, again at the official rate and commission-free. For more info, check a currency converter (such as www.xe.com) or www.europa.eu.int.

Taxes

The **value added tax** (*imposto sul valore aggiunta,* or IVA) is a sales tax levied in EU countries. Foreigners making any purchase over €155 are entitled to an additional 20% VAT refund. Some stores take off 20% on site. Others require that you fill out forms at the customs desk upon leaving the EU and send receipts from home within six months. Not all storefront "Tax-Free" stickers imply an immediate, on-site refund, so ask before making a purchase.

GETTING THERE

How you arrive in Florence will be dictated by where you come from. Florence may have named its Amerigo Vespucci airport after the guy who in turn gave the Americas their name, but that doesn't mean the city has any flights from the US. Those flying across the Atlantic will have to transfer at another European airport. If flying from within Europe, it will probably be cheaper for you to fly into the budget-airline hub that is Pisa Airport. Buses run regularly from Pisa Airport to Florence; they take just over an hour and cost about €10. If coming from within Italy, you will most likely catch a train, which will bring you into Santa Maria Novella station. If traveling locally, buses may be useful.

By Plane

Aeroporto Amerigo Vespucci is Florence's main airport. (V. del Termine 11 ☎055 30 615 main line, 055 30 61 700 for 24hr. automated service; www.aeroporto.firenze.it *i* For lost baggage, call ☎055 30 61 302.) From the airport, the city can be reached via the **VolainBus shuttle.** You can pick up the shuttle on the Departures side. (⇆ Exit the airport to the right and pass the taxi stand. Drop-off is at Santa Maria Novella station. $ €5. ⏰ 25min., every 30min. 6am-11:30pm.) A cab from the airport to the city center costs about €20.

By Train

Santa Maria Novella train station dominates the northwest of the city. (www.grandistazioni.it ⏰ Open daily 6am-midnight.) You can purchase tickets from the fast ticket kiosks or tellers. There are daily trains from: Bologna ($ €25-36. ⏰ 40min., 2 per hr. 7am-11:26pm.); Milan ($ €53. ⏰ 1¾hr., 1 per hr. 7am-9pm.); Rome ($ €45 ⏰ 1½hr., 2 per hr. 8:30am-11:33pm.); Siena ($ €6.30. ⏰ 1½hr., 6 per hr. 5am-9:18pm.); Venice. ($ €43. ⏰ 2hr., 2 per hr. 7:30am-7:30pm.) For precise schedules and prices, check www.trenitalia.com.

By Bus

Three major intercity bus companies run out of Florence's bus station. From Santa Maria Novella train station, turn left onto on V. Alamanni—the station is on the left by a long driveway. **SITA**

(V. Santa Caterina da Siena 17 ☎800 37 37 60; www.sitabus.it) runs buses to and from Siena, San Gimignano, and other Tuscan destinations. **LAZZI** (P. della Stazione 4/6r ☎055 21 51 55;www. lazzi.it ⏰ For timetable info call ☎055 35 10 61.) buses depart from P. Adua, just east of the train station. Routes connect to Lucca, Pisa, and many other regional towns. **CAP-COPIT** (Largo Fratelli Alinari 10 ☎055 21 46 37; www.capautolinee.it) runs to regional towns. Timetables for all three companies change regularly, so call ahead or check online for schedules.

GETTING AROUND

The main thing that you should know is that Florence is a small city. Most visitors simply walk everywhere without any need for public transportation. This is ideal for the budget traveler, as you won't rack up the Metro and bus fares like you do in many other European cities. And if you're going to venture outside the compact city center, Florence has you covered.

By Bus

As the city's only form of public transportation, Florence's tiny orange buses are surprisingly clean, reliable, and organized. Operated by **ATAF** and **LI-NEA,** the extensive bus network includes several night-owl buses that take over regular routes in the late evenings. The schedule for every passing line is posted on the pole of each well-marked bus stop, complete with the direction the bus is going and a list of every stop in order. Most buses originate at P. della Stazione or P. di San Marco. Buses #12 and #13 run to the Piazzale Michelangelo; bus #7 runs to Fiesole. You're unlikely to need to use the buses unless you're leaving the city center. You can buy tickets from most newsstands, ticket vending machines, or the ATAF kiosk in P. della Stazione. (☎800 42 45 00 $ 90min. ticket €1.20, €2 if purchased on board; 24hr. ticket €5; 3-day ticket €12.) Stamp your ticket when you board the bus; you then have the length of time denoted by the ticket to re-use it. Be careful—if you forget to time-stamp your ticket when you board the bus (and can't successfully play the "confused foreigner" card), it's a €50 fine.

By Taxi

To call a cab, call **Radio Taxi.** (☎055 4390, 055 4499, 055 4242, or 055 4798) Tell the operator your location and when you want the cab, and the nearest available car will be sent to you. Each cab has a rate card in full view, and the meter displays the running fare, which is based on the distance traveled and any supplements charged. If you're going far or are nervous, it never hurts to ask for an estimate before boarding. There are surcharges for Sundays, holidays, luggage, and late nights. Unless you have a lot of baggage, you probably won't want to take a taxi during the day, when traffic will make the meter tick up mercilessly. At lunchtime, a 5min. ride from the Duomo to the Oltrarno will cost €7. Nevertheless, cabs are a manageable late-night option if you're outside the city, and especially if you're in a group. Designated cab stands can be found at P. della Stazione, Fortezza da Basso, and P. della Repubblica. Cabs can also often be found at Santa Maria Novella.

By Bike

It takes some confidence to bike in the crowded parts of central Florence, but cycling is a great way to check out a longer stretch of the Arno's banks or to cover a lot of territory in one day. **Mille E Una Bici** (☎055 65 05 295; www.comune.firenze.it/servizi_pubblici/trasporti/noleggiobici.htm) rents 200 bikes that can be picked up and returned at any of its four locations: P. della Stazione, P. di Santa Croce, P. Ghiberti, and Stazione F.S. Campo Di Marte. **Florence By Bike** (V. San Zanobi 91r and 120/122r ☎055 48 89 92; www.florencebybike.it ☒ Open Apr-Oct daily 9am-7:30pm; Nov-Mar M-Sa 9am-1pm and 3:30-7:30pm.) is another good resource. Staff will help renters plan routes, whether it's an afternoon or a multi-day trip outside of town.

PRACTICALITIES

For all the hostels, cafes, museums, and bars we list, we know some of the most important places you visit during your trip might actually be more mundane. Whether it's a tourist office, internet cafe, or post office, these practicalities are vital to a successful trip, and you'll find all you need right here.

- **TOURIST OFFICES: Uffici Informazione Turistica** has its primary office at **Via Manzoni 16.** (☎055 23 320 ☒ Open M-F 9am-1pm.) Other locations include **Piazza della Stazione 4** (☎055 21 22 45 ☒ Open M-Sa 8:30am-7pm, Su 8:30am-2pm.), **Via Cavour 1r** (☎055 29 08 32 ☒ Open M-Sa 8:30am-6:30pm, Su 8:30am-1pm.), and **Borgo Santa Croce 29r.** (☎055 23 40

444 ⏰ Open Mar-Oct M-Sa 9am-7pm, Su 9am-2pm; Nov-Feb M-Sa 9am-5pm, Su 9am-2pm.)

- **CURRENCY EXCHANGE: Best and Fast Change** has offices at V. de' Cerretani 47r (☎055 23 99 855) and Borgo Santa Lorenzo 16r. (☎055 28 43 91)

- **ATMS: BNL** (V. de' Cerretani 6) accepts Visa. **Banca Toscana** (V. dell'Ariento 18) accepts Mastercard.

- **LUGGAGE STORAGE:** At **Stazione Santa Maria Novella.** (🔀 By platform 16. $ 1st 4hr. €4, 5th-12th hr. €0.60 per hr., €0.20 per hr. thereafter. Cash only. ⏰ Open daily 6am-11:50pm.)

- **LAUNDROMATS: Onda Blue.** (V. degli Alfani 24 and V. Guelfa 221r ⏰ Open daily 8am-10pm.)

- **INTERNET: Internet Train** can be found all over the city. For a central location, try **Via de' Benci 36r.** (☎055 26 38 555; www.internettrain.it 🔀 From P. Santa Croce, turn left onto V. de' Benci. $ Wi-Fi €2.50-3 per hr. Internet €3-4.50 per hr. ⏰ Open daily 10am-10:30pm.) Many restaurants and library cafes offer free Wi-Fi. Try **BRAC.** (V. dei Vagellai 18r ☎055 09 44 877 ⏰ Open daily 10am-11pm.)

- **POST OFFICES: Via Pellicceria 3.** (☎055 27 36 481 🔀 South of P. della Repubblica ⏰ Open M-F 8:15am-7pm, Sa 8:15am-12:30pm.) Other locations include V. de' Barbadori 37r (☎055 28 81 75), V. Pietrapiana 53 (☎055 42 21 850), V. de' Barbadori 37r (☎055 28 81 75), and V. Camillo Cavour 71a. (☎ 055 47 19 10)

- **POSTAL CODE:** 50100.

SAFETY AND HEALTH

General Advice

In any type of crisis, the most important thing to do is **stay calm.** Your country's embassy abroad is usually your best resource in an emergency; registering with that embassy upon arrival in the country is a good idea. The government offices listed in the

Emergency

Practicalities are great, but some things are particularly important, and we present those to you here. Hopefully you never need any of these things, but if you do, it's best to be prepared.

- **EMERGENCY NUMBER: Ambulance:** ☎118.

- **POLICE: Polizia Municipale.** (☎055 32 85, 24hr. non-emergency helpline ☎055 32 83 333) Help is also available for tourists at the mobile police units parked at V. dei Calzaioli near P. della Signoria and at Borgo Santa Jacopo in the Oltrarno near Ponte Vecchio. The emergency **Carabinieri** number is ☎112.

- **LATE-NIGHT PHARMACIES: Farmacia Comunale.** (Stazione Santa Maria Novella ☎055 21 67 61 ☼ Open 24hr. Ring the bell 1-4am.) **Farmacia Molteni.** (V. Calzaioli 7r ☎055 28 94 90 ☂ Just north of P. della Signoria.) **Farmacia All'Insegna del Moro.** (P. San Giovanni 20r ☎055 21 13 43 ☂ A little east of the Duomo.)

- **HOSPITALS/MEDICAL SERVICES: Arcispedale Santa Maria Nuova** is northeast of the Duomo and has a 24hr. emergency room. (P. Santa Maria Nuova 1 ☎055 27 581) Tourist medical services can be found at **Via Lorenzo Il Magnifico 59.** (☎055 47 54 11 ☂ In the north of the city, near P. della Libertà. ☼ M-F 11am-noon and 5-6pm, Sa 11am-noon.) **Associazione Volontari Ospedalieri** provides free medical translation. (☎055 42 50 126; www.avofirenze.it ☼ Open M 4-6pm, Tu 10am-noon, W 4-6pm, Th 10am-noon, F 4-6pm.)

Travel Advisories feature at the end of this section can provide information on the services they offer their citizens in case of emergencies abroad.

Local Laws and Police

In Italy, you will mainly encounter two types of boys and girls in blue: the *polizia* (☎113) and the *carabinieri* (☎112). The *polizia* are a civil force under the command of the Ministry of the Interior, whereas the *carabinieri* fall under the auspices of the Ministry of Defense and are considered a military force. Both, however, generally serve the same purpose—to maintain security and order in the country. In the case of attack or robbery, both will respond to inquiries or desperate pleas for help.

Drugs and Alcohol

Needless to say, **illegal drugs** are best avoided altogether, particularly when traveling in a foreign country. In Italy, just like almost everywhere else in the world, drugs including marijuana, cocaine, and heroin are illegal, and possession or other drug-related offenses will be harshly punished.

The legal drinking age in Italy is (drumroll please) 16. Remember to drink responsibly and to **never drink and drive.** Doing so is illegal and can result in a prison sentence, not to mention early death. The legal blood alcohol content (BAC) for driving in Italy is under 0.05%, significantly lower than the US limit of 0.08%.

Specific Concerns

Travelers with Disabilities

Travelers in wheelchairs should be aware that travel in Tuscany will sometimes be extremely difficult. Many cities predate the wheelchair—sometimes it seems even the wheel—by several

Travel Advisories

The following government offices provide travel information and advisories:

- **AUSTRALIA: Department of Foreign Affairs and Trade.** (☎+61 2 6261 1111; www.smartraveller.gov.au)

- **CANADA: Department of Foreign Affairs and International Trade.** Call or visit the website for the free booklet *Bon Voyage, But...* (☎+1-800-267-6788; www.international.gc.ca)

- **NEW ZEALAND: Ministry of Foreign Affairs and Trade.** (☎+64 4 439 8000; www.safetravel.govt.nz)

- **UK: Foreign and Commonwealth Office.** (☎+44 845 850 2829; www.fco.gov.uk)

- **US: Department of State.** (☎888 407 4747 from the US, +1-202-501-4444 elsewhere; http://travel.state.gov)

centuries and thus pose unique challenges to travelers with disabilities. **Accessible Italy** (}378 941 111; www.accessibleitaly.com) offers advice to tourists of limited mobility heading to Italy, with tips on subjects ranging from finding accessible accommodations to wheelchair rental.

Pre-Departure Health

Matching a prescription to a foreign equivalent is not always easy, safe, or possible, so if you take **prescription drugs,** carry up-to-date prescriptions or a statement from your doctor stating the medications' trade names, manufacturers, chemical names, and dosages. Be sure to keep all medication with you in your carry-on luggage. It is also a good idea to look up the Italian names of drugs you may need during your trip.

Immunizations and Precautions

Travelers over two years old should make sure that the following vaccines are up to date: MMR (for measles, mumps, and rubella); DTaP or Td (for diphtheria, tetanus, and pertussis); IPV (for polio); Hib (for *Haemophilus influenzae* B); and HepB (for Hepatitis B). For recommendations on immunizations and prophylaxis, check with a doctor and consult the **Centers for Disease Control and Prevention (CDC)** in the US (☎+1-800-232-4636; www.cdc. gov/travel) or the equivalent in your home country.

KEEPING IN TOUCH

By Email and Internet

Hello and welcome to the 21st century, where you're rarely more than a 5min. walk from the nearest Wi-Fi hot spot, even if sometimes you'll have to pay a few bucks or buy a drink for the privilege of using it. **Internet cafes** and free internet terminals are listed in the **Practicalities** section above. For lists of additional cybercafes in Florence, check out www.cybercafes.com or cafe.ecs.net.

    Wireless hot spots make internet access possible in public and remote places. Unfortunately, they also pose security risks. Hot spots are public, open networks that use unencrypted, unsecured connections. They are susceptible to hacks and "packet sniffing"—the theft of passwords and other private information. To prevent problems, disable "ad hoc" mode, turn off file sharing and network discovery, encrypt your email, turn on your firewall, beware of phony networks, and watch for over-the-shoulder creeps.

By Telephone

Calling Home from Florence

If you have internet access, your best—i.e., cheapest, most convenient, and most tech-savvy—means of calling home is probably our good friend ▧**Skype** (www.skype.com). You can even videochat if you have one of those new-fangled webcams. Calls to other Skype users are free; calls to landlines and mobiles worldwide start at US$0.023 per minute, depending on where you're calling.

For those still stuck in the 20th century, **prepaid phone cards** are a common and relatively inexpensive means of calling abroad. Each one comes with a Personal Identification Number (PIN) and a toll-free access number. You call the access number and then follow the directions for dialing your PIN. To purchase prepaid phone cards, check online for the best rates; www.callingcards.com is a good place to start. Online providers generally send your access number and PIN via email, with no actual "card" involved. You can also call home with prepaid phone cards purchased in Florence.

Another option is a **calling card,** linked to a major national telecommunications service in your home country. Calls are billed collect or to your account. Cards generally come with instructions for dialing both domestically and internationally.

Placing a collect call through an international operator can be expensive but may be necessary in case of an emergency. You can frequently call collect without even possessing a company's calling card just by calling its access number and following the instructions.

Cellular Phones

Sadly, the world refuses to be a simple place, and cell phones bought abroad, particularly in the US, are unlikely to work in Europe. Fortunately, it is quite easy to purchase a reasonably priced phone in Italy. Plus, you won't necessarily have to deal with cell

Essentials

International Calls

To call Italy from home or to call home from Italy, dial:

1. **THE INTERNATIONAL DIALING PREFIX.** To call from **Italy, New Zealand** or the **UK**, dial ☎00; from **Australia,** ☎0011; and from **Canada** or the **US,** ☎011.

2. **THE COUNTRY CODE OF THE COUNTRY YOU WANT TO CALL.** To call **Italy,** dial ☎39, for **Australia,** ☎61; **Canada** or the **US,** ☎1; **Ireland,** ☎353; **New Zealand,** ☎64; and for the **UK,** ☎44.

3. **THE LOCAL NUMBER.** If the area code begins with a zero, you can omit that number when dialing from abroad.

phone plans and bills; prepaid minutes are widely available, and phones can be purchased cheaply or even rented, which removes the hassle of pay phones and phone cards. Some of Italy's biggest providers are TIM, Vodafone, Wind, and 3.

The international standard for cell phones is **Global System for Mobile Communication (GSM).** To make and receive calls in Italy, you will need a GSM-compatible phone and a **SIM (Subscriber Identity Module) card,** a country-specific, thumbnail-size chip that gives you a local phone number and plugs you into the local network. Many SIM cards are prepaid, and incoming calls are frequently free. You can buy additional cards or vouchers (usually available at convenience stores) to "top up" your phone. For more information on GSM phones, check out www.telestial.com. Companies like **Cellular Abroad** (www.cellularabroad.com) and **OneSimCard** (www.onesimcard.com) rent cell phones and SIM cards that work in a variety of destinations around the world.

By Snail Mail

Sending Mail Home from Florence
Airmail is the best way to send mail home from Florence. Write "airmail," or *"per posta aerea,"* on the front. For simple letters or postcards, airmail tends to be surprisingly cheap, but the price will go up sharply for weighty packages. Most post offices will charge exorbitant fees or simply refuse to send airmail with enclosures. **Surface mail** is by far the cheapest, slowest, and most antiquated

way to send mail. It takes one to two months to cross the Atlantic and one to three to cross the Pacific—good for heavy items you won't need for a while, like souvenirs that you've acquired along the way.

Receiving Mail in Florence

There are several ways to arrange pickup of letters sent to you while you are in Florence, even if you do not have an address of your own. Mail can be sent via **Poste Restante** (General Delivery; **Fermo Posta** in Italian) to Florence, and it is generally reliable (though in Italy it's not a surprise for things to be a little untimely). Address Poste Restante letters like so:

> Leonardo DA VINCI
> c/o Ufficio Postale Centrale
> FERMO POSTA
> 50123 Firenze
> Italy

The mail will go to a special desk in the central post office at V. Pellicceria 3, unless you specify a local post office by street address or postal code. It's best to use the largest post office, since mail may be sent there regardless. Bring your passport (or other photo ID) for pickup; there may be a small fee. If the clerks insist that there is nothing for you, ask them to check under your first name as well. *Let's Go* lists post offices in the **Practicalities** section. It is usually safer and quicker, though more expensive, to send mail express or registered. If you don't want to deal with Poste Restante, consider asking your hostel or accommodation if you can have things mailed to you there. Of course, if you have your own mailing address or a reliable friend to receive mail for you, that will be the easiest solution.

TIME DIFFERENCES

Italy is 1hr. ahead of Greenwich Mean Time (GMT) and observes Daylight Saving Time. This means that it is 6hr. ahead of New York City, 9hr. ahead of Los Angeles, 1hr. ahead of the British Isles, 9hr. behind Sydney, and 11hr. behind New Zealand. Don't accidentally call your mom at 5am!

CLIMATE

You'd think that Italy was balmy and beautiful, bordering the Mediterranean as it does. And you'd be right—for some places, some of the time. Surrounded by hills, Florence has pretty consistently hot summers, and, with very little wind, its inhabitants don't get much respite from the humidity. The winter is a little more bearable, but wetter, with a lot of precipitation in late fall and early winter. Long story short, we at *Let's Go* can't really tell you what the weather is going to be like on your trip, so check the forecast before you go. And then don't trust it, because it's probably wrong anyway.

MONTH	AVG. HIGH TEMP.		AVG. LOW TEMP.		AVG. RAINFALL		AVG. NUMBER OF WET DAYS
January	10°C	50°F	1°C	34°F	74mm	3.9 in.	6
February	12°C	53°F	3°C	37°F	69mm	2.7 in.	7
March	15°C	59°F	4°C	40°F	81mm	3.2 in.	7
April	18°C	65°F	7°C	45°F	79mm	3.1 in.	7
May	23°C	74°F	11°C	52°F	74mm	2.9 in.	7
June	27°C	81°F	14°C	58°F	56mm	2.2 in.	7
July	31°C	88°F	17°C	63°F	41mm	1.6 in.	4
August	31°C	87°F	17°C	62°F	76mm	3 in.	5
September	26°C	79°F	14°C	57°F	79mm	3.1 in.	8
October	21°C	70°F	10°C	50°F	89mm	3.5 in.	8
November	14°C	58°F	5°C	41°F	112mm	4.4 in.	11
December	10°C	50°F	2°C	36°F	91mm	3.6 in.	10

To convert from degrees Fahrenheit to degrees Celsius, subtract 32 and multiply by 5/9. To convert from Celsius to Fahrenheit, multiply by 9/5 and add 32. The mathematically challenged may use this handy chart:

°CELSIUS	-5	0	5	10	15	20	25	30	35	40
°FAHRENHEIT	23	32	41	50	59	68	77	86	95	104

MEASUREMENTS

Like the rest of the rational world, Italy uses the metric system. The basic unit of length is the meter (m), which is divided into 100 centimeters (cm) or 1000 millimeters (mm). One thousand meters make up one kilometer (km). Fluids are measured in liters (L), each divided into 1000 milliliters (mL). A liter of pure water weighs one kilogram (kg), the unit of mass that is divided into 1000 grams (g). One metric ton is 1000kg. Again, you should probably just use the chart:

MEASUREMENT CONVERSIONS	
1 inch (in.) = 25.4mm	1 millimeter (mm) = 0.039 in.
1 foot (ft.) = 0.305m	1 meter (m) = 3.28 ft.
1 yard (yd.) = 0.914m	1 meter (m) = 1.094 yd.
1 mile (mi.) = 1.609km	1 kilometer (km) = 0.621 mi.
1 ounce (oz.) = 28.35g	1 gram (g) = 0.035 oz.
1 pound (lb.) = 0.454kg	1 kilogram (kg) = 2.205 lb.
1 fluid ounce (fl. oz.) = 29.57mL	1 milliliter (mL) = 0.034 fl. oz.
1 gallon (gal.) = 3.785L	1 liter (L) = 0.264 gal.

Essentials

LANGUAGE

It is (hopefully) not necessary to inform you that the primary language spoken in Italy is Italian. Prevalence of English-speaking varies wildly. Florence is a heavily touristed city (get ready to join the crowds!), and the locals are intelligent enough to figure out that speaking English is a seriously useful skill. It will generally not be necessary to speak Italian at major sights or large hotels. Once you venture to more out-of-the-way hostels or cozy trattorias, however, don't take it for granted that you'll find someone speaking English. You probably won't. That means it's time to dip into *Let's Go*'s **Phrasebook** and try to adapt your high school knowledge of French and Spanish into passable Italian. And don't discount pointing and hand signals; they can be the source of endless hilarity, numerous misunderstandings, and occasional epiphanies. Read through the pronunciation tips below if you're planning to try to fit in like a local, although you should probably come to terms with the fact that most people will smell your English-speaking blood from miles away, no matter how much effort you put into saying *Ciao* with just the right degree of aloof coolness.

Pronunciation

Vowels

There are seven vowel sounds in standard Italian. **A, i,** and **u** each have one pronunciation. **E** and **o** each have two slightly different pronunciations, one open and one closed, depending on the vowel's placement in the word, the stress placed on it, and the regional accent in which it is spoken. Below are approximate pronunciations:

Essentials

PHONETIC UNIT	PRONUNCIATION	PHONETIC UNIT	PRONUNCIATION
a	"a" as in "father" (casa)	o (closed)	"o" as in "bone" (sono)
e (closed)	"ay" as in "gray" (sera)	o (open)	"aw" as in "ought" (bocca)
e (open)	"eh" as in "wet" (sette)	u	"oo" as in "moon" (gusto)
i	"ee" as in "cheese" (vino)		

Consonants

C AND G. Before a, o, or u, **c** and **g** are hard, as in *candy* and *goose* or as in the Italian *colore* (koh-LOHR-eh; color) and *gatto* (GAHT-toh; cat). Italians soften c and g into **ch** and **j** sounds, respectively, when followed by i or e, as in *cheese* and *jeep* or the Italian *cibo* (CHEE-boh; food) and *gelato* (jeh-LAH-toh; ice cream).

CH AND GH. H returns **c** and **g** to their "hard" sounds in front of i or e (see above): *chianti* (ky-AHN-tee), the Tuscan wine, and *spaghetti* (spah-GEHT-tee), the pasta.

GN AND GLI. Pronounce **gn** like the ni in *onion*, or as in the Italian *bagno* (BAHN-yoh; bath). **Gli** is pronounced like the **lli** in *million*, or as in the Italian *sbagliato* (zbal-YAH-toh; wrong).

SC AND SCH. When followed by **a, o,** or **u**, sc is pronounced as **sk**. *Scusi* (excuse me) yields "SKOO-zee." When followed by an **e** or **i**, sc is pronounced **sh** as in *sciopero* (SHOH-pair-oh; strike). The addition of the letter **h** returns **c** to its hard sound (sk) before **i** or **e**, as in *pesche* (PEHS-keh; peaches).

DOUBLE CONSONANTS. When you see a double consonant, stress the preceding vowel; failure to do so can lead to confusion. For example, *penne all'arrabbiata* is "short pasta in a spicy, red sauce," whereas *pene all'arrabbiata* means "penis in a spicy, red sauce."

Phrasebook

ENGLISH	ITALIAN	ENGLISH	ITALIAN
Yes	Sì	Is there a bed available tonight?	C'è un posto libero stasera?
No	No	With bath/shower	Con bagno/doccia
Stop	Ferma	With hot bath/ shower	Con bagno/doccia caldo/a
Go	Va'	Is there air conditioning?	C'è aria condizionata?
Goodbye	Arrivederci	Does it work?	Funziona?

Hello	Buongiorno	Do you think I'm stupid?	Pensi che io sono stupido?
High	Alto	I would like to buy a ticket/pass	Vorrei comprare un biglietto/una tessera
Low	Basso	One-way	Solo andata
Why?	Perché?	Round-trip	Andata e ritorno
I don't know	Non lo so	I got on the wrong train	Sono salito sul treno sbagliato
Thank you	Grazie	The middle of nowhere	Nel mezzo del nulla
How are you?	Come stai?	Oops, sorry!	Scusi!
I am from the US	Sono degli Stati Uniti	I lost my passport/ wallet	Ho perso il passa-porto/portafoglio
I have a visa/ID	Ho un visto/ carta d'identità	I've been robbed	Sono stato derubato/a
I have nothing to declare (but my genius)	Non ho nulla da dichiarare (ma il mio genio)	Leave me alone!	Lasciami stare!/ Mollami!
I will be here for less than three months	Lo sarò qui per meno di tré mesi	I'm calling the police!	Telefono alla polizia!
No, I swear, I'm not smuggling anything	No giuro, io non ho nulla di contrab-bando	You're going to jail	Si sta andando in prigione
Please release me from jail	Vi prego di liberare dal carcere	Go away, moron!	Vattene, cretino!
Could you repeat that?	Potrebbe ripetere?	And now for something com-pletely different	E ora qualcosa di completamente diverso
I don't understand	Non capisco	You're cute	Sei carino/a (bello/a)
Help!	Aiuto!	Nice dress, it'd look good on my bedroom floor	Bel vestito, sare-bbe guardare bene sul pavimento della mia camera da letto
Leave me alone!	Lasciami stare!/ Mollami!	I've lost my telephone number, could I borrow yours?	Ho perso il mio numero di telefono, potrebbe prestarmi il suo?
I don't want to buy your souvenirs	Non voglio acquistare il souvenir	I love you, I swear	Ti amo, te lo giuro
Hotel/hostel	Albergo/ostello	I only have safe sex	Pratico solo sesso sicuro
I have a reserva-tion	Ho una preno-tazione	The profound mystery of what you just said sets my soul on fire	Il profondo mistero di ciò che stai dicendo mi infuoca il cuore
Could I reserve a single room/double room?	Potrei prenotare una camera sin-gola/doppia?	Not if you're the last man on earth	Neanche se lei fossi l'unico uomo sulla terra

Essentials

Let's Go Online

Plan your next trip on our spiffy website, **www.letsgo.com.** It features full book content, the latest travel info on your favorite destinations, and tons of interactive features: make your own itinerary, read blogs from our trusty Researcher-Writers, browse our photo library, watch exclusive videos, check out our newsletter, find travel deals, follow us on Facebook, and buy new guides. Plus, if this Essentials wasn't enough for you, we've got even more online. We're always updating and adding new features, so check back often!

Florence 101

Epicenter of the Italian Renaissance, home to some of history's most noted artists, scientists, and religious leaders, and the place with the world's highest concentration of dudes named David, Florence has a rich culture all its own. Over the years, the former capital of Italy has amassed an incredible collection of art, including Botticelli's luminescent *Primavera* and, of course, Michelangelo's 17 ft. masterpiece (and its rockin' abs). But Florentine history is not only defined by brush strokes and chiseled marble. Once ruled by the Medici family, the banking barons of Renaissance Italy, Florence has a dark past deep with political turmoil and controversy. Nowadays things have calmed down a bit, giving tourists the perfect opportunity to stroll along the *piazza,* explore more churches than they ever thought possible, and quickly sink into a food coma after overdosing on gelato. Offering something for both newcomers and veterans, Florence still has all the pizzazz and flair that it did centuries ago. Read on to learn some of the dos and don'ts of the Florentine lifestyle, how to stay as chic as the locals (it's not as easy as you think), and the best way to burn off those ever-increasing gelato calories.

Facts and Figures

- **POPULATION:** 370,702
- **STEPS TO THE TOP OF BRUNELLESCHI'S CUPOLA:** 465
- **NUMBER OF CHURCHES:** 60
- **BOTTICELLIS IN THE UFFIZI:** 18
- **RULERS FROM THE MEDICI FAMILY:** 17
- **WORLD-RENOWNED FASHION DESIGNERS NATIVE TO FLORENCE:** 4
- **MUSEUMS DEDICATED TO SHOES:** 1

HISTORY

No Country for Young Men? (59 BCE-700 CE)

Florence was founded in 59 BCE by **Julius Caesar** as a retirement center for his veteran military officials. Keeping with the military theme, the city was first designed to mimic a military camp. With its gridded layout, Florence became a metropolitan *tour de force* in Central Italy and attracted both the **Byzantines** and **Goths** after the Roman Empire fizzled out.

In the sixth century, Florence adopted Christianity as its principle religion and built its very first churches, which were dedicated to patron saint San Giovanni. Now a Christian community, Florence was largely under papal control, as the Pope held serious sway over the city's development and governing bodies.

Cathedrals and Communes (774-1200)

Florence fell under the rule of the **Holy Roman Empire** in 774 when Charlemagne conquered the city. Fearful of Hungarian invasions, the city's ruling counts and countesses built walls to protect Florence. Free from foreign attack, the city prospered, growing from a former military community to a center of religious thought. Under the direction of **Pope Victor II,** the city built up its booming collection of churches.

From 1125 until the turn of the 13th century, Florence's ruling military leaders amassed control over surrounding towns in Tuscany. After winning numerous battles, Florence and its newly acquired territories established a constituted **commune,** a medieval allegiance of defense between neighboring communities. During the city's time as a commune, Florentine leaders took advantage of the protection granted by their allies to develop the city's infrastructure and industries.

Galloping Guelphs and Gibillines! (1200-1348)

By 1215, the city had been divided into two classes: the working class **Guelphs** and the noble **Gibillines.** If you couldn't guess already, the huge gap between the two groups drove the Guelphs to kick some Gibilline butt a la *Braveheart.* With their newfound control of city politics, the Guelphs, who were mostly merchants and artisans, created a new social order that encouraged growth in the agricultural and—you guessed it—arts industries.

The Guelphs' hold on Florence, however, was failing, and the Gibillines took power once again in 1260. After a few more decades of back-and-forth struggle, two new political groups emerged in Florence, the entrepreneurial **Magnati** and laboring **Popolani.** In spite of the political tensions that resulted from the four-way frenzy, Florence continued to develop as one of the most prominent cities in Europe. It was during this time that **Dante Alighieri** began crafting *The Divine Comedy,* a symbol of the booming art scene. And then a few fleas came along.

The Mighty Medici (1348-1737)

The year 1348 marked the beginning of the **Black Plague,** the only period in history during which the world population actually decreased. As the plague drew to a close and society began to get back on its feet again, the conniving **Cosimo de' Medici** seized the opportunity to make some major bucks off of Florence's own little baby boom. The wealth he amassed in his surprisingly long life of 75 years established his family as the de facto rulers of Florence and Tuscany for the next three centuries.

Using their newfound power, the Medici began a campaign to jumpstart the city's less than prospering art scene by commissioning sculptors and other artists to recapture the grandeur of classical antiquity. During their reign, Renaissance royalty like **Leonardo da Vinci** and **Michelangelo** revolutionized the fields of art and science. A good deal of work in the Uffizi Gallery and especially the Palazzo Pitti (the Medici's former residence) were given to the city of Florence when the last Medici, Gian Gastone de' Medici, died. Also during the Renaissance, famed architect Filippo Brunelleschi designed the **Duomo,** Florence's most recognizable church. The emergence of the Italian High Renaissance might not have begun in Florence, or even have happened at all, without the financial backing of the Medici and their affiliates.

The Woes of World Wars (1900-today)

As the 20th century dawned on Italy, so did the country's most devastating political turmoil. Madman **Mussolini** took advantage of Europe's post-WWI disrepair to seize control in 1922. In 1940, convinced that his pal Hitler would easily win the war against Britain and France, Mussolini decided to side with the Axis. The dictator was particularly eager to aid the Germans during the Battle of France so that he could regain control of disputed areas including Nice, Corsica, and Savoy. Once the US entered the war, Italy reaffirmed its alliance with Germany and declared war on America. The decision, though, proved to be extremely unwise, ultimately leading to the worst destruction of Italian cultural property since the Middle Ages.

Florence was occupied by Germany from 1943 to '44, during which time allied fighters continuously bombed the city. As the Germans realized they were losing control of Europe, though, they commenced a full-scale retreat from Italy. On their way out of Florence, they bombed every bridge leading into the city (except for the **Ponte Vecchio,** which was spared) to spite the allied troops.

In 1945 the occupation ended, ushering in the modern era of Italian politics. The current constitution, instituted in 1948, allows for a democratic republic with a president, a prime minister, a bicameral parliament, and an independent judiciary. Though the government has changed nearly 60 times since, one element remains consistent: powerful, bold leaders. Self-made tycoon **Silvio Berlusconi** is the latest in this colorful lineup, elected as prime minister in 1999... and 2001... and 2008, with plenty of corruption scandals as well as two resignations in between. Berlusconi's middle-right stance aligned him with American President George Bush and the Iraq war. Though the unpopularity of this decision opened the doors for the more liberal Romano Prodi to move into power, Italians proved themselves to be more forgiving than the oft-divorced Berlusconi's ex- and estranged wives, as this philanderer once again won the seat as prime minister of Italy.

CUSTOMS AND ETIQUETTE

Florentines exude the typical boisterousness and sociability of any Italian. Despite the metropolitan atmosphere, Florence isn't New York, so lose the "I'm in a constant rush" mentality: slow down and take in all that the city has to offer. Remember that as you're traveling, it's essential to greet anyone you converse with using your best "*buongiorno.*" Greeting people with a smile can do wonders to help ingratiate you with the locals, who may even reciprocate the kindness with an invitation to dinner. Sure, mealtime conversations with Italians tend to be loud and include many indecipherable hand gestures, but don't interpret this boldness as rudeness. Instead, try to be as expressive as the locals—like the old saying goes, "When in Florence, do as the Florentines do." Or something like that.

Save the Short Shorts

During your time perusing Florence's abundant cultural offerings, you will inevitably find yourself exploring at least one of the city's famed cathedrals. Although most churches don't mind visitors during the day, Catholic parishioners in Florence expect the women in their churches to dress more like Mother Teresa than Lady Gaga. While the more popular Duomo and Santa Croce may provide sheaths to cover your shoulders and legs, smaller churches are unlikely to offer this amenity. Don't be caught off guard and have to hike back to your hostel because your shorts are a bit above fingertip length; plan your outfit ahead of time.

Cutting the Queue

Kindness is king in Florence, but that doesn't mean the locals don't know how to get what they want, when they want it. Warning: shopping in Florence is a high-energy, competitive activity, suited only for trained professionals and veterans. Unlike in the United States, cutting in front of a line is not at all uncommon for Italian shopaholics. If you're seriously tempted to knock out the cutter's lights, hold yourself back from causing a scene. The last thing you want is a Florentine fashionista giving you a smack down in the middle of Miu Miu. Besides, every experienced shopper knows Prada is worth the patience. But, if you're in enough of a hurry yourself, give barging a go. The locals may even commend you for your crassness as you leave the store, Versace shoes in tow.

FOOD AND DRINK

Florence is particularly well known for its reliance on rustic, hearty Tuscan staples. As the city has transitioned into the 21st century, chefs have begun to experiment with contemporary haute cuisine, creating dishes that combine the comfort of traditional local foods with innovative ingredients and techniques. Prepare to be adventurous when you start exploring Florentine cuisine, as some dishes may not be exactly what you expect.

Horses and Donkeys and Sheep, Oh My!

Prepare your stomach for an experience unlike any other. Florentines have what some might deem unusual tastes, but you'll discover that shredded horse meat, braised donkey rump, and *trippa* (stewed sheep intestines) aren't really as offensive as they sound. Though these delicacies don't represent the staples of traditional Florence, you're guaranteed to encounter them on the menu of nearly any restaurant nowadays. The dishes date back to Roman antiquity, and, despite the passing of millennia and ever-changing culinary trends, they remain just as popular among Florentines. If you eat meat, each is worth a try; after all, the sale of horse meat for human consumption is illegal in many countries, so when else will you get the chance?

Drink (More Than You Can Actually Remember)

There's nothing more calming than a fine bottle of *vino* after a strenuous day hitting the tourist circuit. Because of its prime location in Tuscany, arguably Italy's finest wine-making region, there's never a lack of Jesus juice in Florence. Whether you're looking for a bold Chianti or a mellower white Trebbiano, you're guaranteed an abundance of locally produced options. So enjoy the city's decadent offerings, and, though you hardly need encouraging, take an excursion out to the surrounding region to develop a better appreciation for Tuscany's wineries and their unique specialties.

ART AND ARCHITECTURE

Florence was the preferred playground of some of Italy's most renowned artists, whose names live on in everyone's favorite crime-fighting amphibians, the ▧**Teenage Mutant Ninja Turtles.** Leonardo, Michelangelo, Raphael, and Donatello, among others, revolutionized Western art, replacing the austere religious iconography of the Middle Ages with highly idealized representations of both religion and man.

The Rockin' Renaissance

Florence was the birthplace of the Italian High Renaissance, boasting such artistic big-wigs as **Botticelli** and **Brunelleschi,** in addition to the TMNT crew. On your visit to the city, make sure to stop at Florence's major venues for Renaissance art—the Uffizi Gallery, Palazzo Pitti, and Galleria dell'Accademia—to see the extensive collections that made these guys famous in the first place. Using newly developed scientific studies of anatomy and physiology, the Renaissance Masters created these sculptures and paintings that accurately represent the human form. Like pre-teen boys discovering their first *Playboy,* the citizens of Florence were fascinated by the explicit nudity of most Renaissance art. Doing what it does best, the Vatican deemed the art morally unsuitable and either castrated statues or covered up their junk with grape leaves.

Stairway to Heaven

No trip to Florence is complete without climbing the hundreds of stairs to the top of **Brunelleschi's Dome** and **Giotto's Campanile** at the Duomo, Florence's largest cathedral. The Cupola's 465 stairs of claustrophobic agony will provide you with an unparalleled view of the city. If you're still looking to burn off the calories from your carb-laden lunch, you can climb the 414 steps to the top of the Campanile adjoining the church.

FASHION

The home of fashion mainstays Guccio Gucci, Emilio Pucci, Roberto Cavalli, and Salvatore Ferragamo, Florence boasts one of the most prominent fashion scenes in modern Italy. Though Florence pales in comparison to Milan in the world of couture, there's no lack of luxury in this city dedicated to the pursuit of happiness in heels.

Fashion Firenze

Florentines are extremely fashion conscious. Because of the higher apparel prices in Italy compared to the US, Italians have adopted the mindset of buying high-quality, fashionable clothing that will last for years. If you're hoping to fare well with the Florentines, make your best effort to choose an appropriate outfit for any occasion, even if it's merely catching a coffee at the local *caffè*. The key to walking the streets (read: catwalks) of Florence is to keep things classy. Don't be shocked to see a woman in 6 in. heels on her way to the flower market, or a grandmother hanging her laundry to dry while sporting the latest Dolce and Gabbana scarf. Most importantly, don't be caught walking around in worn-out kicks in the world's only city with an entire block-long museum dedicated to the world of Ferragamo shoes.

HOLIDAYS AND FESTIVALS

In keeping with the rest of Italy, most Florentine festivals are religiously oriented, often celebrating some facet of Jesus's life. But don't worry if it's been a while since you last went to confession. Florence's events calendar abounds with traditional cultural holidays, most of which, not unlike college frat parties, involve copious amounts of eating and drinking.

HOLIDAY OR FESTIVAL	DESCRIPTION	DATE
Capodanno	Ringing in the New Year receives the royal treatment in Florence. Revelers party in the streets and set off fireworks over the Arno.	January 1
Easter Sunday (Explosion of the Cart)	To get Easter started off with a blast, a mechanical dove lands on a wire above the Duomo's high altar, setting off a cart of fireworks.	late March or early April
Calcio in Costume	This summer festival's hordes of dancing men dressed in outlandish costumes might remind you of a '90s Cher concert.	late June
Festival of San Giovanni	Enjoy plentiful helpings of pasta during this festival dedicated to the patron saint of Florence.	June 24
Festa della Rificolona	This procession of children through the streets of Florence to commemorate the birth of the Virgin Mary will surely bring a tear to your eye.	September 7
Festival dei Popoli	This film festival, though not as well known as Cannes, gives local artists a chance to showcase their independent works.	late November
Burning of the Tree	In preparation for Christmas, Tuscan revelers throw a massive bonfire of evergreen branches. Kind of like Burning Man, but without all the acid.	December 24

Beyond Tourism

If you are reading this, then you are a member of an elite group—and we don't mean "the literate." You're a student preparing for a semester abroad. You're taking a gap year to save the trees, the whales, or the dates. You're an 80-year-old woman who has devoted her life to egg-laying platypuses and what the hell is up with that. In short, you're a traveler, not a tourist; like any good spy, you don't just observe your surroundings—you become an active part of them.

Your mission, should you choose to accept it, is to study, volunteer, or work abroad as laid out in the dossier—er, chapter—below. We leave the rest (when to go, whom to bring, and how many *Arrested Development* DVDs to pack) in your hands. This message will self-destruct in five seconds. Good luck.

STUDYING

If you've always dreamed of spending time in Italy (or even if you haven't), it's no surprise that you're considering Florence. Considered the mecca of American study-abroad programs, Florence is said to attract more college students than any other foreign city. (Doubt us? Keep track of how much English you hear on a Saturday night in the P. Santa Croce.) Students have been flocking to the University of Florence's Cultural Center for Foreigners since 1907, before "studying abroad" was even popular. A word of caution: Florence probably isn't the place to study if you want to escape from Anglo-American culture. Foreigners may not be ubiquitous, but there are quite a few of them, especially in a city with just over 350,000 locals. Regardless, Florence should be at the top of your study-abroad list, despite the difficulty of squeezing into those new leather pants after gorging on pasta. Just make sure that amid countless hours of shopping, eating, dancing, and drinking, you actually find some time to study.

Visa information

Generally, non-EU students staying in Italy for more than three months are required to apply for a visa before they leave their home countries. To apply for a **student visa,** you'll need a valid passport, several recent passport photos, proof of enrollment, records of previous educational history, and a completed application. You may also be asked to provide proof of medical insurance coverage and means of financial support in Italy. EU students are luckier: you do not need a visa to enter or study in Italy. Both non-EU and EU students may be required to apply for a **permesso de soggiorno** (permit to stay) from the local *Ufficio degli Stranieri* (Foreigners' Bureau) when you arrive. The short-term visa fee is €60. For updated visa information, visit the Italian Embassy's website.

Universities

You shouldn't have a hard time finding a program of interest in Florence, no matter what that interest might be. There are a variety of joint Italian- and English-language university programs that offer rigorous academics, but they aren't cheap. Alternatively, there are many smaller language academies that focus primarily on beginning and intermediate Italian studies, with the added bonus of being less expensive.

International Programs

Florence is the hip new place for American universities to set up their own satellite campuses (NYU, Stanford, California State University, Georgetown, Syracuse, and Middlebury: we're looking at you). However, most of these programs are only open to students of their partner universities abroad. Luckily, the programs below welcome applications from all students.

American Institute for Foreign Study (AIFS)

9 W. Broad St., Stamford, CT 06902, USA

☎+1-800-727-2437; www.aifsabroad.com

AIFS offers for-credit university programs through a partnership with the Richmond American International University in London. Courses are conducted in English, but you can brush up on your Italian in language classes.

▶ *i* All students (rising freshmen included) may apply for summer programs. Min. 2.5 GPA for semester-long programs. Ⓢ Summer US$7500; semester US$17,000. Tuition includes airfare, housing, meals, and excursions.

Global Student Experience (GSE)

17752 Skypark Cir., Ste. 235, Irvine, CA 92614, USA

☎+1-866-756-2443; www.gseabroad.com

GSE places students either in the Lorenzo de' Medici or University of Florence. This organization is most helpful if you want to study at an authentic Italian *università* but aren't quite sure how to begin.

▶ *i* Min. 2.5 GPA and at least 1 semester of college-level Italian. Ⓢ University of Florence summer program US$4695; semester program US$9995. Housing, tuition, and insurance included.

Lorenzo de' Medici

3600 Bee Caves Rd., #205B, Austin, TX 78746, USA

☎+1-877-765-4536; www.lorenzodemedici.org

Imagine dropping an American university right down in the center of San Lorenzo. This university basically does just that. The course offerings of this Texas-operated organization run the gamut of liberal arts subjects. The social sciences and arts are taught in English, but the school also offers strong Italian language and culture programs.

▶ *i* Must be university students entering at least sophomore year. Min. 2.8 GPA. Ⓢ Summer US$2825; semester US$11,440; academic year US$22,635. Housing, tuition, and insurance included. Does not include weekly wine tastings with the Slow Drink Club.

Study Abroad Italy (SAI)

7160 Keating Ave., Sebastopol, CA 95742, USA

☎+1-800-655-8965; www.saiprograms.com

SAI offers three different programs in Florence: liberal arts, studio arts, and design; hospitality, cuisine, and wine studies; and Italian culture and language studies. None of these have minimum language requirements and all of the courses may be taken in English, except for the Italian language courses (duh).

▶ *i* Summer programs 3-12 weeks; semester and year programs also available. Students often housed in homestays. $ Summer programs US$4100-13,000; semester US$11,000-18,000. Housing, tuition, insurance, and excursions included.

Italian Programs

If you plan to enroll directly in an Italian university, be prepared for a lot of red tape. Entering a program as a foreigner can be daunting, especially if you're not lucky enough to be an EU student on an Erasmus exchange. Plus, transferring credits to American and UK universities can be tricky. The Ministero dell'Istruzione (Ministry of Education) runs a surprisingly helpful website, **www.study-in-italy.it,** that is a good place to start your quest for Italian fluency.

Università Degli Studi di Firenze: Centro di Cultura per Stranieri

V. Francesco Valori 9

☎055 50 32 703; www.ccs.unifi.it/mdswitch.html

The Cultural Center for Foreigners at the University of Florence offers language courses as well as a dozen Italian cultural courses, all taught *in italiano*. For those used to paying an arm and a leg for tuition, these courses are ridiculously inexpensive (government-funded higher education for the win!).

▶ i University students only. Italian cultural courses open to those proficient in Italian, or who have completed the center's Advanced Intermediate Italian course. $ Summer €500; trimester €650. Housing available for an additional cost.

Language Schools

As renowned novelist Gustave Flaubert once said, "Language is a cracked kettle on which we beat out tunes for bears to dance to." While we at *Let's Go* have absolutely no clue what he is talking about, we do know that the following are good resources for learning *italiano*.

Centro Fiorenza

V. di Santo Spirito 14

☎055 23 98 274 ; www.centrofiorenza.com

If anyone can teach Italian, it's these guys. The Center has 12 levels, from beginner to advanced proficiency. While the focus is on intensive group and one-on-one language courses, Centro Fiorenza also offers internships and cultural enrichment activities. There is also a program on the island of Elba, 2hr. away from Florence—good luck studying verb conjugations while tanning on the beach.

▶ *i* Academic credit may be transferable. Ⓢ 2-week group language course €410; 4-week €748; 12-week €1910.

Eurocentres

P. Santo Spirito 9

☎800 87 52 24; www.eurocentres.com

Part of a British group of international language schools, the Eurocentres Italian Language School in Florence is located in a 16th-century Renaissance palace in the middle of the old town center. If the location doesn't impress you, your classmates might: Eurocentres is known for appealing to 20-somethings from around the globe.

▶ Ⓢ 2 weeks €386; 4 weeks €740; 12 weeks €1848. Homestays from €187 per week; apartments or dorms from €315 per week.

Istituto Italiano

V. de' Martelli 4

☎055 26 54 510; www.istitutoitaliano.it

Just a few steps from the Duomo, this language school focuses on "semi-intensive," "*classico,*" and "super-intensive" language programs (with options to study cinema, wines, and music). The *Istituto* also tries to fit in extracurricular activities and outings to cultural events in the city.

▶ *i* Offers Certificate of Italian as a Foreign Language. Classes 2-8hr. per day. Ⓢ Semi-intensive program €330; classico €480; super-intensive €800.

Koiné

Borgo Santa Croce 17

☎055 21 38 81; www.koinecenter.com

The headquarters of Koinè Italian language organization, this Florence location also offers the widest range of courses. The most popular are group intensives, but there are also refresher courses, internship programs, and specialized language programs for preparation in the arts or photography industries.

▶ *i* Our favorite course? "Cook with an Italian Mamma." Ⓢ 2-week group program €570; 4-week €1060. Additional €150 security deposit.

Beyond Tourism

Schools for the Arts

The birthplace of Botticelli and Leonardo (and, more recently, Gucci and Ferragamo), Florence gives students nearly unlimited access to the arts, with numerous programs in fashion, cuisine, architecture, music, and plain-old oil-on-canvas painting.

Apicius—The Culinary Institute of Florence

V. Guelfa 85

☎055 26 58 135; www.tuscancooking.com

The culinary programs at Apicius are billed as "intensive" cooking experiences, run with the same vigor as the most intensive language schools. Students learn everything from traditional Tuscan gastronomy to cutting-edge winemaking, but the main draw to Apicius is simple: three weeks in a kitchen with unlimited pasta and Chianti.

▸ $ 1 week US$1185-1425; 3 weeks US$600-1300. Intensive language option available: 1 week US$240; 3 weeks US$675. Application fee US$60.

The British Institute of Florence

P. Strozzi 2

☎055 26 77 81; www.britishinstitute.it

The British Institute offers month-long fine arts courses in life- and cast-drawing in conjunction with the Charles H. Cecil Studios. Admit it, the middle initial makes it sound much more prestigious.

▸ *i* All experience levels welcome, but stick figures are generally discouraged. 4hr. class per week. $ Month-long studio program €275.

Florence University of the Arts (FUA)

V. Guelfa 85

☎055 25 68 135; www.fua.it

FUA partners with a variety of study-abroad programs for studio and art history, offering semester, quarter, January, and summer programs. The university comprises a number of schools that include fine arts, digital imaging and visual arts, and fashion and accessory studies.

▸ $ Summer from US$4100; semester from US$12,300. Housing included.

Studio Art Centers International Florence (SACI Florence)

Palazzo dei Cartelloni, V. Sant'Antonio 11

☎055 28 99 48; www.saci-florence.org

SACI Florence offers studio art courses ranging from ceramics to painting conservation. But the best part is that the curriculum centers on field trips to other artistic hotspots like Pisa, Milan, and Rome.

▶ *i* Summer program in archaeology also available. Ⓢ Summer US$7000; semester US$18,000. Housing and excursions included.

VOLUNTEERING

Ready to move beyond the "expand your knowledge while learning a lot of Italian" mindset and give back to your newly adopted city? Volunteering is a great way to satisfy that itch. Strong Catholic service communities have been an Italian cultural symbol for centuries. There are many ways to get involved, but it can be difficult to track down opportunities unless you're well connected to the local non-profit community. Some of the most helpful resources for finding volunteer jobs are online, especially aggregators like **www.idealist.org** and **www.volunteerabroad.com.**

Archaeology

In case you weren't already aware, Florence is full of artistic masterpieces, and they require an army of caretakers. Did you think *David* maintained his chiseled abs all by himself?

Responsibletravel.com

6 Old Steine, Brighton, East Sussex, BN1 1EJ, UK

☎+44 1273 600 030; www.responsibletravel.com

Were you the kind of kid who loved digging up your mom's daisies and generally playing in the mud? Responsibletravel. com provides hundreds of listings for volunteer opportunities around the world, including a week-long archaeology expedition in the Tuscan countryside. Digging up priceless historical artifacts? Pretty awesome, if we do say so ourselves.

▶ *i* Be ready for an "adventurous trip with a purpose." Ⓢ 1 week US$630; 2 weeks US$1765.

The Environment and Animal Care

Outside of the bustling metropolis that is Florence, life in surrounding Tuscany is more laid-back and traditional. While some might pay for expensive ecotours through the area, we know that you, *Let's Go* reader, are much more adept at saving your hard-earned money.

Fondazione Flaminia da Filicaja

V. Poggio all'Aglione 23, Montaione

☎328 62 29 264; www.horseprotection.it

Located an hour outside Florence, the Italian Horse Protection Association works to rehabilitate **horses** that have been abused by their owners. Short- and long-term volunteers help run the daily care of these recovering animals. Sixty horses with adorable names like "Rocket" and "Letizia" need your help!

▶ 🐾 Located in Montaione, 1hr. by car southwest of Florence; accessible by train to Siena and bus to Montaione.

World-Wide Opportunities on Organic Farms (WWOOF Italia)

V. Casavecchia 109, Castagneto Carducci

www.wwoof.it

Part of an international organization of small organic farms, WWOOF Italia compiles a list of local farms that are in need of volunteer work. They give you room and board, and you spend anywhere from a few weeks to a few months working on a family-run organic farm, ranch, or dairy.

▶ *i* Must become a WWOOF Italia member through their website. Ⓢ Membership €25, including insurance.

Urban Issues

With a rapidly aging population (over 20% of Italians are over 65), the elderly are a particularly vulnerable community in Florence. Another long-term issue is that, due to persistent conflicts over immigration, many young immigrants are left out of Italian civic life. You, super(wo)man, can help fix these problems.

United Planet

11 Arlington St., Boston, MA 02116, USA

☎+1-800-292-2316; www.unitedplanet.org

United Planet, a member of the International Cultural Youth Exchange Federation, may help you get over the obstacle of dealing with Italian nonprofit organizations. Their Italian volunteer programs focus on helping the disabled and elderly.

▶ *i* 4-12 weeks. Ⓢ 4 weeks US$1715; 12 weeks US$3315. Housing, food, and insurance included.

WORKING

You're halfway through your six-month stay in Italy and you've run out of cash. Or you're in good fiscal shape but need extra income to subsidize an out-of-control *cappuccino* addiction. The job search in Italy can be rough—with unemployment hovering at around 8.6%, positions aren't always readily available. Connecting with the English-speaking community is a must, especially through centers like the **Tuscan American Association** (V. de' Servi 14; www.toscanausa.org). But with a little advance research, some old-fashioned luck, and these helpful listings, you'll be raking in the dough in no time.

Long-Term Work

The easiest way for young people to secure long-term work in Florence is through established internship programs. Sadly, most of these internships are unpaid. The benefit of this setup is that the organizations will manage the major bureaucratic hurdles. If you want to manage things on your own, here are some places to start.

Teaching English

As an English-speaker, you've got at least one major asset: your language! (Don't worry, we're sure you have many more. This one is just the most relevant.) If you don't already have a Teaching English as a Foreign Language (TEFL) certificate, start looking for a training program that can get you one—most employers will require one of these babies for you to teach in or around Florence. Whether you decide to obtain TEFL certification in Italy or at home, make sure to ask your school to connect you with job placement services.

One obstacle is that there is somewhat of a Brit-bias in and around Florence.Although many organizations actively recruit British college graduates to teach English, visitors from other English-speaking countries are not as lucky. Moral of the story: start watching lots of *Harry Potter* and BBC shows. And try to master your Cockney slang.

The Learning Center of Tuscany

V. Corsica 15

☎055 05 15 035; www.learningcentertuscany.com

The Learning Center of Tuscany is one of many organizations

Beyond Tourism

in Florence that help foreigners become TEFL certified. Seminars for college graduates run three to four weeks, after which the organization will help pair you with a local employer.

▶ *i* Offered on-site or via distance learning. $ 4 weeks €1199. US$500 non-refundable deposit.

Office of Overseas Schools, US State Department

2201 C St. NW, Washington, DC 20520, USA

☎+1-202-647-4000; www.state.gov/m/a/os/

Teach in one of the many primary or secondary schools in Florence that serve the sons and daughters of American diplomats and military personnel. Positions are hard to come by, but if you're lucky enough to snag one, you can count on good pay and benefits.

World Endeavors

3015 E. Franklin Ave., Minneapolis, MN 55406

☎+1-866-802-9618; www.worldendeavors.com

World Endeavors offers paid internships to teach English in Florence, with options to continue working with the organization when your job is over. World Endeavors also plans cultural, language, and pre-professional activities.

More Visa Information

Obtaining a visa to work in Italy can be kind of a pain. If you intend to stay in Florence for fewer than three months, both EU and non-EU citizens can rejoice: a tourist visa will usually suffice, and short-term employment may not require any other work permits (but please be careful: that kind of a situation can easily lend itself to sketchy or illegal dealings, which *Let's Go* does not condone). For commitments longer than three months, EU passport holders do not need a permit to live or work in Italy, though you will need to register for a **permesso di soggiorno per lavoro** (permit to stay) through the local police office. Non-EU citizens aiming to work in Italy must obtain an **autorizzazione al lavoro in Italia** (Italian work permit) and the relevant visas before arriving. Here's where things get messy, so we recommend you check out the perpetually changing requirements on your own. Visit the Italian Ministry of Foreign Affairs website (www.esteri.it) or the US Embassy site (http://italy.usembassy.gov) for more information.

▶ *i* 3- to 6-month-long sessions. Offers TEFL certification. Ⓢ 3-month stay from US$4895. Housing, placement, and language training included.

Au Pair Work

Call them what you will (nannies, babysitters, childcare providers), but au pairs have a pretty sweet setup in Florence. In return for taking care of the kids and light housework, host families generally provide room, board, and a small stipend. These openings can sometimes be hard to find. The easiest way to find a host family is to work through an au pair service, though many charge a fee to connect you with an employer.

Geovisions

63 Whitfield St., Guilford, CT 06437, USA

☎+1-877-949-9998; www.geovisions.org

Geovisions links au pairs from the US, Canada, UK, Australia, New Zealand, and Ireland with families in Florence, most of which have school-aged children. Hosts are required to offer a stipend, at least one day off per week, and the option to take Italian language classes.

▶ *i* 2-10 months. Must be 18-27 and have basic knowledge of Italian. Ⓢ 60-90 days US$950 fee; over 90 days US$1255 fee.

Roma Au Pair

V. Piero Mascagni 138, Rome

☎06 86 32 15 19; www.romaaupair.com

Roma Au Pair links foreign au pairs with Italian families mainly in Rome, but also elsewhere in the country, including Florence. The organization has a rigorous selection process for interested families.

▶ *i* 6-12 month stays.

Short-Term Work

There are usually easy ways to find short-term work in Florence even without previous arrangements. Unless you have a well-connected patron who can secure you a job (and if you do, we are incredibly jealous), your best friend is the web. Check out the English-language publications *The Informer* (www.informer. it) or *The Florentine* (www.theflorentine.net) for a window into the expat community, or use the database on *Corriere della Sera*'s Corriere Lavoro (lavoro.corriere.it). If you still come up short, consider a trip to the local **centro per l'impiego** (employment center)—locations and hours are online at www.provincia.fi.it/lavoro.

Workaway.info

www.workaway.info

This online community links travelers to short-term work abroad. Regular posts range from volunteer positions in wildlife preserves near active volcanoes to part-time work landscaping for jazz musicians (we couldn't make these up).

▶ *i* Must register online as a Workawayer (their name, not ours). $ 2-year membership €22.

Tell the World

If your friends are tired of hearing about that time you saved a baby orangutan in Indonesia, there's clearly only one thing to do: get new friends. Find them at our website, www.letsgo.com, where you can post your study-, volunteer-, or work-abroad stories for other, more appreciative community members to read.

Index

A

accommodations: 32; *see also* Accommodations Index
Amaltea: 147
American Institute for Foreign Study (AIFS): 203
animal care: 207
Antica Enoteca Italiana: 135
Antico Sigillo: 156
Apartamenti Reali: 73
Apicius—The Culinary Institute of Florence: 206
archaeology: 207
architecture: 198
Argini e Margini: 144
art: 198
arts, the: 111
au pair work: 211

B

B and B La Torre: 152
Baptistery of San Giovanni: 51
Baptistery: 131
Bar Piazzetta: 168
Bargello, The: 55
Basilica di San Lorenzo: 64
Basilica di Santa Croce: 69
Basilica di Santa Maria Novella: 60
Basion Contrario: 157
Battistero: 141
Bazeel: 146
Betty Blue Cafe: 158
Beyond Tourism: 201
Boboli Gardens: 72
Botanic Gardens: 67
BRAC: 112
British Institute of Florence, The: 206
Bulldog: 147

C

Caffè Combattenti: 168
Caffè del Corso: 135
Caffè delle Erbe: 168
Campanile and Dome: 50
Camping Siena Colleverde: 127
Camposanto: 141
Casa Buonarroti: 71
Casa di Antonella: 126
Casa di Dante: 58
Centro Fiorenza: 204
Chiesa di San Salvatore a Ognissanti: 61
Chiesa di Santa Maria de' Ricci: 112
Cinema Teatro Odeon: 115
cinema: 115
classical music: 112
climate: 188
communications: 184
consulates: 174
Crypt: 131
culture: 111
customs: 197

DE

Dolce Pisa: 145
Dublin Post: 135
Duomo and Museo di Arte Sacra: 166
Duomo di San Martino: 154
Duomo: 10, 49, 129, 142
East Oltrarno: 13
Elemento: 158
embassies: 174
essentials: 172
Eurocentres: 205
excursions: 124

FG

fashion: 199

festivals: 200

Florence University of the Arts (FUA): 206

Fondazione Flaminia da Filicaja: 208

Fontebranda: 132

food: 76, 198; *see also* Restaurants Index

Foresteria Monastero di San Girolamo: 163

Fortezza Medicea: 130

Galleria d'Arte Moderna: 73

Galleria del Costume: 72

Galleria dell'Accademia: 64

Galleria Palatina: 72

Gelateria di Piazza: 166

Gelateria Veneta: 158

Geovisions: 211

Giardino Scotto: 143

Global Student Experience (GSE): 203

Guesthouse San Frediano: 152

HIJK

health: 181

history: 194

holidays: 200

Hotel Helvetia: 139

Hotel Pisa: 139

Il Baronetto: 145

international programs: 202

Instituto Italiano: 205

Italian programs: 204

itineraries: 14

Jazz Club: 114

jazz: 114

Koiné: 205

L

La Bottega del Gelato: 144

La Cité Libreria Cafe: 111

La Compagnia dei Vinattieri: 133

La Fontana della Frutta: 133

La Gemma di Elena: 151

La Pizzeria di Nonno Mede: 132

language: 189

language schools: 204

Leaning Tower of Pisa: 141

Learning Center of Tuscany: 209

Locando Il Pino: 164

Lorenzo de' Medici: 203

Lucca: 150

Lu.C.C.A.: 155

M

Macchine di Leonardo: 68

Mara Méo: 157

measurements: 188

Medici Chapels: 63

money: 175

Museo Archeologico: 68

Museo degli Argenti: 73

Museo Degli Innocenti: 68

Museo delle Porcellana: 73

Museo delle Sinopie: 143

Museo dell'Opera del Duomo: 143

Museo dell'Opera: 131

Museo dell'Opificio Delle Pietre Dure: 67

Museo di Ferragamo: 59

Museo di San Marco: 66

Museo di Storia Naturale: Zoologia La Specola: 74

Museo Nazionale Alinari della Fotografia: 61

Museo Opera di Santa Maria del Fiore: 50

Museo Stefano Bardini: 75

Music of the Trees: 159

NOP

neighborhoods: 10

nightlife: 95; *see also* Nightlife Index

Office of Overseas Schools, US State Department: 210

Ostello in Chianti (HI): 164

Ostello San Frediano (HI): 151
Osteria i Santi: 145
Palazzo Comunale and Torre
    Grossa: 165
Palazzo Medici Riccardi: 63
Palazzo Pfanner: 155
Palazzo Pubblico and Torre del
    Mangia: 130
Palazzo Strozzi: 59
Palazzo Vecchio: 58
phrasebook: 190
Piazza dei Miracoli: 141
Piazza del Campo: 128
Piazza della Repubblica: 57
Piazza della Signoria: 11, 57
Piazza Napoleone: 153
Piazzale Michelangelo: 75
Piccolo Hotel Etruria: 126
Pisa: 138
Pizzeria Bella Mariana: 156
Pizzicheria di Miccoli: 133
planning tips: 9
police: 182
Ponte Vecchio: 57
Puccini e la sua Lucca: 159
Puccini Opera: 154

QRS

Relais Under The Tower: 140
Responsibletravel.com: 207
restaurants: see food
Ristorante Enoteca il Castello: 167
Rocca di Montestaffoli and Museo
    del Vino: 165
rock music: 114
Roma Au Pair: 211
safety: 181
Sale e Pepe: 134
San Colombano: 156
san gimignano: 162
San Lorenzo: 12
San Marco: 12
San Paolo Pub: 135

Santa Croce: 13
Santa Maria Novella: 12
Savini: 134
schools for the arts: 206
Sei Divino: 114
shopping: 117; see also Shopping
    Index
Siena in Centro: 128
Siena: 125
sights: 48
Spaghetti Lasagne Pizza: 157
spectator sports: 116
Stadio Artemio Franchi: 116
Studio Art Centers International
    Florence (SACI Florence): 206
Study Abroad Italy (SAI): 203
studying: 201
Summer Festival: 160
Sunset Cafe: 146
Synagogue of Florence: 69

TU

teaching English: 209
Teatro della Pergola: 115
Teatro Verdi: 113
theater: 115
time: 187
transportation: 178
Trattoria Chiribiri: 167
Tuscany: 124
Uffizi Gallery: 52
United Planet: 208
Università Degli Studi di Firenze:
    Centro di Cultura per Stranieri:
    204
universities: 202
US State Department (US Citizens
    Only): 176

VWXYZ

visas: 173
volunteering: 207
Walking Street Hostel: 138

Walls, The: 153
West Oltrarno: 13
work permits: 173
Workaway.info: 212
working: 209

World Endeavors: 210
World-Wide Opportunities on
  Organic Farms (WWOOF Italia):
  208
YHA Ostello di Siena: 127

Accommodations Index

Academy Hostel: 33
David Inn: 43
Desiree Hotel: 38
Florence Youth Hostel: 35
Holiday Rooms: 41
Hostel Plus: 42
Hostel Santa Monaca: 45
Hostel Veronique/Alekin Hostel: 37
Hotel Ariston: 44
Hotel Arizona: 44
Hotel Benvenuti: 44
Hotel Bretagna: 35
Hotel Casci: 34
Hotel Consigli: 38
Hotel Dalí: 34
Hotel Ester: 41
Hotel Gioia: 43

Hotel Locanda Orchidea: 34
Hotel San Marco: 44
Hotel Serena: 38
Hotel Stella Mary: 39
Ostello Archi Rossi: 39
Ostello Centrale Euro Students/
  Hostel Central: 42
Ostello Gallo d'Oro: 43
Pensione La Scala: 37
Plus Camping Michelangelo: 46
Residenza Dei Pucci: 35
Soggiorno Annamaria / Katti
  House: 41
Soggiorno Pitti: 46
Villa Alle Rampe: 47
Youth Firenze 2000 Bed and
  Breakfast: 46

Restaurants Index

50 Rosso: 83
Acqua al 2: 81
All'Antico Vinaio: 91
Antica Gelateria Fiorentina: 85
Bar Cabras: 85
Buca Niccolini: 78
Caffè Duomo: 78
Caffè Giacosa: 83
Caffè Pasticceria La Loggia degli
  Albizi: 91
Cibréo Teatro del Sale: 89
Da Vinattieri: 80
Dante: 92
Diner, The: 92
Dioniso: 88

Eby's Bar: 91
Festival del Gelato: 80
Gelateria dei Neri: 90
Gelateria La Carraia: 93
Gran Caffè San Marco: 87
Grom: 79
Gusta Pizza: 94
Gustapanino: 92
I Fratellini: 80
Il Brincello: 85
Il Pirata: 85
Il Vegetariano: 87
La Ghiotta: 90
La Grotta di Leo: 84
Le Botteghe di Donatello: 79

L'Hosteria del Bricco: 94
Little David: 78
Mesopotamia: 77
Nerbone: 84
Oil Shoppe, The: 89
Osteria all'antico Mercato: 86
Osteria del Porcellino: 81
Osteria Santo Spirito: 94
O'Vesuvio: 81
Pizzeria Centopoveri: 82
Pizzeria del Duomo: 78
Ristorante La Spada: 83

Ristorante le Fonticine: 86
Ristorante Pizzeria da Zeus: 87
Ruth's: 90
Trattoria Anita: 91
Trattoria Gusto Leo: 81
Trattoria il Contadino: 82
Trattoria La Madia: 79
Trattoria Mario: 84
Trattoria Zaza: 86
Vestri Cioccolato d'Autore: 77
Vin Olio: 88

Nightlife Index

Amadeus: 97
Astor Cafe: 96
Be Bop Music Club: 106
Blob Club, The: 98
Caffè Sant'Ambrogio: 105
Central Park: 100
ClubHouse, The: 102
Dolce Vita: 108
Dublin Pub: 101
Finnegan Irish Pub: 103
Fish Pub, The: 102
I Visacci Caffè: 107
James Joyce Pub: 109
Joshua Tree Pub, The: 100
Kitsch the Pub: 102
Las Palmas: 104
Lochness Lounge: 104
Mostodolce: 101
Moyo: 97

Naima: 105
Negroni: 110
Oibò: 105
Old Stove, The: 97
One-Eyed Jack: 108
Plaz: 105
Pop Cafe: 108
Public House 27: 100
Rifrullo: 109
Shot Cafe: 96
Slowly: 98
Space Electronic Discotheque: 100
Tartan Jock: 107
Twice: 98
Volume: 108
William, The: 107
Wine Bar Nabucco: 103
Zoe: 109

Shopping Index

Alberto Cozzi: 122
Alice Atelier: The Masks of Prof.
  Agostino Dessì: 121
Farmaceutica di Santa Maria
  Novella: 120
Galleria Michelangelo: 121

Goldenpoint: 119
Made in Tuscany: 123
Mercato Centrale: 118
Promod: 119
San Lorenzo: 118
Santo Spirito: 119

FLORENCE ACKNOWLEDGEMENTS

MICHAEL THANKS: Billy, for being a phenomenal RM and spotting all the mistakes I would have surely missed (and for his sass). Linda, because you and The Cause made every day an adventure—спасибо большой, товарищ. Leah, for being my Editor and Quad buddy, and for being one with the earth. Amy, for bringing the word "y'all" into my vocabulary and being an awesome hostess (TT shall continue). Chris, for fielding thousands of nitpicky questions, and for settling Catan with me. Everyone in LGHQ, for always bringing laughs and lots of food. Sofia, for being a superstar RW, rolling with the punches, and making every copybatch a joy to read. Al's, for feeding me. My awesome parents, who drove back and forth to bring me home for the weekend. Miranda and Kristin, for being the best friends in the world. And Bryan, for absolutely everything.

BILLY THANKS: Sofia her fervor and her puns. Michael for his sass and his sassy editing. Chris for keeping to his schedules and for the Tanjore train. The Soviet/Snuggle Pod for its love, laughs, and coffee (JTR). Google Maps for all its enlightening wisdom. The Format Manual for its insistence on the Oxford comma. NPR for my walks to work. The RLL department for their tutelage. InDesign for always shuttin' down on me. MK for her magical prod abilities. Iya for her humor and noms. Amy and Israel for keeping me sane. Joe for being a #bestie. The residents of 300 Western for laughs, Vinho Verde, and the EBW. Rachel for her coffee breaks. Brandi for being a bee charmer. John for being a beeb. The fam for good ol' support. And Cambridge for a great four years.

ABOUT LET'S GO

The Student Travel Guide

Let's Go publishes the world's favorite student travel guides, written entirely by Harvard students. Armed with pens, notebooks, and a few changes of clothes stuffed into their backpacks, our student researchers go across continents, through time zones, and above expectations to seek out invaluable travel experiences for our readers. Because we are a completely student-run company, we have a unique perspective on how students travel, where they want to go, and what they're looking to do when they get there. If your dream is to grab a machete and forge through the jungles of Costa Rica, we can take you there. If you'd rather bask in the Riviera sun at a beachside cafe, we'll set you a table. In short, we write for readers who know that there's more to travel than tour buses. To keep up, visit our website, www.letsgo.com, where you can sign up to blog, post photos from your trips, and connect with the Let's Go community.

Traveling Beyond Tourism

We're on a mission to provide our readers with sharp, fresh coverage packed with socially responsible opportunities to go beyond tourism. Each guide's Beyond Tourism chapter shares ideas about responsible travel, study abroad, and how to give back to the places you visit while on the road. To help you gain a deeper connection with the places you travel, our fearless researchers scour the globe to give you the heads-up on both world-renowned and off-the-beaten-track opportunities. We've also opened our pages to respected writers and scholars to hear their takes on the countries and regions we cover, and asked travelers who have worked, studied, or volunteered abroad to contribute first-person accounts of their experiences.

Fifty-Two Years of Wisdom

Let's Go has been on the road for 52 years and counting. We've grown a lot since publishing our first 20-page pamphlet to Europe in 1960, but five decades and 60 titles later, our witty, candid guides are still researched and written entirely by students on shoestring budgets who know that train strikes, stolen luggage, food poisoning, and marriage proposals are all part of a day's work. Meanwhile, we're still bringing readers fresh new features, such as a student-life section with advice on how and where to meet students from around the world; a revamped, user-friendly layout for our listings; and greater emphasis on the experiences that make travel abroad a rite of passage for readers of all ages. And, of course, this year's 16 titles—including five brand-new guides—are still brimming with editorial honesty, a commitment to students, and our irreverent style.

The Let's Go Community

More than just a travel guide company, Let's Go is a community that reaches from our headquarters in Cambridge, MA, all across the globe. Our small staff of dedicated student editors, writers, and tech nerds comes together because of our shared passion for travel and our desire to help other travelers get the most out of their experience. We love it when our readers become part of the Let's Go community as well—when you travel, drop us a postcard (67 Mt. Auburn St., Cambridge, MA 02138, USA), send us an email (feedback@letsgo.com), or sign up on our website (www.letsgo.com) to tell us about your adventures and discoveries.

For more information, updated travel coverage, and news from our researcher team, visit us online at www.letsgo.com.

LET'S GO BUDGET

TAKE A LET'S GO BUDGET GUIDE TO EUROPE

LET'S GO BUDGET AMSTERDAM
978-1-61237-015-6

LET'S GO BUDGET ATHENS
978-1-61237-005-7

LET'S GO BUDGET BARCELONA
978-1-61237-014-9

LET'S GO BUDGET BERLIN
978-1-61237-006-4

LET'S GO BUDGET FLORENCE
978-1-61237-007-1

LET'S GO BUDGET ISTANBUL
978-1-61237-008-8

LET'S GO BUDGET LONDON
978-1-61237-013-2

LET'S GO BUDGET MADRID
978-1-61237-009-5

LET'S GO BUDGET PARIS
978-1-61237-011-8

LET'S GO BUDGET PRAGUE
978-1-61237-010-1

LET'S GO BUDGET ROME
978-1-61237-012-5

ALL LET'S GO BUDGET GUIDEBOOKS ARE $9.99.
*Let's Go also publishes guides to individual countries
that are available at bookstores and online retailers.*

For more information: visit **LETSGO.COM**
JOIN THE DISCUSSION WITH LET'S GO ON **FACEBOOK** AND **TWITTER**

HELPING LET'S GO. If you want to share your discoveries, suggestions, or corrections, please drop us a line. We appreciate every piece of correspondence, whether a postcard, a 10-page email, or a coconut. Visit Let's Go at www.letsgo. com or send an email to:

feedback@letsgo.com, subject: "Let's Go Budget Florence"

Address mail to:

Let's Go Budget Florence, 67 Mount Auburn St., Cambridge, MA 02138, USA

In addition to the invaluable travel advice our readers share with us, many are kind enough to offer their services as researchers or editors. Unfortunately, our charter enables us to employ only currently enrolled Harvard students.
Maps © Let's Go and Avalon Travel
Interior design by Darren Alessi
Production by Amber Pirker
Photos © Let's Go, Sofia, Marykate Jasper and Liz Weinbloom, photographers

Distributed by Publishers Group West.
Printed in Canada by Friesens Corp.

ISBN-13: 978-1-61237-007-1
ISBN-10: 1-61237-007-1
First edition
10 9 8 7 6 5 4 3 2 1

Let's Go Budget Florence is written by Let's Go Publications, 67 Mt. Auburn St., Cambridge, MA 02138, USA.

Let's Go® and the LG logo are trademarks of Let's Go, Inc.

LEGAL DISCLAIMER. For 50 years, Let's Go has published the world's favorite budget travel guides, written entirely by students and updated periodically based on the personal anecdotes and travel experiences of our student writers. Although every effort was made to ensure that the information was correct at the time of going to press, the author and publisher do not assume and hereby disclaim any liability to any party for any loss or damage caused by errors, omissions, or any potential travel disruption due to labor or financial difficulty, whether such errors or omissions result from negligence, accident, or any other cause.

ADVERTISING DISCLAIMER. All advertisements appearing in Let's Go publications are sold by an independent agency not affiliated with the editorial production of the guides. Advertisers are never given preferential treatment, and the guides are researched, written, and published independent of advertising. Advertisements do not imply endorsement of products or services by Let's Go, and Let's Go does not vouch for the accuracy of information provided in advertisements.

If you are interested in purchasing advertising space in a Let's Go publication, contact Edman & Company at 1-203-656-1000.

QUICK REFERENCE

YOUR GUIDE TO LET'S GO ICONS

[icon]	*Let's Go* recommends	☎	Phone numbers	[icon]	Directions
i	Other hard info	$	Prices	⏰	Hours

IMPORTANT PHONE NUMBERS

EMERGENCY: ☎112			
Amsterdam	☎911	London	☎999
Barcelona	☎092	Madrid	☎092
Berlin	☎110	Paris	☎17
Florence	☎113	Prague	☎158
Istanbul	☎155	Rome	☎113

USEFUL PHRASES

ENGLISH	FRENCH	GERMAN	ITALIAN	SPANISH
Hello/Hi	Bonjour/Salut	Hallo/Tag	Ciao	Hola
Goodbye/Bye	Au revoir	Auf Wiedersehen/ Tschüss	Arrivederci/Ciao	Adios/Chao
Yes	Oui	Ja	Sì	Sí
No	Non	Nein	No	No
Excuse me!	Pardon!	Entschuldigen Sie!	Scusa!	Perdón!
Thank you	Merci	Danke	Grazie	Gracias
Go away!	Va t'en!	Geh weg!	Vattene via!	Vete!
Help!	Au secours!	Hilfe!	Aiuto!	Ayuda!
Call the police!	Appelez la police!	Ruf die Polizei!	Chiamare la polizia!	Llame a la policía!
Get a doctor!	Cherchez un médecin!	Hol einen Arzt!	Avere un medico!	Llame a un médico!
I don't understand	Je ne comprends pas	Ich verstehe nicht	Non capisco	No comprendo
Do you speak English?	Parlez-vous anglais?	Sprechen Sie Englisch?	Parli inglese?	¿Habla inglés?
Where is...?	Où est...?	Wo ist...?	Dove...?	¿Dónde está...?

TEMPERATURE CONVERSIONS

°CELSIUS	-5	0	5	10	15	20	25	30	35	40
°FAHRENHEIT	23	32	41	50	59	68	77	86	95	104

MEASUREMENT CONVERSIONS

1 inch (in.) = 25.4mm	1 millimeter (mm) = 0.039 in.
1 foot (ft.) = 0.305m	1 meter (m) = 3.28 ft.
1 mile (mi.) = 1.609km	1 kilometer (km) = 0.621 mi.
1 pound (lb.) = 0.454kg	1 kilogram (kg) = 2.205 lb.
1 gallon (gal.) = 3.785L	1 liter (L) = 0.264 gal.